D1486404

The Bedside
Guardian 2020

The Bedside Guardian 2020

EDITED BY
KATHERINE BUTLER

guardianbooks

Published by Guardian Books 2020

2 4 6 8 10 9 7 5 3 1

Copyright © Guardian News and Media Ltd 2020

Katherine Butler has asserted her right under the Copyright,
Designs and Patents Act 1988 to be identified as the editor of this work
This book is sold subject to the condition that it shall not, by way of
trade or otherwise, be lent, resold, hired out, or otherwise circulated
without the publisher's prior consent in any form of binding or
cover other than that in which it is published and without a
similar condition, including this condition, being
imposed on the subsequent purchaser.

First published in Great Britain in 2020 by
Guardian Books
Kings Place, 90 York Way
London N1 9GU

www.guardianbooks.co.uk

A CIP catalogue record for this book is available from the British Library

ISBN 978-1-9162047-1-3

Cover design by Guardian News & Media Ltd
Typeset by seagulls.net

Printed and bound in Great Britain by
CPI Group (UK) Ltd, Croydon CR0 4YY

Contents

WINTER

SPRING

Foreword

BERNARDINE EVARISTO

What drama, what madness, what tragedy, what a year we've had. Coronavirus, Black Lives Matter, Brexit and the ticking time bomb in the background, a climate every day made less stable and more dangerous by our ongoing abuse of the planet.

I want to think the human race will be able to survive whatever the world throws our way. The sorry truth, though, is that a great many individuals didn't survive the year because of our government's mishandling of the Covid-19 pandemic. Only some of us can now look back at the past 12 months and reflect on how this virus completely blindsided us. One minute an outbreak was happening somewhere far away – as usual – with no chance of it reaching these shores. The next it was here; we had become its unwitting hosts, helping it to proliferate. OK, so this is the nature of modern pandemics, but political leaders such as Boris Johnson and his older doppelgänger, Trump, made things so much worse.

Early March 2020 now feels as if it belongs to a very distant past, when we could carry on our normal daily lives jostling up against each other without risking fatal illness. The coronavirus crisis elbowed out Brexit, the issue that had dominated the national conversation for so long, dividing us into those who thought leaving the European alliance was a foolhardy rupture and those who believed in 'making Britain great again'; some of these are also people who like harking back to the good old days when the British empire controlled a quarter of the world's countries, exploiting the natives and stealing their resources.

My low expectations of Boris Johnson, the man who pops up throughout the dramas covered by this book, were confirmed this year, and they chime with the sentiments in the opening article, 'The *Guardian* view on Boris Johnson: let no such man be trusted'. It's easy to blame his favourite ideologue, Dominic 'lockdown cheat' Cummings, for pulling the strings, but that lets his paymaster off the hook.

Nearly a year after the warning in that editorial, Johnson, unchastened by his own illness, is still at it. The book's concluding article, by Fintan O'Toole, highlights this braying patrician's populism even as it continues to hoodwink those for whom authority comes packaged in the guise of upper-class men.

Johnson would not still be 'mis-leading' this country today if he were someone from a working-class background. He would be exposed for what he is – unreliable, childish, disingenuous, shambolic, mendacious. He would also be facing an inquiry into the deaths of tens of thousands of people.

The tragic outcome of his mis-leadership is brought home most movingly by the NHS doctor Rachel Clarke. Clarke writes from the hospital frontline about an elderly patient with coronavirus called Winston, who is in the last hours of his life. She knows his death is unnecessary and her account reminds us that, far from protecting the elderly in care homes, the government actively endangered them. When she hears Boris Johnson declare his government's coronavirus strategy a success, in spite of England having the highest number of excess deaths in Europe and one of the worst in the world, she feels physically sick. Her piece brought me to tears.

The pandemic continues to cast a dark cloud over our lives. Science may eventually remove or lessen the threat. Long into the post-coronavirus age, though, I fear we will still be dealing with that other pandemic that 2020 cast into the spotlight, the brutality of racism in majority-white countries. The killing, or rather 21st-century lynching, of George Floyd in Minneapolis by Derek Chauvin, a policeman, inspired unprecedented global protests in support of Black Lives Matter. As a consequence, many institutions in the UK promised to look into their own discriminatory practices and to promise corrective action.

I was particularly struck by Afua Hirsch's powerful piece, 'The racism that killed George Floyd was built in Britain', because it gets to the heart of what's wrong with how Britain remembers its past and curates its own history. It's so easy to profess moral outrage at how racism is manifested in America without connecting it to the origins of racism in British history, or acknowledging that Brits imported it across the Atlantic to its colonies there.

Likewise, David Olusoga is right to argue that the removal of a 120-year-old civic statue of slave trader Edward Colston from its plinth in Bristol is a necessary counteractive to the egregious systemic racism of today's Britain. Colston was up to his neck in the murder and enslavement of thousands of Africans.

I am hopeful that this second wave of Black Lives Matter will be more impactful in the long run than the first. But I also take the view that it's all well and good promising institutional change when the streets are teeming with protesters and the media is headlining racism, but what happens when everything quietens down and it's just easier to perpetuate the status quo?

We might think we know how racism pans out in our society, but why, for example, has there been such a disproportionate number of black and Asian deaths from coronavirus? There is no mystery, as Angela Saini points out writing about racial health inequalities; the answer is not race, it is racism.

I'm sorry to see Gary Younge leave his official role as a *Guardian* journalist, because I've enjoyed his essential articles for the entire 26 years he's been on the staff. We were both at the Ake Festival in Nigeria last October, and I remember thinking, as he took to the stage, how vitally important he has been as the rare – often only – black mainstream cultural commentator, who has always spoken up for black folk.

In his final column, 'In these bleak times, imagine a world where you can thrive', he pays homage to his Bajan mother who raised him and shaped his political consciousness. Unlike Johnson, who was also a journalist, albeit an often flippant and untruthful one, Younge was not born into an entitled elite, but his brilliant, serious and stirring journalism has been amplified by determination rooted in integrity. Unlike Johnson, he is a true intellectual who is aware of how systemic racism operates and discriminates. 'Sing yourself up,' he wrote, even before this summer's protests inspired many young black people into imagining a more equal future. It is something he has been doing for black people his entire career.

This anthology balances light and dark; from Suzanne Moore's clear-sighted and compassionate take on desperate migrants crossing the English Channel, to marmalade-making, to the cultural phenomenon that is Michaela Coel, author and star of the (sadly) groundbreaking drama about black millennials, *I May Destroy You*, there is so much to read and enjoy here.

I felt nostalgic, too, reading Michael Billington's swansong after nearly 50 years as the *Guardian*'s theatre critic. I have seen him at press nights over the years, and always wished I was seated right behind him in order to sneak a peek at his notes. The last time was at a Bush Theatre production two summers ago. He is an incredible repository of theatre history but, as he himself admits, there are very few critics of colour, and his replacement, Arifa

Akbar, is a long-overdue appointment. She herself has written a fascinating piece, taking a job as a tea lady in her father's care home during lockdown in order to keep an eye on him.

The climate crisis is amplified by the very young Greta Thunberg, who never stops banging the drum and telling older generations that we need to cut carbon emissions. She reminds us in her uncompromising article ahead of the Davos summit that the older generation is letting her generation down and that we need to act now. She's right, of course.

If one good thing came out of lockdown, it was the measurable, if temporary, reduction in global pollution. As our climate fast turns from relatively benevolent to dangerously malevolent, we need to heed Thunberg's pleas and take action – today. Our warming planet won't go off the boil until we stop heating it up.

There is so much work to do in the journey towards egalitarianism, and thank goodness the *Guardian* continues to champion so many important issues and highlight injustices, digging deep into cause and effect and advocating for social change. Many of us turn to its pages in order to make sense of our challenging and changing times. In doing so we feel more energised to harness the collective power to work towards creating a better world. And we feel less alone.

Introduction

KATHERINE BUTLER

At 11pm on 31 January, the leavers were celebrating in Parliament Square. As Jonathan Freedland wrote of the scene, they were 'beaming, proud in their tops bearing the slogan: "Job Done"'. They had the prize. The UK had just left the EU. From Downing Street, Boris Johnson, frontman of the 2016 leave campaign, hailed 'the dawn of a new era'.

Earlier that day, reports about a new strain of pneumonia moved onto the UK's news radar with two cases identified in Britain. Five hundred people in the Chinese province of Hubei were already dead and the city of Wuhan had been sealed off.

Within weeks of the union jack being lowered in Brussels, that Eurosceptic prize could not have felt more pointless.

A virus that stopped at no borders was in our midst, half of humanity would soon be in lockdown, daily life changed beyond recognition.

How does an anthology of journalism covering the dystopia of 2020 do justice to it without inducing despair?

Ever since the first annual *Bedside Guardian* in 1951, its editors have said 'their' year contained a rare amount of turbulence. For all our sakes, I hope 2021 bucks that trend.

This book isn't a history or a review, it's a curation of *Guardian* journalism as it happened: without the wisdom of hindsight but with all the immediacy, sometimes urgency, of how writers saw events at the time.

You're back, for example, to the April moment we heard that the prime minister had been moved to intensive care. A dispatch from Trump's America crackles with tension as the curfew hour approaches in Minneapolis and riot police emerge from a side street, baton-charging protesters after the death of George Floyd.

The Covid-19 pandemic, inescapable as it is, dominates from 6 February when Lily Kuo so vividly conveys the fear felt in locked-down Wuhan. But another rare historic moment would appear with the Black Lives Matter protests and the glorious realisation, as David Olusoga wrote, 'that things can never go back to how they were'. The two themes overlapped, most poignantly in Sirin Kale's piece on the life and death of rail worker Belly Mujinga.

Brexit, the thing that obsessed British political life for the previous four years, receded from view. Yet it was, to borrow that chilling bit of health policy jargon that entered our language in 2020, an underlying condition.

The promise to 'get Brexit done' was, after all, what secured a landslide for Boris Johnson in the December general election. So, when calamity struck, power was in the hands of a careerist known for his lack of interest in detail and want of respect for either expertise or the rule of law.

Brexit too had amplified an exceptionalism which manifested again in Johnson's early refusal to learn public health lessons from Britain's European neighbours, stop shaking hands, or close the pubs. It would be weaponised by his Eurosceptic culture warriors as they invoked wartime sacrifice, jingoistically boasting about their 'world-beating' pandemic response, yet, as Nesrine Malik writes, 'shifting the responsibility entirely onto the public'.

Freedom-loving England would end up with the highest excess death rate in Europe and facing the worst recession in 300 years.

Scenes from across Europe still filled the *Guardian*'s pages in the weeks after Britain's departure. Not in the ways we'd imagined when we resolved to deepen the newspaper's engagement with the continent this year. The sense of shock is captured here as an ice rink is turned into a mortuary in Madrid and grieving Italians go from singing defiant Gloria Gaynor anthems to more complex emotions.

Each piece in the collection works as a stand-alone read – I hope that, taken together, they connect bigger questions. Why it took a pandemic for us to see systemic ills: that low-paid migrants were doing the 'essential' jobs with only the flimsiest protections, and, as Aditya Chakrabortty asks in an essay about his mother's death, whether the lives of people with non-Covid conditions were cut short to save the NHS.

I feel reassured that scientists such as William Hanage spoke out in mid-March, when Johnson was still dithering, about the reckless flirtation with 'herd immunity'. And, if Dominic Cummings' Barnard Castle jaunt, which came to light at the end of May, was the low point of Downing Street's disregard for the collective national sacrifice, we had potent satire. I hope John Crace's sketch made Classic Dom wince.

Here too is the indomitability of the human spirit and our need for each other. People can only take so much isolation and paralysing fear before personal epiphanies and new ways of coping emerge. Grace Dent confronts mortality in a column ostensibly about going to Morrisons; Adrian Chiles shares his soda bread recipe and the man who taught PE to the nation's locked-down children opens up about his tough past. Simon Hattenstone longs for a footie hug.

Starting in October 2019, the book covers the last months of the old normal: Prince Andrew seals his own downfall; a boy appears in youth court for the theft of a McFlurry. The electoral rout was perhaps in the runes for Labour when, in a former Durham mining stronghold, Julian Coman meets a young labourer, furious Brexit wasn't done by Halloween, who says he is going to vote Conservative although he also notes: 'They all talk a load of shite.'

Trouble was brewing in other ways. The climate emergency became real for Brigid Delaney as Sydney filled with smoke; while Donald Trump risked a dangerous new chapter in the Middle East by assassinating one of Iran's most powerful figures.

We know now, too, that even during a plague, life goes on. Harvey Weinstein was convicted. Harry and Meghan moved to America. Jürgen Klopp's Liverpool shrugged off history – and won the league. People in Hong Kong and Belarus defied repression – their courage, covered in these pages, was one of the year's few bright lights.

If we learned anything from 2020 it was to expect uncertainty. So hope makes as much sense as despair. Naomi Klein argues powerfully for slowing down, rejecting a return to the pre-Covid normal, only worse, and without the close relationships that sustain us. If a progressive economic agenda emerged while the Second World War was still raging, argues Larry Elliott, it can be done now. And, as Jonathan Watts found, communities are crying out for new ways to live that are more in tune with nature and ecological balance.

Editing this much-loved institution is an honour and I'm grateful to Katharine Viner, the *Guardian*'s inspiring editor-in-chief, for giving me the opportunity. Reading so much good journalism brought joy to a dark year. Having to omit so much of it brought pain. I wasn't in the end able to squeeze in a piece from the remarkable Empty Doorway series by Simon Hattenstone and Daniel Lavelle, but I still want everyone to go online and read all of it.

Previous *Bedside Guardian* editors Aditya Chakrabortty, Claire Armitstead and Hugh Muir generously shared their wisdom and reassurance.

Lindsay Davies's patience, skill and good humour throughout were invaluable.

Conditions were especially trying this year for section editors so I'm doubly grateful for their thoughts and nominations.

Thanks too to Francesca Melandri for kindly letting me include her essay: 'A letter to the UK from Italy'.

The pandemic is still shaping our lives. Perhaps in the bleakness it helps to know that *Guardian* journalism will be trying to change the world too – as it has done through pandemics, wars and dark times over the last 200 years – making sure that some things can never go back to how they were.

Autumn

The *Guardian* view on Boris Johnson: let no such man be trusted

GUARDIAN EDITORIAL

Visiting Watford, Boris Johnson made it commendably clear yesterday that he opposes the self-interested abuse of a process laid down by treaty and law. Asked about an American spy's wife who has claimed diplomatic immunity after being involved in the death of a British motorcyclist, Mr Johnson could not, for once, have spoken more plainly. 'I must answer you directly,' he said. 'I do not think that it can be right to use the process of diplomatic immunity for this type of purpose.'

The remarks were welcome and to the point. But such rigour is rare coming from this prime minister's mouth. The problem with Mr Johnson's brief tenure of 10 Downing Street is the exact opposite of the point he made yesterday. He is not a consistent upholder of proper process at all. On the contrary, he is a shameless and serial abuser of it. This week, the damage being done to this country by this most untrustworthy of prime ministers is scattered as far as the eye can see.

Only two weeks ago, do not forget, Mr Johnson suffered probably the most humiliating constitutional reprimand ever inflicted on a British prime minister, when the supreme court unanimously dismissed his five-week prorogation of parliament as unlawful. The judges found that his move breached the principle that a government must be held to account by a sovereign parliament. The embarrassing implication was that Mr Johnson had misled the Queen.

It is a mark of the unprecedented lack of trust which this prime minister now inspires that a Scottish court was asked yesterday to issue an order requiring him to uphold the law. In Edinburgh the court of session declined to issue such an order, which would have ensured compliance with the Benn act's requirement for a Brexit extension if there is no new deal with the EU on 19 October. But it only did so on the basis that Mr Johnson's lawyers had pledged in court that he would comply. Not to accept that pledge, the court said, 'would be destructive of one of the core principles of constitutional propriety and of the mutual trust that is the bedrock of the relationship between the court and the crown'.

On his visit to Watford, the Conservative leader insisted again that Britain will leave the EU on 31 October. This will not be possible, under the Benn act, unless there is a deal in Brussels in under two weeks. That looks unlikely. Mr Johnson's proposals for a deal fall well short of EU positions on multiple counts. President Macron wants everything sorted by Friday. Without an agreement, the Benn act comes into force, compelling Mr Johnson to do what he has always said he will not do. We shall see all too soon if the Scottish court was right to trust Mr Johnson.

The signs are not good. Today, the government plans to prorogue parliament until a Queen's speech next Monday. It is true that the 2017–19 session is now the longest since the Long Parliament. But a Queen's speech normally either follows an election or portends a new legislative programme.

This one is the opposite. It coincides with Mr Johnson's plan to call an election and will thus contain nothing that will reach the statute book before the poll. In effect, as Professor Robert Hazell of the UCL Constitution Unit has argued powerfully, the speech is thus not a legislative programme but an election manifesto.

'The Queen will have been used,' the professor says, 'to make a Conservative party political broadcast.'

All this is entirely of a piece. Mr Johnson took office in July as head of a Tory faction. He has bulldozed precedent, propriety, parliament, his opponents and the country's allies with Trumpian disdain. Most have fought back. They must go on doing so. Mr Johnson must be stopped from gaming with the Commons, the courts and the country. And, until a no-deal Brexit is off the table, he must be denied the general election he seeks.

10 OCTOBER

Streets make communities. Have architects realised at last?

SIMON JENKINS

Wonders never cease. The Royal Institute of British Architects has just given a prize to a street. Not to a vainglorious skyscraper, or an 'iconic' bunker museum or a luxury pad in a field, but a living, breathing street. This street is not just a street but a 'council street'. Norwich council's chief executive, Laura McGillivray, claims no higher ambition than that 'new social housing should be a fabulous place to live'. She did not seek some architectural 'statement', just a neighbourhood like the thousands that – at least in the private sector – have retained their popularity among Britons who have had choice in the matter for some three centuries.

I have championed streets all my life and find it painful to hear Goldsmith Street's new residents say why they so like it. 'The place just seems safe ... To see my little girl playing outside the front door made me cry ... We made instant friends across the street ... I feel like I don't rent it, I own it.' Why should such sentiments be surprising from council tenants?

Goldsmith Street is composed of 105 flats and houses, with no visible separation between the public and the limited number of private-tenure properties. Traffic is not banned but demoted. The estate is high-density and among the most energy-efficient in the country. The architects, Mikhail Riches and Cathy Hawley, stress the social impact of their design, such as 'placing front doors opposite front doors', aligning facades with street views and having private balconies overlooking public spaces. This was hailed by the Stirling prize chair Julia Barfield as a 'modest masterpiece' – as if it was new.

The language used by Riches and Hawley comes straight from the 1960s American sociologist Jane Jacobs, and her epic *The Death and Life of Great American Cities*. She meticulously analysed the streets of Greenwich Village in New York, noting how their layouts enabled them to be 'self-policing' and secure. They were overlooked from end to end by front rooms, doorsteps and stoops, 'semi-private domains'. People were thus empowered and responsible for their surroundings. The built form itself created a sense of community.

If Jacobs had been a medical expert, her analysis would have translated into professional practice. Architects knew better and treated it as nostalgic rubbish. Her message ran counter to Corbusian orthodoxy, in which public architecture was about scale and social control. Jacobs relegated architects to virtual conservationists. Students were duly taught to evict neighbourhoods, demolish streets and stack people high, where they would be dependent on a distant council. Public-sector architecture was about social disruption. It has been that way for half a century.

The resulting devastation of British cities has long been charted, from 1950s east London, studied by Peter Willmott and

Michael Young, to Lynsey Hanley's masterful 'intimate history' of Birmingham's estates. By the 1970s, high-rise towers were out of favour, following the collapse of Ronan Point in east London. But council architecture's response was a new grandiosity, with slab estates such as London's now-demolished Heygate. Crime-ridden balconies and corridors replaced broken-down lifts.

The return of the street is exciting. In Liverpool, a council long dedicated to demolishing its historic legacy was recently forced to retain the Victorian Welsh streets area – so run-down it was used as a film set – and restore it to its original purpose: housing local people. Streets are returning to life in Birmingham's Jewellery Quarter, Manchester's Northern Quarter and London's Hackney, Bow and Bermondsey.

New, as opposed to reinstated, streets have so far been hard to come by. The consultancy Create Streets has been leading the charge. It proposed a traditional grid for the Mount Pleasant site in Islington, north London, but was inexcusably blocked by Boris Johnson as mayor, in favour of conventional blocks of flats, actually at lower residential densities. The Olympic legacy authority at Stratford rejected extending the streets of Hackney Wick across their site in favour of towers set round a park. It preferred vanity to community.

The customary claim that cities need to build high to cram in more people is simply untrue. Except at Hong Kong densities, towers rarely house more people than 'high-density low-rise'. London's new council estates in the 1960s and 70s housed fewer, not more, people than what they replaced. Most of London's highest densities remain in the Victorian seven-storey terraces of Kensington and Bayswater. But planning should never pursue density at the expense of community. Community should be the sole arbiter of urban renewal. Without it, cities default to *Blade Runner*.

The fashion for high-rise urban living has passed from public housing to towers of luxury flats. These are sold not to families – let alone neighbourhoods – but to transient single people and overseas investors seeking anonymous bolt-holes. Such ugly structures do nothing to house people or promote communities.

Norwich offers what the Create Streets chief, Nicholas Boys Smith, hails as 'walkable, gentle density'. Its message is not just that the public sector can, at last, take some initiative in local housing. It is that an age of architectural brutalism is at long last passing. One more civilised and sensitive to the stress of urban living is taking its place.

25 OCTOBER

Lured from Vietnam by the promise of work in UK nail bars

AMELIA GENTLEMAN

What might make a young Vietnamese woman leave her home and family to make a dangerous trip across the world for a new life in the UK? Most likely, trafficking experts say, it was the promise of work in one of Britain's proliferating high-street nail bars.

Reports that a young Vietnamese woman was one of the 39 people who died this week in a refrigerated trailer have not been confirmed by police, but anti-slavery organisations have been trying to raise the alarm for years about the growing problem of Vietnamese children and young adults being trafficked into the UK. Boys are usually sent to work in cannabis farms, locked inside converted houses and forced to tend the plants day and night, while the girls and young women are dispatched to nail bars. Both sexes are also frequently forced into sex work.

It is a phenomenon that is hidden in plain sight. Because those trafficked are aware that they are in the UK illegally, they are wary of the police and extremely unlikely to report their own exploitation. Some may not even recognise they are victims of trafficking, since they may have chosen to travel to the UK in search of work, and will often have paid a people-smuggler to organise the journey and find them a job.

The cost of reaching Europe typically ranges between $10,000 and $40,000 (about £8,000 to £30,000) according to 'Precarious Journeys', a report on people-trafficking from Vietnam, published earlier this year by anti-slavery charities. The brother of Pham Thi Tra My said she had paid £30,000 to people-smugglers to get her to the UK, and that some money had been returned to the family overnight as news of the tragedy emerged, according to the BBC.

The line between smuggling and trafficking becomes blurred on the journey. Most Vietnamese working in cannabis farms or in nail bars know that their families at home are heavily in debt to their traffickers for the cost of their journey, and remain trapped in this debt-bondage for years, trying to repay the money and too frightened to seek help.

While it is hard to get accurate statistics about the real numbers of trafficked Vietnamese people, because most remain hidden and undocumented, new figures from the Salvation Army, which works with victims of trafficking, show that more Vietnamese men were referred to the charity between July 2018 and July 2019 than any other nationality.

The charity worked with 209 people from Vietnam over that period, a 248 per cent increase on the number referred five years earlier. The charity Ecpat, which works with child-trafficking victims, has also seen a steep rise in the number of Vietnamese referrals, from 135 in 2012 to 704 in 2018.

In her final texts, sent from the container as she was dying, Pham says she is from the Ha Tinh province of Vietnam, which is the site of the country's worst environmental disaster, a chemical spill from a steel factory in 2016 that poisoned up to 125 miles of the northern coastline and devastated the local fishing industry.

Mimi Vu, who has been working in Vietnam on trafficking and slavery issues for the past seven years and is a leading expert on trafficking of Vietnamese young people to Europe and the UK, said she had met a higher than usual number of people from Ha Tinh province during visits to migrant camps in northern France last week. 'The Ha Tinh environmental disaster has been very problematic for fishermen whose livelihood was taken away. They need money immediately and that has been the push factor for migration,' she said. 'She will probably have come willingly. Her family will have paid for her to go, thinking she will get a job and training in a nail bar in the UK.'

This kind of trafficking is precisely the problem that the Modern Slavery Act, introduced by Theresa May in 2015, was supposed to tackle, but anti-slavery organisations have been disappointed at the lack of funding for its key measures. Debbie Beadle, the director of programmes at Ecpat and co-author of a study into victims of trafficking from Vietnam to Europe, said: 'The resources haven't come to put it into effect. Many police forces and local authorities are still not trained or equipped to identify these victims of trafficking.'

Because victims are not regularly being identified, there have been fewer successful prosecutions under the new human trafficking legislation than expected. The first successful nail bar prosecution was last January, when three people were convicted of conspiring to facilitate the movement of people for labour exploitation. Police found two Vietnamese girls working at the Nail Bar Deluxe in Bath. Both were working 60-hour weeks; one was paid around £30 a month, the other was not paid and slept on a mattress in the attic of the nail bar owner's home. They had been smuggled into the UK in the back of a lorry.

Beadle said most of the victims the charity worked with had travelled to the UK hidden in lorries. 'They usually describe it as one of the most traumatic experiences of their lives.'

27 OCTOBER

End for cornered Isis leader Baghdadi comes with thunderous blast in tunnel

MARTIN CHULOV

Cornered in a dead-end tunnel as a robot crept towards him, Abu Bakr al-Baghdadi had nowhere left to run. Dogs barked in the darkness, a US soldier called out, then came the thundering explosion that killed the world's most wanted man and three terrified children he was using as human shields.

The end for the Islamic State leader was as murderous as his six-year reign, and no less gruesome. In a remote hamlet of north-west Syria, the US military had finally caught up with Baghdadi, who detonated a suicide vest strapped to his body as special forces troops disgorged from helicopters and crouched near the frugal stone house in which he was hiding.

Forensics specialists stood by, carrying samples of Baghdadi's DNA and the means to compare it with remains at the scene. They quickly matched what they had with what soldiers retrieved from the underground blast. Two hours into the raid the attackers were able to confirm that they had found their man. Soldiers secured what remained of Baghdadi in sealed bags, another group ushered 10 children to the home of a bewildered neighbour, and yet more carried items from the home they had destroyed to eight helicopters.

Just before 3.30am Syrian time the helicopter fleet started off for the return journey to Erbil, a 70-minute flight over regions of Syria where the organisation that Baghdadi had led for more than six years still cast its shadow. Crossing briefly into Turkey, then to north-east Syria, where the vanquished US Kurdish partners were this month forced into retreat, and then to the Kurdish north of Iraq, from where much of the long hunt for Baghdadi had been run, the troops finally unloaded their cargo.

Baghdadi had been a prize which had eluded all his pursuers, and the best technology the world's intelligence agencies could muster. He had long understood the perils of being a fugitive in a digital age and the hunt for him began and ended using the old-fashioned ways of spycraft – a person carrying a secret.

Iraqi officials say that in mid-September they identified a Syrian man used to smuggle the wives of two of Baghdadi's brothers, Ahmad and Jumah, to Idlib province via Turkey. The same smuggler had earlier helped move Baghdadi's children from Iraq. Iraqi intelligence officers say they were able to co-opt the man and a woman believed to be his wife, as well as one of Baghdadi's nephews, into providing information about the route he used and the destination of those travelling with him. It was a break like no other, and was soon passed to the CIA.

By mid-October a plan to catch or kill Baghdadi was in full swing. The operation was given the name Kayla Mueller, the US national security adviser, Robert O'Brien, revealed yesterday. It was in honour of the aid worker from Arizona who was enslaved by Baghdadi and who died in Raqqa in 2015.

Iraqi officials say they provided real-time information to Washington as Baghdadi moved about in Idlib. Paranoid, slowed down by war wounds and stricken with diabetes, the 48-year-old was nevertheless used to changing locations. He had done so regularly throughout his life on the run, shifting between eastern Syria and western Iraq before – according to the Iraqi National Intelligence Service – settling in a small pocket of Idlib province.

It was a long way from home for a man who trusted few outside Iraq and no one outside his inner circle. And it was an unlikely place to end up, according to European intelligence officials who had last tracked him to the eastern Syrian town of Baghuz in January.

By early last week American and Iraqi officials were growing more confident that Baghdadi was indeed in Idlib province, moving between homes in a hamlet named Barisha, not far from the border with Turkey. At this point Washington's technical capabilities took over, establishing who Baghdadi was with, and where he was staying. One man was Abu Mohammed al-Halabi, the leader of a rival Salafi jihadi group called Hurras al-Dein – an unlikely bedfellow for the leader of Isis. The groups had been at odds. Only weeks before, Hurras al-Dein members had been rounding up and killing those they suspected of being Isis sympathisers.

According to regional officials, the house Halabi was staying in was built early last year above a tunnel complex. It was an ideal hideout for a fugitive and it required a formidable force to assault it.

'By Thursday afternoon the president and I were informed there was a high probability he would be at the compound in Idlib province,' Mike Pence, the US vice-president, told *Face the Nation* on Sunday.

In a press conference to announce Baghdadi's death, Donald Trump said he had given the order to go ahead with the raid on Saturday in Washington. Shortly afterwards, special forces based in Erbil were given orders to leave for Idlib. It was their biggest and most dangerous operation of the war against Isis – and that was just in getting there. Russia, which controls the airspace over Idlib, was given notice, so too Turkey, with which the US has been at odds in recent weeks. Syrian Kurds in the north-east of the country were also briefed.

The attack force arrived just after 1am and faced a barrage of gunfire from the ground. The fierce clashes that followed killed at least nine members of Isis, in addition to Baghdadi, many of whom were relatives. Halabi was among those to die, as were two of Baghdadi's wives, believed to have detonated suicide vests. The cornered Isis leader is believed to have dropped through a hatch into a tunnel network. Trump said the attack planners knew exactly where it was and how to breach its walls. 'He reached the end of the tunnel as our dogs chased him down. [Baghdadi] ignited his vest, killing himself and three [of his] children. Test results gave ... totally positive identification, it was him.'

Children in handcuffs: a month reporting from youth court

HELEN PIDD

Straining to hear the judge from behind the bulletproof glass in the dock of court one, the 16-year-old pleaded guilty to a crime with the hallmarks of being committed by a child. He had burgled a McDonald's and been caught by police helping himself to a McFlurry. The other charges, all admitted, were more serious: 12 sexual assaults, molesting younger girls from his school and youth club – 'You've got big breasts for a year 8,' he told one – and groping a shop worker who had spotted him trying to steal another ice-cream.

His lawyer told the district judge there were mitigating circumstances. His client had learning difficulties and was 'some years behind his chronological age'. Last Christmas he was sectioned with psychosis and had since been taking a drug for schizophrenia. The boy scarcely remembered the assaults, perhaps because he had been smoking cannabis and the addictive, formerly legal drug spice.

The lawyer pleaded for the boy not to be sent to jail: 'We are all aware of the effects on young men, particularly vulnerable young men, when they are in custody with older boys.' It was then for the judge to decide whether the boy should be kept off the streets and sent to prison, where statistics show he would have a 65 per cent chance of reoffending after mixing with the worst-behaved boys in the north of England, or rehabilitated in the community. How best should a half-hour hearing address the problems of a child with such complex needs?

That question matters to everyone. But every day in youth courts across England and Wales, the fate of some of the most vulnerable – and occasionally dangerous – children in society is decided behind closed doors. The public are not allowed in, even those who accuse the defendants of robbing, assaulting or defrauding them. Journalists rarely visit, deterred by restrictions banning identification of the young people involved.

Yet the secrecy masks what the children's commissioner, Anne Longfield, says is a 'chaotic and dysfunctional' system – an environment she believes is actively child-unfriendly and fails to rehabilitate so many who pass through it.

There has been a dramatic fall in the number of children who end up in the criminal justice system, as the police and youth offending services have increasingly sought to deal informally with minor offending by children: 26,881 children aged 10–17 received a caution or conviction in England and Wales in 2018 compared with 225,000 in 2007, an 88 per cent drop.

But among this smaller cohort, children from minority ethnic backgrounds are disproportionately likely to end up in court and custody and are four times more likely than white children to be arrested. Looked-after children are also vastly overrepresented. Those in care are 13 times more likely to be criminalised than all other children, according to the Children's Rights Alliance for England. ADHD and autistic spectrum disorders abound, along with communication impairment and other learning difficulties.

The *Guardian* spent a month covering every case in one of England's busiest youth courts, in Greater Manchester. From 9.30am to 4.30pm each day, our reporters watched as 128 children – 10 girls and 118 boys – came into contact with an adversarial criminal justice system, accused of everything from joyriding and knife possession to violent disorder and rape. Trials are rare:

most children get caught red-handed and plead guilty, like the McFlurry thief.

The youth court is within the adult magistrates court. To get there, one must go through airport-style security – outsourced, like so much of the public sector, to a private company, G4S in this case. The glass-walled waiting room outside often resembles a messy creche: crisps or drink cartons on the floor, bored toddlers bouldering about as they wait for their older siblings. Some will be there all day: the courts are always running late and 10 or more defendants will often have been given the same start time.

Sometimes the defendants know each other, for better or worse. Occasionally they are from rival gangs. Sometimes they are friends from school, or more often a pupil referral unit. Some of the mothers – and, less often, fathers – are on first-name terms with the staff. 'We're becoming part of the fixtures and fittings,' said one, attending her son's 11th hearing for a string of moped robberies, and filling a cup with cider when the ushers were not looking.

The mother of one boy in the dock, a 16-year-old whose baby-face belied his list of charges – from witness intimidation to knife-point robbery – was not there to see him sent to prison. Earlier in the year she had been fined £100 for not sending him to school for five months.

It can be shocking to see a child behind bulletproof glass, brought up from the cells in handcuffs by dock officers employed by another private company, Amey. They are supposed to always have an 'appropriate adult' in tow – usually a parent, grandparent or social worker – but it does not always work out that way.

Before 2010, when the coalition began closing courts in the name of austerity, nine of Greater Manchester's 10 boroughs had youth courts. Now there are four, with only Manchester open full-time. The result is that children travel further for their hearings, making journeys that can require three buses and two hours. In August, 17 out of 128 children failed to show.

Sometimes children appeared more than once. A number had to come back because of problems with Greater Manchester police's new £27 million computer system, which did not seem able to do something as basic as list a person's previous offences. Some reoffended within the month, including the sexual offender who stole the McFlurry. He had been given the most stringent community sentence: a referral order with intensive supervision and surveillance from his local youth justice service. Two days later, the boy allegedly went into a sports shop and groped a shop assistant. Back in the secure dock of court one, he denied it but was remanded into custody, 65 miles away at HMP Wetherby in West Yorkshire.

Custody is supposed to be the last resort. In 2018, of 22,996 sentences given to children, 1,585 were custodial. More than 70 per cent of juveniles who receive a prison sentence of six months or less reoffend within a year.

'I just don't think it works,' said one youth court solicitor. She had just defended a 15-year-old with learning difficulties who had been found with two kitchen knives, which he had started carrying after being attacked last year. 'They're coming back before the courts time and again on the same offences.'

There had to be another way. 'They come from violent backgrounds a lot of the time, so it's what they know. It's learned behaviour. So why aren't we dealing with that? Why aren't we getting them to speak to people? Why aren't we giving them therapy for what they've seen? Teaching them about alternatives, teaching them how to handle difficult situations? Education is what it comes down to.'

7 NOVEMBER

Boarding schools warp our political class – I know because I went to one

GEORGE MONBIOT

There are two stark facts about British politics. The first is that it is controlled, to a degree unparalleled in any other western European nation, by a tiny, unrepresentative elite. Like almost every aspect of public life here, government is dominated by people educated first at private schools, then at either Oxford or Cambridge.

The second is that many of these people possess a disastrous set of traits: dishonesty, class loyalty and an absence of principle. So, what of our current prime minister? What drives him? What enables such people to dominate us? We urgently need to understand a system that has poisoned the life of this nation.

I think I understand it better than most, because there is a strong similarity between what might have been the defining event of Boris Johnson's childhood and mine. Both of us endured a peculiarly British form of abuse, one intimately associated with the nature of power in this country: we were sent to boarding school when we were very young.

He was slightly older than me (11, rather than eight), but was dispatched, as so many boys were, after a major family trauma. I didn't think a school could be worse than my first boarding school, Elstree, but the accounts that have emerged from his – Ashdown House – during the current independent inquiry into child sexual abuse, suggest that it achieved this improbable feat. Throughout the period when Johnson was a pupil, the inquiry heard, paedophilia was normalised. As the journalist Alex Renton, another ex-pupil, records, the headmaster was a vicious sadist who delighted in beating as many boys as possible, and victimised those who sought to report sexual attacks.

Johnson was at first extremely hostile to the inquiry, describing it as money 'spaffed up a wall'. But he later apologised to other former pupils. He has accepted that sexual assaults took place at the school, though he says he did not witness them. But a culture of abuse affects everybody, one way or another. In my thirties, I met the man who had been the worst bully at my first boarding school. He was candid and apologetic. He explained that he had been sexually abused by teachers and senior boys, acting in concert. Tormenting younger pupils was his way of reasserting power.

The psychotherapist Joy Schaverien lists a set of symptoms that she calls 'boarding school syndrome'. Early boarding, she finds, has similar effects to being taken into care, but with the added twist that your parents have demanded it. Premature separation from your family 'can cause profound developmental damage'.

The justification for early boarding is based on a massive but common misconception. Because physical hardship in childhood makes you physically tough, the founders of the system believed that emotional hardship must make you emotionally tough. It does the opposite. It causes psychological damage that only years of love and therapy can later repair. But if there are two things that being sent to boarding school teach you, they are that love cannot be trusted, and that you should never admit to needing help.

On my first night at boarding school, I felt entirely alone. I was shocked, frightened and intensely homesick, but I soon discovered that expressing these emotions, instead of bringing help and consolation, attracted a gloating, predatory fascination.

The older boys, being vulnerable themselves, knew exactly where to find your weaknesses. There was one night of grace, and thereafter the bullying was relentless, by day and night. It was devastating. There was no pastoral care. Staff looked on as the lives of the small children entrusted to them fell apart. They believed we should sink or swim. (The same philosophy applied to swimming: non-swimmers were thrown into the deep end of an unheated pool.)

I was cut off from everything I knew and loved. Most importantly, I cut myself off from my feelings. When expressions of emotion are dangerous, and when you are constantly told that this terrible thing is being done for your own good, you quickly learn to hide your true feelings, even from yourself. In other words, you learn the deepest form of dishonesty. This duplicity becomes a habit of mind: if every day you lie to yourself, lying to other people becomes second nature.

You develop a shell, a character whose purpose is to project an appearance of confidence and strength, while inside all is fear and flight and anger. The shell may take the form of steely reserve, expansive charm, bumbling eccentricity, or a combination of all three. But underneath it, you are desperately seeking assurance. The easiest means of achieving it is to imagine that you can dominate your feelings by dominating other people. Repressed people oppress people.

In adulthood you are faced with a choice: to remain the person this system sought to create, justifying and reproducing its cruelties, or to spend much of your life painfully unlearning what it taught you, and learning to experience your own emotions without denial, to rediscover love and trust. You must either question almost nothing or question almost everything.

Though only small numbers of people went through this system, it afflicts the entire nation. Many powerful politicians are drawn from this damaged caste. We will not build a kinder, more inclusive country until we understand its peculiar cruelties.

19 NOVEMBER

Are the people of Blackhall Colliery the most honest in Britain?

JOSH HALLIDAY

From the butcher's to the hairdresser's and from the playground to the pub, a tiny pit village has been gripped by a baffling mystery. Detectives in County Durham have revealed that at least 13 meticulously prepared bundles of cash, totalling £26,000, have been left at random places in Blackhall Colliery since 2014. The latest – a wad of 100 £20 notes, amounting to £2,000 – was discovered on Monday morning and was the fourth handed in to police this year.

The mystery has stumped detectives. They have carried out numerous interviews, interrogated bank and Post Office staff and even tested the cash for fingerprints, but the circumstances remain a riddle. Speaking outside the village pub yesterday, hoping to crack the case on his day off, DC John Forster said: 'I am hoping this is some sort of purposeful benefactor who is showing some kindness towards the village. I would rather that than someone who is vulnerable in some way or that it was connected to criminality.'

Forster praised the honesty of the 13 people who had found the £2,000 bags and handed them in, adding that they had been found in a 'very tight' geographical area in the centre of the village. 'One lady who handed it in was shaking – I don't think she had ever been in a police station before,' he said, adding that police had asked those who handed the money in to keep quiet in the hope that detectives would solve the case. One theory is that the money could be the ill-gotten gains of a local drug dealer, although Forster said that did not tally with his knowledge of criminals being ultra-watchful with money.

At Grace Hair and Beauty, on the high street where most of the cash has been found, the mystery behind the cash was the hot topic with customers. 'It could be one of these secret millionaires who wants to do good for the people,' said Doris Huntington, 88, as she had her nails done. 'You'd think he would leave it where a certain kind of people could find it rather than random. It's very honest they've handed it in. Money's no good to me now anyway.'

Lorraine Hall, 43, said the village had been abuzz with rumours and theories since the news broke. 'I think it's somebody that's trying to do something nice – maybe someone who's lived in the village all their life and they haven't got family. A mystery Black-hall Santa,' she said, after serving the lunchtime rush in the cafe.

But in the village community centre, the whispers began seven weeks ago when one of the coffee-morning regulars said she knew someone who had chanced upon a bag of £20 notes. 'I think it's really weird,' said the manager, Alison Paterson, 52. 'I watch too many movies and I wonder if it's someone who's got people coming after him and he's got too much money.'

She initially thought some of the money might have been stolen during a break-in at her community centre in September – but then realised the mystery deposits began in 2014. 'It just feels like someone's done it to create some interest. Maybe it's going to turn into a good-news story – a secret millionaire who's dishing it out. I hope there's a fairytale ending.'

Gaynor Crute, the chair of Monk Hesleden parish council, which includes Blackhall, said she had been scratching her head to think of lottery winners or businesspeople with a local connec-tion who might want to give back to the village, but was at a loss. 'It's from the youngest to the oldest – everyone is talking about it.

· It's all around the village – people have got their own little theories. It will be keeping people going for a while.'

Crute said the area had suffered from hard times since the closure of its colliery in 1981 but it was nice to know that people who maybe needed the money were instead handing it in. 'It's heartwarming to know your neighbours have got so much honesty and integrity,' she said, adding that her local running club would keep their eyes peeled on their next village jog.

Like many former pit villages, Blackhall Colliery has struggled in recent times. Unemployment is nearly three times the national average, with one in 10 people out of work and almost one in three classed as 'economically inactive', mostly long-term sick or retired.

Putting up Christmas decorations in the village hall, Alyson Anderson, 30, said she hoped Blackhall would be known as 'the most trustworthy village in the country' for the people who handed the money in. 'It's not a run-down area but nothing ever that good really happens around here. It might be someone trying to help – a Santa's little elf. I hope it's that.'

20 NOVEMBER

My beloved Hong Kong has become a war zone

VERNA YU

The ongoing political crisis in Hong Kong is probably the biggest challenge of my life. I don't remember having lost sleep and appetite and not being able to think about anything else for months on end ever before.

Like many other Hongkongers, I have been overwhelmed by an acute sense of helplessness and anxiety during the past five months as I have watched our home descend into a war zone every few days. Each time I go out to report, my children's voices sound a note of caution: 'Take care, Mummy!' It feels like I am going to a battlefield whenever I pack a helmet and a gas mask into my bag.

I have been riding an emotional rollercoaster since June as peaceful protests to fight an extradition bill that would have allowed people to be sent for trial in China morphed into a broader and increasingly radical anti-government movement. It has unleashed years of bottled-up anger and frustration at a Hong Kong government under Chinese rule that has no mandate from its people but is answerable to Beijing.

When the government introduced its emergency law to ban face masks in October, it signified to many the start of authoritarian rule to bypass the legislature and impose further restrictions on civil freedoms. It was an ominous signal; perhaps a turning point.

When the metro was shut down by the authorities, a surreal sense of unease took hold in the city. Shops were shuttered. Children's weekend activities were cancelled. All public leisure facilities were closed.

My family took a taxi to the seaside, where there was no lifeguard on the beach. We were held up on our way back by roadblocks set up by protesters. Our children were terrified at the prospect of riot police coming with tear gas, so we got out of the taxi and scrambled away as quickly as we could.

We did not know at the time that this sort of unpredictability would become the new normal. Last week, after conflict escalated when a policeman shot a protester during morning rush hour and police entered university campuses and engaged in violent clashes with students, much of the city was paralysed. Roads were blocked by protesters and police, while many bus routes, metro stations and lines were closed.

Each flare-up means many people are stranded at home, unable to get to work. Schools are shut. Universities ended term early. Even those who manage to get to work worry about whether they can get home. Many who work in the financial district daren't go out to lunch after police threw tear gas at protesting office workers early last week. Social lives grind to a halt as restaurants and shops close early and concerts and events are cancelled or have to end early. For many, it's effectively a curfew.

As everyone's life is disrupted, emotions run high and relationships are strained, causing family rifts and splitting friendships. Casual conversations escalate into blazing rows – are you in the yellow (pro-democracy) camp or the blue (pro-China/government) camp is the dividing line. Couples become estranged. Parents and children stop talking to each other. Families and friends try to avoid mentioning politics over the dinner table but often fail.

Many of my friends, especially those with families, are planning to emigrate – driven by fears that their children will have to grow up in a society where Hong Kong's core values are lost. As schools across the city have been suspended over the past few days, Hong Kong's rigorously academically drilled children are enjoying rare days of free play in parks. I don't know whether I should laugh or cry when I see them play 'black cops' and 'protesters' and throwing 'tear gas' at each other. I guess the recent unrest has already made an indelible mark on them and will remain in their memories for the rest of their lives.

It's particularly poignant given that most people in Hong Kong are the children or grandchildren of refugees who fled China during war, famine or political upheaval. My own grandparents fled with their seven children in a crowded train to Hong Kong in 1949, just months before the Communist party took control of China. My father recounted how they slept on tables and chairs at a school when they first arrived.

The international metropolis and regional financial hub we see today was built in just decades after the second world war through the hard work of my forebears, and refugees like them. Just a generation or two later, will their offspring have to flee again?

The majority of Hongkongers, especially the young, cannot afford to emigrate. And they know very well that China is a powerful regime that they have no means to fight against.

I have asked many protesters why they continue to engage in endless street battles with the police where they only get injured and arrested – with riot charges carrying a maximum sentence of 10 years – when there is little hope of winning further concessions. I asked whether they have considered that, after five months of resistance, the escalated actions have given the authorities justification to impose draconian policies and Hong Kong people are left with less civil freedom than we had to start with.

They say peaceful protests have got them nowhere and they are not afraid of sacrificing their lives in one last fight for Hong Kong. 'If we burn, we burn together!' many say. 'Hong Kong is dying anyway, so we might as well make a last struggle.'

I was pained by their hopelessness but I warned them that history is full of examples of violent revolutions overthrowing one dictatorship, only to see it replaced by another.

'So what is your solution then?' they asked. I was speechless.

21 NOVEMBER

The toxic prince: how one question in a TV debate sealed Andrew's fate

ESTHER ADDLEY AND BEN QUINN

After years successfully shrugging off questions about his judgment, his business relationships and, more seriously, his association with the sex offender Jeffrey Epstein, Prince Andrew was finally undone not by a newspaper headline or law enforcer but by a woman called Sue from Leeds.

It was Sue – whose surname is as yet unknown – who submitted a question to ITV's leaders' debate on Monday, asking: 'Is the monarchy fit for purpose?' Julie Etchingham, chairing the debate involving Jeremy Corbyn and Boris Johnson, put the question to the party leaders. And with that, the *Guardian* has learned, the fate of the Duke of York was sealed. It was one thing for news commentators and Twitter observers, following the prince's calamitous interview on Saturday with *BBC Newsnight*, to savage his performance, to call his position untenable. But the moment when the value of the monarchy itself was challenged in a general election debate was the point when Buckingham Palace could stand by no longer. The debate was the critical tipping point at which it finally became clear that the Duke of York had to be jettisoned.

On Tuesday, as universities, charities and firms distanced themselves from the prince and his charity-linked activities, Andrew met the Queen at the palace, where he was told his role as an active, publicly funded royal was over 'for the foreseeable future'. He issued the statement in his own name, maintaining the fiction that he had requested the demotion himself – a shaming instance of the royal crest on paper appearing above the name of a sex offender, since Epstein was named in his statement. But no informed observer believes this was something that Andrew either wanted or would have submitted to very willingly.

By the following day the palace was rowing back somewhat, saying Andrew would continue in his association with the business mentoring initiative Pitch@Palace as a private individual. Quite how an organisation that explicitly trades on the prince's royal residences could be operated as a private enterprise is something which, palace insiders conceded, had yet to be worked out. One idea considered was that rooms might be hired in palaces such as Blenheim or Eltham that were not owned by the crown.

Even as scrutiny of the prince's actions intensified after the death of Epstein in August and a wave of further allegations arose against the billionaire, Andrew saw no reason to scale back his activities. Within the royal households' army of more than 1,000 staff, the prince had been building a small fiefdom, which had been planning as recently as last week to take on new employees to help drive forward a focus on technology. The office is still advertising a role for a project assistant with a background in technology to work on the Inspiring Digital Enterprise Award (iDEA) initiative, which has now been thrown into doubt since BT said it was reviewing its involvement. The prince's office has also been looking in recent weeks for designers to work on the brief. The recruits would join what is described as a 'dedicated team of professionals' who manage the prince's official programme and initiatives founded by him. Central to the team has been his private secretary, Amanda Thirsk, a former banker who joined his office in 2012 and is seen as the driving force behind the *Newsnight* interview.

The prince's confidence in his position may lie in part with the way he has been indulged in the past. In March 2011, as controversy over his association with Epstein swirled, prompting questions in parliament over his suitability as a British trade envoy, the Queen responded by awarding him a knight grand cross of the Royal Victorian Order, the highest possible honour for 'personal service' to the monarch.

Ingrid Seward, editor of *Majesty* magazine, said: 'Andrew was born in 1960 and was the second in line to the throne after his brother for 22 years, until the birth of Prince William. That's a long time to be a pampered favourite child and a prince and war hero. And I think he slightly got it into his head that he could do what he liked.'

His abrupt removal from public life is not an indication of the Queen's waning affection, observers said, but of the reality of where power lies inside the household. 'He was sacked and he didn't go willingly,' said Peter Hunt, the former BBC royal correspondent, 'and even though the Queen will have handed him the royal equivalent of a P45, the form was filled out by Prince Charles. I see Charles as absolutely the driving force behind it.'

Palace protocol might insist the Queen is behind all significant decisions, noted Hunt, but with the monarch now 93 years old, Charles was in effect the shadow king. 'Charles would absolutely have been front and centre in that decision,' Hunt said. 'Fundamentally, Prince Andrew was toxifying the House of Windsor, and their desperate, desperate hope is that that toxicity will reduce over time. But they are not in control of events – that is the crucial thing.'

2 DECEMBER

Clive James and Jonathan Miller trusted our wits

JOHN MULLAN

Death is usually good for sales. The assistants in the largest London branch of Waterstones report that, last Wednesday afternoon, almost all the fairly small stock of books by Clive James disappeared from the shelves. It was as if a certain generation of readers had suddenly remembered how entertaining he was. The coincidence of his death being reported on the same day as that of Jonathan Miller (though in fact they died three days apart) struck many as significant. As a letter to this newspaper put it, 'In a world increasingly populated by charlatans and idiots, we have just lost two outstanding, intelligent, funny and talented individuals in one day.'

Were they the last representatives of a special kind of public intellectual, the polymath as entertainer? There are still plenty of public intellectuals, but they are not often funny and not so often on TV. What James and Miller shared was a habit of cultural irreverence that was only possible because of their love of culture. Both flourished in part because British TV at the time had more confidence in the wits of its viewers.

And what did the schedule, as reported by James the TV critic, look like? An hour-long interview with Harold Pinter rubs elbows with a report on the lyrics of leading contenders in the Eurovision song contest. A Ken Russell film about Wordsworth and Coleridge is found more absurd and less entertaining than an episode of the current affairs programme *Nationwide* featuring child impersonators. Of course, it took James to find the incongruities. Analysis of the latest episode of *Dallas* (of whose delicious absurdities he was a connoisseur) would be illustrated by an epigraph from Nietzsche. And through it all James's prose had a kind of deadpan poetry in which you always heard his voice.

TV made them famous for their voices and their faces and their bodies: James, a genial retired prop forward; Miller, a performance artist of long, tangled limbs. Watching Miller in *The Body in Question* convey lessons about medicine and health even as he sickeningly experienced increased gravity in a looping plane, you wondered whether the comic aspects were intentional or not. He was confident that TV could give us Shakespeare or a multi-part inquiry into the nature of language or an engaging history of atheism. James, the natural TV aficionado, ended up seeming more doubtful. His 1995 address to the Royal Television Society was titled 'Bring Back the Overqualified'. You get the drift.

None of the undergraduates whom I asked last week had heard of either man – but that is hardly surprising. Clive James and Jonathan Miller lived for the fizz of their own cultural moment. Miller's productions of plays and operas live on in the memories of those who saw them. You can read James's collections of TV reviews today, but if you read them first in the newspaper then they have done their work. If the two men belonged to a lost age of 'the overqualified', it was because both knew enough to think that they were hardly qualified at all.

John Mullan is professor of English at University College London.

4 December

Bishop Auckland weighs a once unthinkable Tory revolution

JULIAN COMAN

Four years ago in Shildon, County Durham, Michael O'Neill stumbled upon a long-forgotten piece of local heritage. In a corner of the small town's railway museum, tucked away in storage and forgotten, was an old Bishop Auckland Railway Union banner, believed to date to 1915. A classic of its genre, this piece of labour movement iconography depicts uniformed railway workers gazing towards a utopian future. Below is a version of the final paragraph of *The Communist Manifesto*: 'Workers of the world unite! You have nothing to lose but your chains. You have a world to win.'

O'Neill, 44, is from Bishop Auckland. Over the years he has been involved in numerous community projects, most recently raising funds for a memorial to Cpl Lee Brownson, a local boy who was killed in Afghanistan in 2010. Through his efforts, the railwaymen's banner is now proudly on display at the Four Clocks Centre, alongside a small exhibition telling the story of the world's first steam locomotive railway line, which passed through the area.

For a lifelong Labour voter, this was an act of loving commemoration. But in less than two weeks, O'Neill will vote Conservative. 'I've been a Labour member and my family has always voted Labour,' he says, 'but the party around here has turned nasty in my opinion since the Brexit referendum. I voted to leave, but leave voters are being called racist and far right, which is not how it is. We have a local Labour MP in Helen Goodman who should be standing up for democracy. It shouldn't matter that she voted remain.'

The significance of what would amount to a political revolution in the town everyone calls 'Bishop' is not lost on him: 'Ten years ago, a Conservative MP wouldn't get the time of day on the doorstep around here. This place is steeped in memories of the Thatcher era and the mines and the steelworks. But I'm not alone in turning against Labour.'

Last week, the most comprehensive poll of the election campaign so far predicted that Goodman's majority of 502 over the Conservatives will be swept away on 12 December, which would make 25-year-old Dehenna Davison the first Tory ever to represent the area. Bishop Auckland voted 61 per cent in favour of leave and Davison's Twitter handle incorporates the Boris Johnson mantra: 'Get Brexit done'. Though a Brexit party candidate is standing, the seat is regarded as a two-horse race.

In a region that feels its collective voice and concerns have been ignored since the mines closed and other industries went the same way, Labour leave voters saw Brexit as carrying the possibility of social renewal. The failure of the party to full-throatedly endorse the referendum result is seen by former supporters like O'Neill as both dishonourable and as a sign the party has moved away from its working-class roots. Goodman's much-diminished majority – in 2005, it was over 10,000 – also suggests that Labour is paying the price of long-term local incumbency in an era of deepening disillusionment.

From Bishop Auckland itself to the former mining town of Spennymoor and the surrounding pit villages, this constituency was part of one of the richest, most culturally vibrant coalfields in Europe. Twenty-five years after the last pit closed, there is a palpable longing to restore a lost sense of purpose and cohesion, and an anger at the way that the infrastructure of communal life has been allowed to corrode and decay.

The high street, one of Britain's longest, has been in steep decline for a while. This month, Bernadette Rush will vacate No 136, where she has run Image, a bridal shop, for eight years. 'There's been a huge dip in sales,' she says. 'People are either buying online or from out-of-town suppliers who are manufacturing dresses offshore.' For the past few years, Rush has made her living from making alterations to dresses bought elsewhere. She now plans to work from home, reducing her overheads.

In the town centre, 20 per cent of business units are vacant, including the distinguished Victorian co-op building which, until 2017, housed a Beales department store. The site has recently been earmarked for either a hotel or apartments. The huge fascia carrying the famous old name has been removed, exposing rotting wooden slats.

Like many other locals, Rush hopes a singular turn of events might yet change Bishop's fortunes. Last month, Auckland Castle, the medieval home of the Prince Bishops of Durham, was opened to the public. It displays masterpieces by the Spanish artist Francisco de Zurbarán, which have hung in the castle since 1756. Visitors can also see Nicolas Poussin's *The Triumph of Pan*, on loan from the National Gallery.

The Auckland Project is the £150 million brainchild of Jonathan Ruffer, a City investor from Stokesley, near Middlesbrough. Ruffer bought the Zurbaráns from the church commissioners, the body that manages Church of England assets. As well as restoring the castle, he is regenerating the adjacent marketplace, where a miners' art gallery and a 29-metre viewing tower were opened last year. A Spanish art gallery, in homage to Zurbarán, is planned and the market square's pubs have been bought and closed, prior to conversion into hotels and restaurants. Ruffer has also funded the annual Kynren, a lavish outdoor pageant chronicling 2,000 years of English history.

The tower, in particular, has been greeted with bemusement by some. But in the Fifteas Vintage Tea Room, which looks out on Auckland Tower, John Phelan is happy to sing Ruffer's praises. Phelan is a local historian who lives in Howden-le-Wear, four miles away in the neighbouring constituency of North West Durham. 'He's turning Bishop Auckland into a place of culture … History might be the new thing to bring some hope and a feeling of community back to Bishop.'

A sense of renewal, he says, is desperately required. This year Phelan is sending out Christmas cards which carry a photograph of the FA Amateur Cup final in 1954, when Bishop played their local rivals, Crook Town, in front of a Wembley crowd of 100,000. His father took him, aged four, to the match on a train that went directly from Crook to London. But these days, Phelan says, echoing a theme that comes up continually in the area, the local transport possibilities are very different. 'The buses have been cut and you barely get any after six o'clock. That impacts on people's lives. There are villages that are practically cut off in the evening now, for people who don't drive. And the cuts to street lighting have meant that rural areas are pitch-black at night. I know a woman who is frightened to walk her dogs because it gets so dark. Austerity has chipped away at the quality of life.'

He will vote Labour but is not holding out much hope. 'I won't be surprised if the Conservatives tip it … I tell people who are thinking of voting Conservative, "You're shooting yourself in the foot. Look at the cuts! The Conservative governments haven't done anything for this area." But the Brexit issue has been very bad. If I'd have voted for Brexit I'd be angry with Labour. They've dillied and dallied on it. It's been weak. A Labour leader should have said: "People have voted to leave and that's it."'

Whether that would have won the vote of Ryan Lamb, a 23-year-old labourer from Spennymoor, is doubtful. Lamb voted leave in 2016 and Conservative a year later. He intends to do so again this time, though he has no faith in the pledges being made on either side. 'They all talk a load of shite,' he says. 'I don't believe Boris Johnson is going to put my wages up. I don't believe he's going to put more money into the NHS. But Corbyn's crap. Someone sent me a Piers Morgan interview on Facebook. He showed Corbyn up. In the end, we were meant to leave on Halloween and we didn't. It comes down to that.'

Andrew Smith is an 80-year-old former National Union of Mineworkers activist who worked at the Mainsforth and Ferryhill pits. He now volunteers at Spennymoor's mining museum, sometimes assisted by 81-year-old Ernie Foster, who was also active in the union. Smith views the election, and the fraying of loyalty to Labour, with sadness. 'It makes you angry,' he says, 'it makes you frustrated that people who have gone through the times that you went through are thinking like this. It's not just the young. It takes a lot to get through to people, to explain what the real problems are. The media don't help with their bias, people say they don't like Corbyn. But when you ask them, they don't really know why.'

A December election is not ideal for octogenarian activists: 'We'd like to get out leafleting,' says Smith. 'But we're getting on now.' Foster chips in: 'The main thing is that we can't have that lot in round here – the Tories. That can't be allowed.'

4 DECEMBER

What I've learned from 10,000 nights at the theatre

MICHAEL BILLINGTON

What has changed? Are things better or worse? These are the questions I am asked constantly as I prepare to give up my job as a nightly aisle-squatter after some 10,000 nights at the theatre. They are difficult to answer. British theatre is incredibly resilient, yet radically different from when I took up my post at the *Guardian* in 1971. Even the job of being a critic has altered in all sorts of ways.

When I joined the paper, a review was normally transmitted in one of two ways. Either you rushed back to the office straight after a show and banged out your copy on a typewriter by 11pm, or you frantically sought a working phone box and spelled out your 350 words to an easily bored copy-taker. (This helps to explain why my predecessor woke up one morning to find his review of *The Merchant of Venice* featured a character called Skylark.) Now, you tap out the review on a laptop and it whizzes through the ether in a fraction of a second. The deadline has also shifted – unless the show is extremely hot news, as when a Cumberbatch or Branagh plays Hamlet – to 9.30 the morning after the first night. That means I seem to write much of the review in my sleep, something that may not come as a surprise to regular readers.

But if the process – and the people who write the reviews – has changed, the role of the critic remains much the same: you still have to describe, interpret and evaluate a theatrical event for readers who were not there and may have no chance of going. You are not writing for scholars, posterity or the cast of the show, although it would be nice if they all read your words. You are addressing that morning's reader with as much clarity and elegance as you can muster, and seeking to put a transient event in its theatrical and social context. It is a constant challenge that has kept me going for nearly half a century and that has left me feeling that all you can do, in Samuel Beckett's words, is 'fail better'.

If the critic's role has several constants but has changed in multiple ways, the same goes for the theatre. Some things have got better, some worse. If I had to pick out one thing I regret, it would be the virtual disappearance of the regional rep company. Time was when many theatres boasted a permanent ensemble: the most famous was the Liverpool Everyman of the 1970s, when Julie Walters, Bill Nighy, Jonathan Pryce, Antony Sher and Pete Postlethwaite were part of a dazzling troupe. Financial constraints and cultural fragmentation make it hard to assemble that kind of team today.

I would rather, however, accentuate the positive. One thing that has emerged in my lifetime is the move towards gender equality. In the first year of my job, I salivated at the prospect of reviewing new plays by Tom Stoppard, Edward Bond, Alan Bennett, David Storey and Alan Ayckbourn. One fact was obvious: they were all men. One of the first features I wrote asked why there were so few female playwrights. I blush now to reread the piece, which offered all kinds of phoney explanations, but at least I felt I was posing the right question. It is one that seems redundant today. I would attribute that partly to Caryl Churchill, who, from early work such as *Owners* and *Objections to Sex and Violence*, has acted as a guiding light to aspiring dramatists.

Gender equality now affects casting, too. There have long been striking examples of gender-flipping. I saw Frances de la Tour play

Hamlet in 1980; other performers of the moody Dane include Angela Winkler, Maxine Peake and Ruth Negga, with Cush Jumbo still to come. I have also seen, and admired, Kathryn Hunter and Glenda Jackson as King Lear, as well as a number of single-sex productions, such as the recent *Richard II* at the Sam Wanamaker Playhouse in London, cast entirely with women of colour.

It may be a reflection of my age, but I find an inflexible quota system, with a 50/50 gender split, more problematic, especially in Shakespeare. A play such as *Troilus and Cressida*, which explores the latent homoeroticism of male combat, loses more than it gains from gender parity, as a recent RSC production proved. I am, however, always open to persuasion.

What I have no hesitation in saying is that greater sexual equality has given criticism a long-overdue shake-up. When I started out, the theatre critics were like a travelling male club, trundling from stall to stall in baggy, egg-stained suits. Today, on any first night, you will see as many female critics as men. I once had the temerity to ask a female colleague if she thought gender made a difference: she suggested that reviews by women were more impressionistic, those by men more conventionally linear. Be that as it may, the glass ceiling in criticism has cracked irrevocably. What is sorely lacking is critics of colour, which is why the appointment of Arifa Akbar as my successor takes on extra significance.

In the theatre at large, diversity has made huge advances. There have always been outstanding plays by writers of colour: take *Moon on a Rainbow Shawl* by Errol John, *Skyvers* by Barry Reckord and *Play Mas* by Mustapha Matura. What is striking today is that plays by BAME writers are taking place on main stages, are wide-ranging in theme and derive from a large talent pool: I could make a long list, but Bola Agbaje, Gurpreet Kaur Bhatti, Tanika Gupta, debbie tucker green, Kwame Kwei-Armah and Roy Williams represent a rising new generation.

There would be shock and outrage today if you saw a classic revival with an all-white cast. The days when black actors were confined, in Shakespeare, to playing Othello or Aaron the Moor in *Titus Andronicus* are long gone. I have seen actors such as Sophie Okonedo, Sharon D Clarke, Cecilia Noble, Hugh Quarshie, Adrian Lester, David Oyelowo and Chiwetel Ejiofor prove they can play anything and everything. All this represents real progress.

I am often asked how playwriting has changed in my time. The most radical change has been in dramatic form. When I started out, there was a rough consensus as to what constituted a play. Admittedly, some writers were pushing the envelope: Ayckbourn showed in *How the Other Half Loves* that you could put overlapping action in two households on to a single stage; John McGrath in *The Cheviot, the Stag and the Black, Black Oil* used the form of a ceilidh to promote a message about the exploitation of Scotland's resources.

Who today can say, with total and unshakeable confidence, what a play is? Harold Pinter pointed the way, showing in *One for the Road* (1984) that in slightly more than 30 minutes you could offer as powerful a portrait of tyranny as anything in Arthur Koestler. Now, the pungent one-act piece that provides a metaphor for the wider world is everywhere: Churchill's *Far Away*, Mike Bartlett's *Cock*, Sarah Kane's *4.48 Psychosis* and Jez Butterworth's *The River*, to name just a few. What is true of Britain is also true of the US. F Scott Fitzgerald said there are no second acts in American lives and now there are few second acts in American plays.

Yet you can immediately contradict that by pointing to our corresponding appetite for the inordinate. Matthew Lopez's *The Inheritance* is in two parts, lasting six and a half hours. Butterworth can also write long, as he proved in *Jerusalem* and *The Ferryman*. Right now, April De Angelis's two-part version of Elena Ferrante's *My Brilliant Friend* is playing at the National Theatre.

The old rule that a play was an event lasting 150 minutes, with an interval, has been thrown out of the window. Today, form follows function; a play can be as long or as short as its subject dictates.

One of the pleasures of a critic's job – as well as one of its greatest challenges – is trying to describe performances. I have been lucky to have seen some unforgettable ones. It is impossible to list them all, but I would like to mention a few that remain part of my imperishable memory: John Wood, and later Tom Hollander, relishing the intellectual acrobatics of Henry Carr in Stoppard's *Travesties*; Ian McKellen and Judi Dench as the Macbeths in Trevor Nunn's grippingly intimate production; Eileen Atkins as the fiercely independent Maddy Rooney in Beckett's *All That Fall*; Maggie Smith capturing the piercing recollections, as well as the moral evasiveness, of the heroine in *A German Life*; Simon Russell Beale conveying the troubled testiness of Shakespeare's Prospero and Mark Rylance the whimsical passion of Olivia; Paapa Essiedu and David Tennant both highlighting the quick-wittedness and humour of Hamlet in different RSC productions. I could go on and on. One of British theatre's prime assets is its ability to produce, decade after decade, new generations of exciting actors.

I count myself lucky to have been witness to an amazing period in British theatre. I shall probably go on haunting play-houses until I fall off my perch. We hear a lot about the death of criticism, but I believe passionately in its unending mission to record, interpret and evaluate what happens on stages. The means of communication may change in the light of evolving technology, but the function remains the same. I have been priv-ileged to do the job for the past 48 years, but, as I move from the world of daily deadlines to that of periodic commentary, I can only wish my successor the same good fortune I have enjoyed. In the words of Hector in Bennett's *The History Boys*, I am happy to pass the parcel.

13 December

This was a stunning victory for the bullshit-industrial complex

MARINA HYDE

Well. A new dawn has shat, has it not? Shortly after 7am, Boris Johnson slipped into the costume Dominic Cummings has been sewing for him out of the skins of missing statesmen. 'I am humbled that you have put your trust in me,' announced the nation's foremost liar in front of a backdrop reading 'the people's government', as though this ideally axiomatic concept was an innovation.

With the emphasis on 'a sacred trust', this government's senior personnel are immediately keen to stress it will be a servant of the people. I assume the specific servant it's modelled on is Paul Burrell. They've already dragged the Queen into it, and will soon begin amassing the nation's property in their attic 'for safekeeping'. Brexit will be done for Christmas, with Johnson scoring a stunning victory for the bullshit-industrial complex. From the outset, the Tories decided it was more effective to pretend you're listening to people who have doubts about you, than to invite them to fuck off and join the Labour party. But hey – everyone's a strategist after the event.

In financial news, the pound pounded exuberantly to its money shot, and I imagine there were big moves on the US chlorine markets. Back in Westminster, the UK's prime minister took to the podium like a gelatinous Sith, introduced by Michael Gove as part of the Conservative scheme to rehabilitate former knife-wielders. Three and a half years ago, Michael was telling the world that Boris Johnson was unfit for leadership; now he was giving a community theatre performance worthy of *The League of Gentlemen*'s troupe, Legz Akimbo. Solemnly, Gove announced that Britain's Jews 'should never have to live in fear again'. Britain's Muslims, not so much, given the prime minister's multiple racisms on that and other fronts, and a grotesque TV riff merely hours earlier on burqa-wearing fighter pilots, from the world's worst stage dad, Stanley Johnson.

Still, where there is discord, let Boris sow his wild oats. And then leave you to raise them. The point is: Johnson is world king now. And so to what happens next.

The Tory programme for government was not so much a manifesto as a Mumsnet 'Am I being unreasonable?' thread. It also stopped after the first year, with the only clue for Act 2 being plans for voter suppression, and the so-called page 48 material, paving the way for the government to dismantle judicial and even parliamentary constraints on itself. As for the 2019 Tory intake, you may find yourself gripped by a hunch that the party has spent about 15 minutes vetting half the newbies, whose moral eccentricities will gradually unfurl themselves to us like so many exquisite lotus blossoms.

Johnson announced his intention to bring the country back together, presumably by walling us in and forcing us to till his sunlit uplands. Speaking of which, Ashfield was won by a Tory named Lee Anderson, who put out a video during the campaign stating that 'nuisance' council tenants should be made to live in tents in the middle of a field, where they would be woken at 6am and forced to pick vegetables until the end of the day, when they'd get a cold shower, then 'back in the tent'. Labour came third – THIRD – here.

A historic triumph for the Tories, then. Less so for the others, bar of course the SNP. Even hopes that Dominic Raab would soon be spending more time with the contents of his lock-up were misplaced. For their part, Labour line-takers were keen to concentrate on the differences between the 2017 and 2019 elections, but would arguably benefit more from accepting the similarities. Which are that they lost both times. This one was the real bed-shitter, though. Jeremy Corbyn has announced he will not fight the next election, but will stay in post to preside over the process of dealing with its fallout. This feels a bit like BP pitching for the contract to clean up the Gulf of Mexico after the Deepwater Horizon spill.

Unfortunately, Corbyn's promise of a 'period of reflection' did not seem to be politician-speak for looking at himself in the mirror. Instead, a period of reflection led by a man who hasn't changed his mind since 1970 seems an inevitable act of political Dadaism.

In reality, though, the timing doesn't much matter, with the scale of this victory likely to take a decade to turn around. Corbynism has turned out to be for the very, very few. Which is to say, nobody at all. Yet. There was some talk this morning of it being a 30-year project, suggesting the plan will come to glorious fruition just in time for the moment we're living, *Children of Men*-style, in Britain's catacombs. At that point, Corbynism will sweep to power with an ambitious programme of nationalising the urine distilleries via which we obtain our drinking water. If you totally agree they shouldn't be in the hands of the private militias, make a calendar note to get very excited about this bold and transformative vision in 2045.

Today? Well, according to a range of senior Labour figures, 'the real fight starts now'. No rush, of course – though it would be nice to get a heads-up on whether they think it'll be a fight for medicines or fuel. On the other hand, some people are just about beginning to tire of Labour fights starting after the knockout, when someone else has won the belt, and the party's woken up in the head-trauma unit.

18 DECEMBER

My father paid four times his weekly wage for the greatest gift of my life

PETER WHITE

It's eight o'clock on Christmas morning, and Uncle Tom wants to hear the news. My 11-year-old self is wondering why on earth grownups want to hear the news on Christmas Day when there are vital things to be done, such as handing out presents. And then, while I am only half-listening, something weird happens: the Greenwich time pips start. Surely we have already heard those? And then the boring man with the plummy voice begins going on about a Christmas message to the world from the Vatican. Surely that's been on already, too?

It's my older brother, Colin, who gets it! 'Pete, Pete, it's a tape recorder, you idiot! We've got our tape recorder.'

The penny drops: Uncle Tom and my dad have recorded the headlines, and are playing them back.

I think it's often quite rare to experience real excitement over a present: in my experience, children are as good as adults at knowing what is expected of them and simulating joyful surprise, even when they don't feel it. But for me this was one of those rare moments when my insides gave an involuntary lurch and the world did a little somersault.

Colin and I had both been blind from birth, and at this point were spending most of our time at a special boarding school, Worcester College for the Blind (now called New College

Worcester). In the late 1950s, Britain had just reached the point when exciting consumer goods were coming within reach of the not-really-rich, and at Worcester reel-to-reel tape recorders were definitely the consumer gizmos of choice. For blind kids, they would trump cameras every time, especially at this moment when rock'n'roll was more of a religion than a pastime. For us, you could identify the better-off kids not by the clothes they wore, or the holidays they boasted about, but by the tape recorders they owned. So, in our class, Iain Hopkin was marked out as something of a plutocrat by his Brenell recorder. Still, a recorder of your own was the height of aspiration, and Colin – more realistic about family finances than me – had no real expectations.

I realised, much later, that at this time my dad, a very good joiner and carpenter, was probably earning about £8 a week. The tape recorder my parents had bought us, although nowhere near top-of-the-range, would have cost more than four times his weekly wage. My parents could only afford it by borrowing the money from Uncle Tom, who had a thriving grocery business. Family or not, I know my mum and dad would have thought long and hard before incurring the debt.

The new toy, mains-powered and the size of a small suitcase, dominated the rest of Christmas Day and the remainder of the holidays. Once we had mastered the controls, we recorded everything in sight: each other, our parents, the milkman, the dog ... And we very quickly learned the fun to be had at catching people unawares.

Uncle Tom, at whose house we were staying over the holiday, got an early reward for his generous loan. Some friends he regarded as a little pretentious were coming over for Boxing Day; my aunt and uncle always referred to the husband as 'the mayor of Romford'. (Whether that was because he was or just talked as if he was, I'm not sure I ever learned.) Uncle Tom was keen Bill should be made to listen to his chirpy cockney accent, which he claimed he didn't have. (Things like this mattered 60 years ago.) My task was to record them when they arrived and then at a quiet moment play it back to set Bill straight. Delighted to be trusted in this adult conspiracy of inverted snobbery, I set the machine going as they came up the path. The reaction was more than Uncle Tom could have hoped for; I think he decided at that point that his £30-odd investment had already been more than repaid.

It wasn't the first time I had been entranced by a tape recorder. I vividly remember, aged four, coming into a room and hearing a child singing, tunelessly, and raucously. I stopped dead. 'It's you,' Dad said. 'Noisy, aren't you?' I didn't understand. It turned out that he'd borrowed a tape recorder because he and some friends were writing and performing songs and sketches for his former school's annual concert. And so, for the first time, in the same way that a sighted child might react to seeing themselves in a mirror or a photograph, I got the sense of myself as a separate person, existing outside my head and experienced by other people. It was exciting and embarrassing – not a bad summing-up of my later life as a broadcaster.

I really took my first steps down that path when I got back to school after the holidays ended. I was lucky to be in a class of imaginative and creative boys (yes, sadly, Worcester was single-sex then) and it wasn't long before – all of us radio-obsessed – we started to make our own embryo radio programmes. While studio managers at the BBC were still banging coconuts together to represent horses' hooves, we were using the little oblong pieces of lead we needed to represent numbers when doing sums to recreate shrapnel for our first world war battles. And very effective they were, dropped on to a desk from a great height.

Meanwhile, I would wander round the school, commenting in the voices of my radio idols – the hushed, reverential tones of Richard Dimbleby, the gravel-voiced war correspondent René Cutforth and, favourite of all, the mellow Hampshire burr of John Arlott.

Most of what I described was pure imagination, although occasionally we would stage real events to heighten the excitement. Particularly memorable was a boxing match between Mick and Geoff (respectively the strongest and the gamest boys in the class, both totally blind. The commentary came from the only one of us with a little bit of sight, in a very passable imitation of the boxing commentator Raymond Glendenning). The strong boy beat the game boy, by the way.

The acquisition of the tape recorder coincided with the formation of our own band: Reg Webb, Andy Woods and – yes – Peter White, imaginatively called the W Brothers and destined to be the greatest group ever, had not the Beatles come along and pinched our best material. Reg and Andy were good musicians, and went on to have professional careers. I wasn't in their musical class, but made up for it with what I thought at the time was my witty banter to introduce our songs. At one of our concerts a girl actually screamed – although it could have been that someone trod on her foot.

In fact, the biggest challenge was not finding things to do with the tape recorder but wrestling it away from Colin – it was, after all, a joint present. His generosity on the first day we got it did not extend to his handing it over to his ham-fisted brother at school. I can still hear the phrases: 'You'll break it; you'll lose it; you'll scramble up all the tapes.' And, annoyingly, I did do all of those things. On one fraught occasion, trying in front of an open window to disentangle the hopelessly knotted tape that contained my latest radio gem, I managed to get yards of the stuff enmeshed in an overhanging tree.

But 10 years later, by which time I had begun and abandoned a university law course, it was the confidence gained from those early excursions into sound that had me walking into the local radio station in Southampton, trying to sell myself as the next Robin Day. It all nearly ended there, as the receptionist told me there were no vacancies, and that I'd have to apply to the BBC in London 'through the normal channels'.

Luck intervened. A producer charged with putting together a weekly programme for blind people saw me and my white cane being ushered into the lift. As I prepared to hitchhike my disillusioned way back to university, he rang me at home, and asked if I would go back to Southampton to see him.

Twenty-five years after that, I presented my first report for BBC TV's *Six O'Clock News*, a date with the telly my dad had never missed. Although by then he'd been dead for more than a decade, I like to think he'd have realised that his inspired Christmas present really had not just changed, but shaped my life.

Peter White is the BBC's disability affairs correspondent.

19 DECEMBER

2019 wasn't just protests and *Fleabag*: it was the year a climate truth bomb dropped

BRIGID DELANEY

When I think about 2019, there is one scene that springs to mind, something that sums up the milieu so perfectly that it almost seems art-directed.

There we were two weeks ago at Rose Bay on the water's edge, waiting for a private boat to take us to a harbourside mansion for a wine tasting. It was one of those days when Sydney's air quality was among the worst in the world. The boat emerged from the pea soup gloom with the letters 'VIP' on the side. We were all in our party dresses and chunky trainers, phones fully charged to maximise the Instagrammable location, only coughing a little bit, although people's eyes were red and I noticed some fellow guests pulling on Ventolin inhalers.

At the mansion there was a DJ, sommeliers and a chef, who explained in great detail the origin of the scallops on the canapes and a recent, inspirational trip to Oaxaca. Later there was a wine tasting where we gathered around to swirl and spit. Every varietal had notes of bushfire. Various people wandered up to us and said, 'Great day for it!', and 'Beautiful weather', without irony.

How could they say that? The sun was (there was only one word for it) demonic, a burning red eye in a thick smoky sky. The Sydney Harbour Bridge and the Opera House were out there ... somewhere, obscured in a brown haze.

We stood near the pool, eating tiny food, drinking wine from large balloon glasses while ash flew from the sky, some of it landing in my drink. The DJ played on but the tunes – Tones and I, Mark Ronson – were nervy, jangly and strangely discordant. The smell of the smoke had an almost chemical taint, and in between trying the pinot and moving on to the tempranillo, I wondered about the alchemy at work in this commingling of the elements: the ancient forests and its animals turned to columns of ash, collapsed and drifting through the air, settling on the water and soil; and later in and on my body after swimming in the dirty sea that morning and now swallowing particles of ash floating in my wine at the party on the harbour's edge. ('At the end of the world,' my friend and I nervously joked.)

More wine was poured and more people commented on the great weather (except for a sommelier who confessed sotto voce that he felt afraid), and influencers posed in the gloom on the jetty and by the swimming pool, seeing but refusing to see what was all around them: this red-raw sun, that dirty brown sky.

The cognitive dissonance would have been funny had I not been so scared. It brought to mind F Scott Fitzgerald, a writer who understood more than most that decadent parties prefigure societal collapse. Had his novel *The Great Gatsby* been written now, the scene that day in Point Piper would not be out of place.

Returning to shore in the haze, we could have been excused for thinking we were crossing the Styx – the mystical Greek crossing into the Underworld – and in this heightened state the day seemed more than the sum of its parts. Instead it served as both an elegy for the lost world that had disappeared beyond the haze and a portent of the world to come.

That is what 2019 has come to mean to me: not the landslide elections and the global protests and *Fleabag* season 2. But the year some undeniable bomb dropped and dispersed its truth all around us in the form of dark particles in the air that didn't just sit around us – but entered our bodies in unholy communion, its fine matter an anti-sustenance that made us sick and afraid.

The truth bomb came in various forms: in the form of a girl (Greta Thunberg) whose eloquent rage finally caught the world's attention and inspired millions around the globe to strike for climate action. The truth also came in the form of heat, smoke and fire. Even then, some people tried to ignore it.

Ernest Hemingway had this famous line from his 1929 book *The Sun Also Rises*, which speaks to me of where things washed up in 2019:

'How did you go bankrupt?' Bill asked.

'Two ways,' Mike said. 'Gradually, then suddenly.'

Two thousand and nineteen is the year of suddenly. Many of us were shaken awake from our cognitive dissonance this year as our weather patterns and climate conditions become ever more extreme. When wine turns to ash in your mouth, you can't deny the new reality any more.

Yet some still live in a land of cognitive dissonance: the lump of coal brought to parliament; the haze over the city obscuring the flashing Christmas lights; dead bats falling from the sky because their sophisticated and highly evolved sonar systems are over-heating and confused; beekeepers being traumatised and needing counselling after hearing the sounds of animals screaming as they burn to death; new types of megafires devouring entire ecosystems; the NSW premier opening a new zoo during these megafires with a commitment to 'protecting wildlife'; and the prime minister disappearing without a word about the climate catastrophe – last seen boarding a business-class Jetstar flight bound for Hawaii; the Instagrammers posing on the jetty under the eye of Sauron, hoping that with the right filters, we can pretend the sky is blue.

Cognitive dissonance is natural – it can make you feel safer, like the world is a more orderly, stable place than the reality, which is chaos. The end of this year makes me wonder how much during the years prior we have been engaged in uninten-tional acts of disassociation and dissonance. Maybe we had to, to survive the barrage of nonstop news – the dozen major scandals that emerge each week from Trump's White House, the way that Brexit is important, boring and confusing all at once. It's all too much so we just disassociate.

It's no wonder the hot illegal drug of 2019 – ketamine – is an anaesthetic, numbing your body and making you feel separate from your environment. People disappear, aptly, into the k-hole, the chemical equivalent of our political situation. 'Like you're watching your own life happen instead of living it,' said *New York* magazine, calling it 'the party drug for the end of the world'.

But 2019 was in many ways, for many of us, Year Zero. It was the year many of us stopped disassociating, woke up and realised the party is over.

Winter

Qassem Suleimani's death threatens to open grisly new chapter in Middle East

JULIAN BORGER

In his long military career, Qassem Suleimani left the Middle East littered with corpses. Now he has finally joined them. His death has closed one gruesome chapter in the region's endless conflicts, only to open another, which could well prove even worse. No one can predict how this will turn out.

Nothing about Donald Trump's actions in the Middle East until now suggests that Suleimani's assassination by drone outside Baghdad airport was part of a considered plan. And the leadership in Tehran, for its part, has clearly been shocked by Trump's dramatic leap up the escalation ladder.

In the latest tit-for-tat round of the proxy war in Iraq, an American contractor had been killed in a rocket attack a week ago, triggering retaliatory airstrikes against Iranian-supported militia camps. This in turn led to the storming of the US embassy compound by pro-Iran militiamen, in which no one appears to have been hurt.

The Suleimani killing dispensed with proxies and aimed a direct dagger thrust at the heart of Iranian power. Trump may have thought ordering this hit would bring the same plaudits, with as little blowback, as hunting down Abu Bakr al-Baghdadi, the leader of Islamic State. He would be wrong.

The Isis caliphate had collapsed and its fighters had scattered. The leader of the Revolutionary Guards' Quds force, on the other hand, was a bearded icon of the Islamic Republic, arguably its second most powerful figure after the supreme leader, Ayatollah Ali Khamenei. Killing him was a blunt act of war against a substantial regional power. Its half-million-strong armed services are the most potent military force the US has faced since confronting the Chinese people's volunteer army more than 60 years ago in Korea.

There was nothing inevitable about this conflict. Six years ago the legacy of loathing left by the Islamic Revolution began to fade. There was a multilateral agreement to curb Iran's nuclear programme in 2015, and an unspoken mutual non-aggression pact with Suleimani during the shared campaign against Isis in Syria and Iraq. 'For a while when we were doing counter-Isis operations, we essentially had a gentleman's agreement with him, that his forces wouldn't target us and we wouldn't target him,' said Kirsten Fontenrose, the former senior director for the Gulf in Trump's national security council.

But with Trump's abrogation of the 2015 nuclear deal and the collapse of the Isis caliphate, which largely removed a common foe, it was Suleimani who emerged as the US's arch-enemy. 'He was a target of opportunity,' Fontenrose said.

Fontenrose, now at the Atlantic Council, predicted that, while the Iran-backed militias in Iraq might lash out immediately, in revenge for one of their own top commanders killed alongside Suleimani, Tehran would wait and pick the time, place and manner of its retribution – and then strike again and again. 'I think they'll probably try to hit us in other parts of the world, maybe west Africa, maybe Latin America, to send the message that they could get us anywhere,' she said. 'And I think the US is going to ... try to spread out our assault in a similar way.'

There are few good reasons to assume that this new raised level of conflict, halfway between cold and hot wars, will be stable, and will not erupt into all-out war. Both sides have a long history of misreading each other's intentions.

While the consequences of the killing are unclear, what is almost certain is that Trump has not thought them through. Since his election, the national security decision-making process, by which the pros and cons of US action were once assessed, has been gutted. The independent thinkers in Trump's orbit have left the stage, leaving a president who ultimately trusts his gut instincts above any expert.

It is those instincts, more than any other single factor, that have led the US and Iran to this point, and in particular Trump's visceral hatred of his predecessor, Barack Obama, and his diplomatic legacy, the 2015 nuclear deal. Destruction of the deal and the economic strangulation of Iran became a central imperative of Trumpian foreign policy.

The decision to kill Suleimani is likely to have been made with the US presidential election in November in mind – how it might play as a punchline on the campaign trail, finally eclipsing, perhaps, Obama's conquest of Osama bin Laden. But it will be a story that will almost certainly be told against a backdrop of more attacks, greater uncertainty and a deepening sense of dread.

10 JANUARY

At Davos we will tell world leaders to abandon the fossil fuel economy

GRETA THUNBERG

We have just entered a new decade, where every day will be absolutely crucial in deciding what the future will look like. Towards the end of January, chief executives, investors and policymakers will gather in Davos for the 50th anniversary of the World Economic Forum. Young climate activists and school strikers from around the world will be present to put pressure on these leaders.

We demand that at this year's forum, participants from all companies, banks, institutions and governments immediately halt all investments in fossil fuel exploration and extraction, immediately end all fossil fuel subsidies and immediately and completely divest from fossil fuels.

We don't want these things done by 2050, 2030 or even 2021, we want this done now – as in *right now*.

We understand and know very well that the world is complicated and that what we are asking for may not be easy. But the climate crisis is also extremely complicated, and this is an emergency. In an emergency you step out of your comfort zone and make decisions that may not be very pleasant. And let's be clear – there is nothing easy, comfortable or pleasant about the climate and environmental emergency.

Young people are being let down by older generations and those in power. To some it may seem like we are asking for a lot. But this is just the very minimum of effort needed to start the rapid sustainable transition. The fact that this still – in 2020 – hasn't been done already is, quite frankly, a disgrace.

Yet, since the 2015 Paris agreement, 33 major global banks have collectively poured $1.9 trillion (£1.5 trillion) into fossil fuels. In 2017 alone, the world spent $5.2 trillion subsidising fossil fuels. This has to stop.

The world of finance has a responsibility to the planet, the people and all other species living on it. In fact, it ought to be in every company and stakeholder's interest to make sure the planet they live on will thrive. But history has not shown the corporate world's willingness to hold themselves accountable. So it falls on us, the children, to do that. We call upon the world's leaders to stop investing in the fossil fuel economy. Instead, they should invest in existing sustainable technologies, research and in restoring nature. Short-term profit should not trump long-term stability of life.

The theme of this year's gathering in Davos is 'stakeholders for a cohesive and sustainable world'. According to the forum's website, leaders will meet to discuss ideas and improve our global progress on climate change. Anything less than immediately ceasing investments in the fossil fuel industry would be a betrayal of life itself. Today's business as usual is turning into a crime against humanity. We demand that leaders play their part in putting an end to this madness. Our future is at stake, let that be their investment.

10 JANUARY

In these bleak times, imagine a world where you can thrive

GARY YOUNGE

As a child my mother used to put on the song 'Young, Gifted and Black', by Bob and Marcia, put my feet on hers and then dance us both around the living room. 'They're playing our song,' she'd say. It was the early 1970s, she was barely 30 and I was the youngest of three children she was raising alone. Struggling to believe there was a viable future for her children in a country where racism was on the rise and the economy was in the tank, she had seriously considered returning to Barbados. But after a six-week family trip back she decided we'd struggle to keep up academically: at school in England I played; in Barbados we sat in rows and recited times tables. I think this was partly cover for the fact that, after more than a decade of self-reliance and relative anonymity, fitting back into island life would have been diffi-cult. So we danced around the living room, singing ourselves up: imagining a world in which we would thrive, for which we had no evidence, but great expectations.

In my interview for a *Guardian* Scott Trust bursary to study a postgraduate course in journalism, I was asked what kind of job I would aspire to if I ever got to work at the paper. 'A columnist, like Hugo Young,' I said.

'There's only room for a handful of columnists on a news-paper,' I was told.

'And why shouldn't one of them be me?' I asked.

From another applicant that question might have come from a sense of entitlement. But it was a genuine inquiry. I was merely articulating the logic that had got me that far: imagining a world in which I might thrive for which I had no evidence.

This is my last column. After 26 years as a staff writer and 20 years – on and off – as a columnist, I'm leaving the *Guardian*. In April, I take up a post as professor of sociology at Manchester University. I have not given up journalism. I may appear in this paper (if they'll have me) and others, very occasionally. But I will be liberated from having to have a thought every Thursday, and you will be liberated from having to read or avoid, enjoy or be enraged by them every Friday.

Much of the politics that has informed my writing in this space comes from my mother. It is partly rooted in her experi-ence. She came to Britain just a month after the Commonwealth Immigrants Act 1962 – branded by the then Labour leader Hugh Gaitskell a piece of 'cruel and brutal anti-colour legislation' –

was passed. She came because the then health minister, Enoch Powell, had embarked on a colossal programme of NHS restructuring that required more nurses. She was living proof of the immigrants that the British economy needs but that its political culture is too toxic to embrace. For her, sex, race and class were not abstract identities, but the forces that converged to keep her wages low and her life stressful.

But my politics is also rooted in what she made of those experiences. She was an anti-colonialist and an anti-racist, an internationalist and humanist who would have never used any of those words to describe herself. Race-conscious as she was, most of her community activism – youth clubs, literacy classes, discos in the church hall – took place in the working-class white community. They were her people, too.

She made me stay up and watch the *Holocaust* miniseries (which freaked me out) when I was 10 and took me to watch *Gandhi* (which was way too long) during the holidays when I was 13. Both times she told me: 'This is your story, too.' She believed the world she wanted to create was never going to come to her, so she would have to take the fight to it. I saw her confront the local National Front candidate, the police and her union – to name but a few. She took me on my first rally (Help the Aged) when I was four, my first demonstration (Campaign for Nuclear Disarmament) when I was 14, and first picket (the South African embassy) at 17.

Even in her sudden and untimely death there were valuable lessons: that life is too short to waste time on people you don't care about, but long enough to make a difference if you want to. She was 44; I was 19. She never got to read my columns. My presence on these pages would have been, I think, as unlikely to her as anything else she hoped I might achieve.

No amount of self-image reinforcement could have defied those odds. The space where those politics could be shared and the route through which I would come to it were paved by others whom I didn't know and (mostly) never met. 'Men make their own history,' wrote Karl Marx. 'But they do not make it as they please; they do not make it under self-selected circumstances, but under circumstances existing already, given and transmitted from the past.'

The bursary I was awarded emerged in the early 1990s and was a response to the uprisings among black youth in the 80s. Black people were always in the news, but rarely in the newsrooms. The Scott Trust wanted to offer a correction and so gave bursaries to under-represented groups in journalism. Without it I would have chosen another profession.

In 1999 the Macpherson report, into the racist murder of Stephen Lawrence, made the concept of institutional racism mainstream. That was the year my first column appeared, my first book was published, and Steve McQueen won the Turner prize. The year before, Chris Ofili won the Turner prize; the year after, Zadie Smith's *White Teeth* came out. The relationship between these events was not causal but contextual. This detracts not one iota from their creative abilities or the hard work that made their success possible. (Only the privileged and the naive believe people's achievements are purely the product of their own genius.) It simply acknowledges that there have been others who were similarly able and hardworking for whom space had not been cleared.

'Ingratitude' is the accusation launched by racists at black people in the public eye who have the audacity to highlight the racial injustice they experience. So I'd like to take this opportunity to express my gratitude to the youth who took to the streets, and bereaved families who took to the courts, to make my career possible.

I sign off from this column at a dispiriting time. With racism, cynicism and intolerance on the rise, wages stagnant and faith that progressive change is possible declining even as resistance grows. Things look bleak. The propensity to despair is strong, but should not be indulged. Sing yourself up. Imagine a world in which you might thrive, for which there is no evidence. And then fight for it.

Forget 'wellness'. Marmalade is the key to a long, healthy life

READERS' LETTERS

13 JANUARY

My wife has just made 18lb of marmalade. She is 77 and I am 78. Which of the three of us will last the longest?
Terry Swann, Sheffield

15 JANUARY

Congratulations to Mr and Mrs Swann on their optimism in making marmalade at the ages of 77 and 78. I, too, have just made 18lb. I live on my own and shall be 84 next month. Hope triumphant?
David Hitchin, Welwyn Garden City, Hertfordshire

16 JANUARY

At just 82 years old, after years of delicious homemade Seville orange delight, changed circumstances recently forced the purchase of a single 350g jar of marmalade. Should I be worried or would buying a whole case improve my prospects?
Valerie Lewis, Wantage, Oxfordshire

20 JANUARY

A mere 77-year-old making a piffling 15lb of marmalade (Letters, 17 January), I accidentally sliced into my finger, and as I am on blood thinners and was alone in the house, I did have doubts whether I might not get to the end of the process, or the process might outlive me.

Deb Masters, Portchester, Portsmouth

30 JANUARY

I don't like marmalade. How should I occupy myself in my declining years?

Anne Cowper, Llandeilo Ferwallt, Gower

1 FEBRUARY

Can I join the search to find the oldest marmalade-making *Guardian* readers? At 92 and a half, I have just made enough marmalade to last a year – with help in lifting a heavy jam pan! I use a family recipe older than me, originating in 1926.

Elizabeth Green, Brockenhurst, Hampshire

1 FEBRUARY

Forget printing articles about 'wellness'. It seems that marmalade holds the key to a long, healthy life.

Pat Wakeling, Nottingham

8 FEBRUARY

My dear husband, who at 80-plus makes delicious marmalade (Letters, 7 February), has just labelled this year's batch 'The Last Hurrah'. Oh dear.

Hazel Harrison, Norwich

23 JANUARY

Royals for rent: will Harry and Meghan become the world's biggest influencers?

ELLE HUNT

The Duke and Duchess of Sussex were never going to be king and queen of the United Kingdom. And now they have been relieved of their royal responsibilities, a new empire stretches before them, limitless, lucrative and theirs for the taking: the kingdom of sponsored content.

Thanks to the intense interest in their love story on social media, Prince Harry and Meghan have been dabbling in the 'influencer' space for as long as they have been a couple. Before marrying Harry, Meghan ran the lifestyle/fashion blog The Tig, which gave her one foot in the world of influencers (the name given to the broad church of people who create and often monetise original content on social media). So perhaps it is no surprise that, in April last year, @SussexRoyal broke Instagram's record for the fastest one million followers (less than six hours). Now it has 11 million and is the couple's platform of choice for personal announcements – including the one they made on 8 January, revealing their intention to step back from royal duties (1.85 million likes).

Now that the royal purse strings have been cut, how will they make a living? Monetising their celebrity through brand partnerships, sponsorship deals and social media seems the most likely path. Ted Sarandos, chief content officer for Netflix, summed it up when asked if he would be open to working with them: 'Who wouldn't be interested?'

But not everyone is so sure. Although they have stepped down from their duties, they will still be answerable to the Firm, says Stephen Bates, the *Guardian*'s royal correspondent from 2000 to 2012 and author of *Royalty Inc: Britain's Best-Known Brand*. 'Clearly, they are still royal, but they can't profit from their association – and their association, via their name, is chiefly what they have,' he says. 'All this stuff about huge marketing opportunities, and people talking up "their brand" and how much it will earn them ... Obviously their celebrity will carry them so far – but in a year or two's time, what are they going to do?'

Perhaps Bates's outlook says less about Harry and Meghan's prospects than the gulf between regal precedent and the current influencer economy. With the *Sunday Times* forecasting influencing to be worth £8 billion globally this year, the sky is the limit when it comes to how much someone can make from their social media followers.

The Obamas, who have signed a deal with Netflix, have been pointed to as role models for Harry and Meghan's new life. There is a key difference, though, because part of the reason the former Potus and Flotus were able to secure such lucrative opportunities post-White House was their impressive careers, demonstrable passions and interests.

'Obama wasn't a hereditary president – or, worse, a hereditary president's younger brother,' says Bates. Though Netflix would surely throw money at a real-life *The Crown*, Bates points out that through the 90s, a glut of royal documentaries produced by Prince Edward's television production company caused headaches for the palace. 'I can see a lot of parties with Harry standing in the corner and people saying: "There's the bloke who used to be in the royal family,"' says Bates.

Influencers can be traced back to the 2000s and socialite Paris Hilton. Hilton may have been 'famous for doing nothing' but she made a lot of money doing it, selling everything from handbags to hair extensions. While she was a pioneer, her one-time best friend Kim Kardashian perfected this. Famous for a sex tape, she monetised this through strategic alignments and business savvy to become one of the most famous – and, though you may hate to hear it, most powerful – women in the world.

This is the upper echelon of influencing, where Harry and Meghan will hope to be coming in – joining the Kardashian-Jenner clan, models Gigi and Bella Hadid, pop stars Selena Gomez and Ariana Grande, and the other most-followed people on Instagram. At this level, there is little to distinguish them from other celebrities.

'They're not any different,' says Sara Flanagan, who set up the 'digital talent' books at the global modelling agency IMG in Sydney, and now works as a media consultant in London. And while Harry and Meghan are world-famous, influencers don't always rely on mainstream name recognition. YouTuber Tana Mongeau has 5.2 million followers and is thought to make up to five figures a month, but is barely known beyond the digital world.

So what do influencers do for the money? Deals can be as small as a one-off payment for a single post on Instagram. This is what we typically think of as sponsored content, or 'spon', and tends to be the more tawdry end of the spectrum. Or they can be hugely lucrative, prestigious 'partnerships' where a brand might ask an influencer to design a product, or front a social media campaign.

The idea is that the brand can target an engaged audience – the influencer's social media followers – more directly than it could with a general ad campaign and with the endorsement of someone they trust. For the influencer, a deal of this type gives them credibility to get more.

In the past five years, an entire industry has emerged to facilitate the influencer economy. There are now ways to buy social media followers, or to artificially inflate your impact so you can get sponsorship, and agencies to broker deals between influencers and brands.

At that structural level, it seems influencing is too big to fail unless, of course, the platforms on which it trades change significantly. The vast majority of influencers depend on Facebook, Instagram, YouTube, the gaming platform Twitch and, to a lesser extent, Twitter for their livelihoods, leaving them vulnerable. Changes to the algorithm, whether real or rumoured, can cause platform-wide panic.

So where do Harry and Meghan fit in? 'In the short-term they could absolutely clean up,' says Flanagan. 'They could be doing single posts for sums in the hundreds of thousands. But it would be very foolish of them, and very short-term.'

Harry Hugo, co-founder of The Goat influencer marketing agency, is left a little breathless by the possibilities for Harry and Meghan. In a few years' time, he says, he can picture the couple working on a documentary 'about breaking away from the royal family. Or a classic brand endorsement with a brand like – this isn't the right brand, but a brand like Coca-Cola.'

It isn't the right brand? 'I'd never rule anything out,' says Hugo. 'But I'd highly doubt it.'

Because more important than money to the long-term success of the Duke and Duchess of Sussex's influencing will be integrity and authenticity, both regarded as north stars that can make or break an influencer's success. So, enjoyable as it may be to picture, there will be no time spent paying their dues on the Instagram coalface with sponsored posts about detox teas and blue-light teeth-whitening kits for Harry and Meghan. They will be able to name their price with the world's biggest brands: Amazon, Netflix and Disney are names already in the mix.

Flanagan predicts that Harry and Meghan (and, let's not forget, a probably sizeable team) will move slowly, in search of 'high-value deals, and only a few of them, and giving a fair percentage of it back to the community and charity work'.

Meghan has already indicated what 'Sussex Royal' might come to stand for with her royal engagements: pushing diversity in *Vogue*, a capsule wardrobe to support women returning to work, and feminist advocacy through the UN. Elaine Lui, a presenter for the Canadian television network CTV and a blogger for Lainey Gossip.com, suggests Meghan could follow Angelina Jolie in combining serious philanthropic work with fashion and beauty endorsements. Harry's charitable interest in sustainable travel, meanwhile, may present opportunities to monetise in future.

Even product lines are not out of the question, says Flanagan, pointing to the Prince of Wales's Duchy Originals range of organic foods – for Meghan in particular. 'There's no doubt that she has the Midas touch.'

The style of Finlay & Co sunglasses that Meghan wore to the Toronto Invictus Games in September 2017 – the first official event she and Harry attended together – account for 80 per cent of the brand's total sales. Meghan's impact on these often little-known, ethical and independent brands – by design, Flanagan says – came to be known as 'the Markle Sparkle'. Now freed up, she will be able to dust a little over herself.

'Before Meghan was a royal, she was an influencer,' says Flanagan. 'What will be new is these hurdles they're going to have to get over as far as being royal, and not being seen to cheapen the royal brand.'

This may prove a difficult line to tread. Taking that Coke dollar (for instance) risks cheapening not only their brand, but also the royal family's – and no one wants to be called on to explain their Instagram activity to their grandma.

The Firm has a track record of coming down hard on members seen to be exploiting their association, says Bates. Sophie, Countess of Wessex, 'got her fingers very badly burned' for seeming to be selling access to royals in the *News of the World*'s 'fake sheikh' sting of 2001. Marion Crawford – the beloved long-time 'Nanny Crawfie' to the Queen and her sister, Princess Margaret, when they were children – was cut off by the royal family for publishing her memoirs after her retirement in 1950. 'They were incredibly anodyne, as you can imagine – all about these lovely little girls and what wonderful children they were – but, as Princess Margaret said: "She ratted",' says Bates. 'The poor old woman was incredibly hurt. And she was just an employee.'

Bates paints a dark picture of the fate that befalls rudderless royals, left to court celebrity friends who match them in status but probably outstrip them in worth. 'Prince Andrew is an awful warning in this, because he lost his purpose in life.'

The importance of royalty to Harry and Meghan's popularity has been overstated, says Lui. 'If anything, the Duke and Duchess are even more famous and intriguing to people now than they were six months ago.' Princess Diana was also without a title, she says – 'and it didn't stop her from maintaining her status as the most famous woman in the world'.

It is an influencers' world, more than it is a royals'. The family you were born into matters less than how many people are paying attention to you – and Meghan and Harry have the world transfixed. Lui says: 'From the very moment that they revealed their relationship, they have been a worldwide obsession, and the only way that we collectively and culturally become bored by an obsession is when they become boring. And when, in the last two years, have they been boring?'

The day we said goodbye

JONATHAN FREEDLAND

How does a nation say goodbye to its neighbours? With a lump in its throat and a poignant song of farewell – or with cheers and a raised middle finger of defiant good riddance? The answer that Britain gave at 11pm on Friday 31 January 2020 was: both.

The UK broke from the European Union on a late winter's night with jubilation and regret, as divided on the day of leaving as it had been in deciding to leave. For some Britons, this was Independence Day. For others, it was a national bereavement.

In Westminster Nigel Farage exulted with his fellow Brexiters in Parliament Square, delighted that a prize they had sought for a quarter of a century, and that once seemed laughably improbable, was in their hands at last.

In Downing Street, a countdown clock beamed on to the outside walls as if impatient for the moment, like children waiting for Christmas. Inside, Boris Johnson – who had been the face and totem of the Vote Leave campaign of 2016 – hailed 'the dawn of a new era', the curtain going up on 'a new act in our great national drama'. Surrounded by cabinet colleagues and veterans of the referendum campaign, the prime minister toasted their success with English sparkling wine, washing down a Brexit day feast of roast beef, Yorkshire pudding and Shropshire blue cheese, a spread pointedly free of the taint of the dreaded continent. Along the Mall, union jacks fluttered brightly.

There was merch for those who wanted it: you could buy a 'Got Brexit Done' tea towel, perhaps using a handful of commemorative

Brexit 50p pieces. If you were in Morley, you could join Andrea Jenkyns's Big Brexit Bash, to celebrate what the West Yorkshire MP called an end to 'a hellish four years' and the start of what was sure to be 'a golden decade', with Britons at last in charge of their own destiny, free of the shackles of Brussels. Sunderland, first to declare for leave in 2016, had the joy of hosting a special Brexit day meeting of the cabinet.

But for others, 11pm was, as Johnson acknowledged in his TV address to the nation, a moment of grievous loss. A YouGov poll, asking remain voters at which of the five stages of grief they now found themselves, registered only 30 per cent who had reached acceptance of the fact of Britain's departure from the EU: 19 per cent are in denial, 16 per cent are angry and 25 per cent are depressed. Alastair Campbell doubtless spoke for many when he said that part of him just wanted to retreat to his bed at 11pm, pulling the duvet over his head.

Melancholy was the mood of a procession yesterday afternoon from Downing Street to the London offices of the European commission, staged, said the organisers, 'to say goodbye to our old friend'. Clad in blue and gold, they numbered just a few hundred; hard to believe that a million or more marched in their cause a matter of months ago.

In Frome, Somerset, they gathered for a late-night vigil at an installation known as the European Community of Stones, a semicircular henge of 12 boulders, one quarried from each of the EU's 12 members when it was built in 1992. They sang the EU anthem, 'Ode to Joy', in recognition of the 'sense of excitement, of opportunity, the EU represented', said Martin Dimery, a local Green party councillor. For him, the EU was 'the greatest international project for peace, prosperity and progress' and now Britain will play no part in it. What was the point of a ceremony to mark that fact? 'Every death deserves a funeral.'

That elegiac quality has been a constant note sounded through these final days of UK membership, expressed most intensely in that widely shared footage of the European parliament rising to its feet to sing 'Auld Lang Syne' to a departing Britain (confirming this is a wrench for them as well as us).

It was the sadness of saying goodbye not to an institution, but to an idea – of friendship across the sea, of harmony between nations, of a resolve that a continent riven by the bloodiest of wars would live out its future in peace. So, while Downing Street had its clock, remainers had a projection of their own: a film beamed on to the white cliffs of Dover, featuring two veterans of the second world war, both in their nineties, speaking of their sadness at the coming of this hour. They would miss the 'comradeship' of the European Union, they said, adding the hope that 'we will be back together before too long'. The film, the work of the Led by Donkeys group, ended with an image of a single gold star from the European flag. 'This is our star,' said the message. 'Look after it for us.'

And that was the plea contained in so many remainer goodbyes, the hope this is not for ever. That afternoon procession in Whitehall was headlined: 'À bientôt EU, see you soon.' A Scottish MEP asked the EU27 'to leave a light on, so we can find our way home'. Farage was having none of that. 'Once we have left we are never coming back and the rest is detail,' he had said in his parting shot to the European parliament, before, in a metaphor made flesh, he had his microphone cut off: Brexit party MEPs had broken the rules by waving union flags. 'Put your flags away ... and take them with you,' the chair said. 'You are leaving.'

So, for all Johnson's talk of 'healing', there was no agreement at the moment of parting – except on one thing. Both sides saw 11pm as chiming in an epochal shift in the history of these islands. True, nothing material altered at that moment. The UK that wakes up this morning will still have to stick to EU rules and pay into the EU budget, albeit without any say, until 31 December. Britons can still go through the EU citizens line at the airport. Things will only get real on the first day of 2021.

In that sense, 11pm ushered in a period of Brexit nirvana for Boris Johnson. For the next 11 months, he will have the best of both worlds: he can say he's got Brexit done, and enjoy the benefits of EU membership. All the political gain, with none of the economic pain.

Truly, he will have his cake and eat it.

Still, leaving the EU marks the biggest change in our national life since 1973, when Britain joined, if not since 1945, given that today's EU is so much larger and more significant than the Common Market of 47 years ago. The new political landscape will be wholly different. The pressure for Scottish independence will be greater than ever: at 11pm, Scotland was taken out of the EU against its will. Irish unification will have a new, pressing logic, one that will only increase as Britain diverges from the EU, thickening that border down the Irish Sea. Meanwhile, Westminster, and especially Conservative, politics will have lost its perennial bogeyman, its reliable scapegoat for all ills: Brussels.

Some remainers believe – and maybe even hope – that the shine will come off Brexit pretty soon. They point to new government advice warning citizens that, come next year, they could face roaming charges when they use their phones on the continent; that they'll need health insurance or a special driving licence or a visa to work or study; that they'll have to queue in the slower, non-EU lane at the airport. Remainers still have their charts, projecting a UK economy turned anaemic once Britain goes it alone. They are poised, ready to declare: 'I told you so.'

But all that is over the horizon. For now, Britain has made one of its periodic shifts away from the continent, in a relationship that has blown hot and cold for at least 1,200 years. Even the eighth-century king Offa of Mercia fretted about trading links across the Channel. In that long sweep of history, the 47 years we spent as Britain-in-Europe may come to look like a blip. Alternatively, so may Brexit. Those draped in blue-and-gold flags could be right: Britain may one day be back, even if all but the most optimistic rejoiners believe that day is decades away.

In Parliament Square, site of hoarse slanging matches for four years, the crowds in the lead-up to 11pm were thinner on both sides. The leavers were beaming, proud in their tops bearing the slogan: 'Job Done'. They believe spring is coming. The remainers were wrapped up against the cold, braced against a January night which, to them, felt like the bleakest midwinter.

6 FEBRUARY

Locked down in Wuhan: 'I'm afraid I will collapse. I called every number, but no one cares'

LILY KUO

Li Lun is desperate. On Tuesday her husband was confirmed to have the Wuhan coronavirus, after weeks of suffering with a fever. They have not been able to get him admitted to a hospital or find space for him to quarantine himself. Li, her husband, her in-laws and the couple's two children, both disabled, live in a three-bedroom apartment in Wuhan.

They sent the children to an aunt on Monday. Li and her mother-in-law have developed symptoms and both have confirmed lung infections, which some doctors say should be reason enough to be quarantined. Li has been vomiting and has had diarrhoea.

They have had no instructions from Wuhan's centre for disease control (CDC), or from the neighbourhood committee that is in charge of communicating with health authorities and hospitals to arrange for treatment and follow-ups. Li posted on the microblog Weibo pleading for help, one of hundreds of posts in the past few days. 'I'm afraid I will collapse. I have called almost every number, everywhere,' Li said. 'Wherever we go, no one cares about us.'

More than 24,000 people have been infected with the coronavirus, which has killed almost 500 people. Most of the infections and deaths have been in China's central Hubei province, which has a population of 50 million that has been in a state of lockdown for the past two weeks. Infected residents and their relatives described a sense of helplessness and mounting outrage as they tried to get help for sick family members and shield healthy ones, often children.

One woman said she had taken her elderly parents to three hospitals searching for space for them. By the time they reached the last one, which had no free beds, her parents were so feverish they were unable to make the journey home. She put blankets on the floor outside the observation ward and they slept there.

The majority of deaths have been among people over the age of 60, but the virus has also affected the middle-aged and young, with symptoms ranging from coughing, fevers and aches to fainting, coughing up blood, extreme difficulty breathing, chest pain and weakness.

For some, the hardest part has been the isolation. It has been nine days since Yan, 37, last saw her husband and two children, an 11-month-old girl and an 11-year-old boy. After Yan developed a fever in late January, she separated herself from them and moved into her mother's apartment. A few days later, she and her mother tested positive for the virus.

Yan and her mother spend their days in separate rooms. Yan reads the news and sits on the balcony. When they go into the common area to get food, they wear masks. Their symptoms have been mild. Yan said she hoped that soon another test would show that her immune system had overcome the virus. 'Then I can reunite with my husband and my baby,' she said.

Several patients described being sent home from hospitals that have been unable to find space for them, and being ordered to quarantine themselves and 'observe' their situation.

Pan, in his mid-fifties and diagnosed this week, had chosen to go to an outside isolation ward arranged by his neighbourhood committee. His wife had just tested negative for the virus and he did not want to infect her or the children. His wife's mother died from the virus on Saturday.

There were about 20 people in the ward, he said, each in their own room. Every day three meals were delivered. There were no doctors or health workers to tend to them. Any medicine they wanted to take they had to buy and bring themselves. 'Before, for a few days, nurses would come, but now no one comes. They said they can't provide medical help,' Pan said.

Experts have said too many infected patients are being sent home, causing a growing number of family clusters of the virus. Few regular citizens know how to effectively self-quarantine, according to Zhang Xiaochun, the chief physician in the imaging department of Wuhan University Zhongnan hospital. 'Preventing the epidemic is a matter of human life. We can't rely on people staying at home and looking after themselves,' Zhang said, according to the magazine *Beijing News*.

The government has depicted the epidemic as a battle to be fought by the people, especially those in Wuhan, and has worked to reassure the public with sweeping measures such as a traffic lockdown and the construction of two new hospitals in little more than 10 days.

Residents in Wuhan, already distrustful of authorities who waited weeks before sounding the alarm about the virus, have grown more angry with the system. As Li's husband's condition worsens and she worries about her own health, she has become increasingly frustrated about being bounced between different government institutions. The hospitals tell her she must go through her local neighbourhood committee to arrange treatment. The neighbourhood committee, if anyone answers the phone, says all it can do is report to the higher-ups.

The more senior health authorities of the Wuhan CDC do not usually answer the phone. When they do, they say to go back to the local community committee. Over and over, Li is told to wait. 'It's getting worse. He can barely hold himself up,' Li said of her husband. 'This is a person's life – how can we wait any longer?'

Additional reporting by Lillian Yang and Pei-Lin Wu.

13 FEBRUARY

How ultra-processed food took over your shopping basket

BEE WILSON

Nearly three decades ago, when I was an overweight teenager, I sometimes ate six pieces of sliced white toast in a row, each one slathered in butter or jam. I remember the spongy texture of the bread as I took it from its plastic bag. No matter how much of this supermarket toast I ate, I hardly felt sated. It was like eating without really eating. Other days, I would buy a box of Crunchy Nut Cornflakes or a tube of Pringles: sour cream and onion flavour stackable snack chips, which were an exciting novelty at the time, having only arrived in the UK in 1991. Although the carton was big enough to feed a crowd, I could demolish most of it by myself in a sitting. Each chip, with its salty and powdery sour cream coating, sent me back for another one. I loved the way the chips – curved like roof tiles – would dissolve slightly on my tongue.

After one of these binges – because that is what they were – I would speak to myself with self-loathing. 'What is wrong with you?' I would say to the tear-stained face in the mirror. I blamed myself for my lack of self-control. But now I feel I was asking myself the wrong question. It shouldn't have been 'What is wrong with you?' but 'What is wrong with this food?'

Back in the 90s, there was no word to cover all the items I used to binge on. Some – crisps or chocolate or fast-food burgers – could be classified as junk food, but others, such as bread and cereal, were more like household staples. These various foods seemed to have nothing in common except for the fact that I found them very easy to eat a lot of, especially when sad. I had no idea that there would one day be a technical explanation for why I found them so hard to resist. The word is 'ultra-processed' and it refers to foods that tend to be low in essential nutrients, high in sugar, oil and salt, and liable to be overconsumed.

Which foods qualify as ultra-processed? It's almost easier to say which are not. I got a cup of coffee the other day at a station cafe and the only snacks for sale that were not ultra-processed were a banana and a packet of nuts. The other options were: a panini made from ultra-processed bread, flavoured crisps, chocolate bars, long-life muffins and sweet wafer biscuits – all ultra-processed.

What characterises ultra-processed foods is that they are so altered that it can be hard to recognise the underlying ingredients. They are concoctions of concoctions, engineered from ingredients that are already highly refined, such as cheap vegetable oils, flours, whey proteins and sugars, which are then whipped up into something more appetising with the help of industrial additives such as emulsifiers.

Ultra-processed foods (or UPFs) now account for more than half of all the calories eaten in the UK and US, and other countries are fast catching up. UPFs are now simply part of the flavour of modern life. These foods are convenient, affordable, highly profitable, strongly flavoured, aggressively marketed – and on sale in supermarkets everywhere. The foods themselves may be familiar, yet the term 'ultra-processed' is less so. None of the friends I spoke with while writing this piece could recall ever having heard it in daily conversation. But everyone had a pretty good hunch what it meant. One recognised the concept as described by the US food writer Michael Pollan – 'edible food-like substances'.

You might say that ultra-processed is just a pompous way to describe many of your normal, everyday pleasures. It could be your morning bowl of Cheerios or your evening pot of flavoured yoghurt. It's savoury snacks and sweet baked goods. It's chicken nuggets or vegan hotdogs. It's the doughnut you buy when you are being indulgent, and the premium protein bar you eat at the gym for a quick energy boost. It's the long-life almond milk in your coffee and the Diet Coke you drink in the afternoon. Consumed in isolation and moderation, each of these products may be perfectly wholesome. The question is: what happens to our bodies when UPFs become as prevalent as they are at the moment?

Evidence now suggests that diets heavy in UPFs can cause overeating and obesity. Consumers may blame themselves for overindulging in these foods, but what if it is in the nature of these products to be overeaten?

In 2014, the Brazilian government took the radical step of advising its citizens to avoid UPFs outright. The country was acting out of a sense of urgency, because the number of young Brazilian adults with obesity had risen so far and so fast, more than doubling between 2002 and 2013. These radical new guidelines urged Brazilians to avoid snacking, and to make time for wholesome food in their lives, to eat regular meals in company, to learn how to cook and to teach children to be 'wary of all forms of food advertising'. One of the first rules was to 'avoid consumption of ultra-processed products' – no government guidelines had ever categorised foods this way before. They condemned at a stroke not just fast foods or sugary snacks, but also many foods which have been reformulated to seem health-giving, from 'lite' margarines to vitamin-fortified breakfast cereals.

From a British perspective – where the official NHS Eatwell guide still classifies low-fat margarines and packaged cereals as 'healthier' options – it looks extreme to warn consumers off all ultra-processed foods (what, even Heinz tomato soup?). But there is evidence to back up the Brazilian position. Over the past decade, large-scale studies from France, Brazil, the US and Spain have suggested that high consumption of UPFs is associated with higher rates of obesity. When eaten in large amounts (and it's hard to eat them any other way) they have also been linked to a whole host of conditions, from depression to asthma to heart disease to gastrointestinal disorders. In 2018, a study from France – following more than 100,000 adults – found that a 10 per cent increase in the proportion of UPFs in someone's diet led to a higher overall cancer risk. 'Ultra-processed' has emerged as the most persuasive new metric for measuring what has gone wrong with modern food.

Why should food processing matter for our health? 'Processed food' is a blurry term and, for years, the food industry has exploited these blurred lines as a way to defend its products. Unless you grow, forage or catch all your own food, almost everything you consume has been processed to some extent. A pint of milk is pasteurised, a pea may be frozen. Cooking is a process. Fermentation is a process. Artisanal, organic kimchi is a processed food, and so is the finest French goat's cheese.

But UPFs are different. They are processed in ways that go far beyond cooking or fermentation, and they may also come plastered with health claims. Even a sugary multicoloured breakfast cereal may state that it is 'a good source of fibre' and 'made with whole grains'. Bettina Elias Siegel, the author of *Kid Food: The Challenge of Feeding Children in a Highly Processed World*, says that in the US, people tend to categorise food in a binary way. There is 'junk food' and then there is everything else. For Siegel, 'ultra-processed' is a helpful tool for showing new parents that 'there's a huge difference between a cooked carrot and a bag of industrially produced, carrot-flavoured veggie puffs' aimed at toddlers, even if those veggie puffs are cynically marketed as 'natural'.

The concept of UPFs was born in the early years of this millennium when a Brazilian scientist called Carlos Monteiro noticed a paradox. People appeared to be buying less sugar, yet obesity and type 2 diabetes were going up. A team of Brazilian nutrition researchers led by Monteiro had been tracking the nation's diet since the 1980s, asking households to record the foods they bought. One of the biggest trends to jump out of the data was that, while the amount of sugar and oil people were buying was going down, their sugar consumption was vastly increasing, because of all of the ready-to-eat sugary products that were now available.

To Monteiro, the bag of sugar on the kitchen counter is a healthy sign, not because sugar itself has any goodness in it, but because it belongs to a person who cooks. Monteiro's data suggested to him that the households still buying sugar were also the ones that were still making old Brazilian dishes such as rice and beans.

When Monteiro looked at the foods that had increased the most in the Brazilian diet – from cookies and sodas to crackers and savoury snacks – what they had in common was that they were all highly processed. Yet he noticed that many of these commonly eaten foods did not even feature in the standard food pyramids of US nutrition guidelines, which show rows of different whole foods according to how much people consume, with rice and wheat at the bottom, then fruits and vegetables, then fish and dairy and so on. These pyramids are based on the assumption that people are still cooking from scratch, as they did in the 1950s. 'It is time to demolish the pyramid,' wrote Monteiro in 2011.

Once something has been classified, it can be studied. In the 10 years since Monteiro first announced the concept, numerous peer-reviewed studies on UPFs have been published, confirming the links he suspected between these foods and higher rates of disease.

As Monteiro sees it, there are four basic kinds of food, graded by the degree to which they are processed. Taken together, these four groups form what he calls the Nova system. The first category – group 1 – is the least processed, and includes anything from a bunch of parsley to a carrot, from a steak to a raisin. He named this group 'unprocessed and minimally processed foods'.

The second group is called 'processed culinary ingredients'. These include butter and salt, sugar and lard, oil and flour – all used in small quantities with group 1 foods to make them more delicious: a pat of butter melting on broccoli, a sprinkling of salt on a piece of fish, a spoonful of sugar on a bowl of strawberries.

Next in the Nova system comes group 3, or 'processed foods'. This category consists of foods that have been preserved, pickled, fermented or salted. Examples would be canned tomatoes and pulses, pickles, traditionally made bread (such as sourdough), smoked fish and cured meats. Monteiro notes that when used sparingly, these processed foods can result in 'delicious dishes' and nutritionally balanced meals.

The final category, group 4, is unlike any of the others. Group 4 foods tend to consist largely of the sugars, oils and starches from group 2, but instead of being used sparingly to make fresh food more delicious, these ingredients are now transformed through colours, emulsifiers, flavourings and other additives to become more palatable. They contain ingredients unfamiliar to domestic kitchens such as soy protein isolate (in cereal bars or shakes with added protein) and 'mechanically separated meat' (turkey hotdogs, sausage rolls).

Group 4 foods differ from other foods not just in substance, but in use. Because they are aggressively promoted and ready to eat, these items have vast market advantages over the minimally processed foods in group 1. Monteiro and his colleagues have observed that these group 4 items are liable to 'replace freshly made regular meals and dishes, with snacking anytime, anywhere'. For Monteiro, there is no doubt that these ultra-processed foods are implicated in obesity as well as a range of non-communicable diseases such as heart disease and type 2 diabetes.

Not everyone in the world of nutrition is convinced by the Nova system of food classification. Some critics of Monteiro have complained that ultra-processed is just another way to describe foods that are sugary or fatty or salty or low in fibre, or all of these at once. If you look at the UPFs that are consumed in the largest quantities, the majority of them take the form of sweet treats or sugary drinks. The question is whether these foods would still be harmful if the levels of sugar and oil could be reduced.

The first time the nutrition researcher Kevin Hall heard anyone talk about ultra-processed food, he thought it was 'a nonsense definition'. It was 2016 and Hall – who studies how people put on weight at the National Institute of Diabetes and Digestive and Kidney Diseases at Bethesda, Maryland – was at a conference chatting with a representative from PepsiCo who scornfully mentioned the new Brazilian directive to avoid ultra-processed foods. Hall agreed that this was a silly rule because, as far as he was concerned, obesity had nothing to do with food processing.

Anyone can see that some foods are processed to a higher degree than others – an Oreo is not the same as an orange – but Hall knew of no scientific proof that said the degree of processed food in a person's diet could cause them to gain weight. When he started to read through the scientific literature on ultra-processed foods, he noticed that all of the damning evidence against them took the form of correlation rather than absolute proof. Like most studies on the harmful effects of particular foods, these studies fell under the umbrella of epidemiology: the study of patterns of health across populations. Hall finds such studies less than convincing. Correlation is not causation, as the saying goes.

Just because people who eat a lot of UPFs are more likely to be obese or suffer from cancer does not mean that obesity and cancer are caused by UPFs, per se. 'Typically, it's people in lower economic brackets who eat a lot of these foods,' Hall said. He thought UPFs were being wrongly blamed for the poor health outcomes of living in poverty.

At the end of 2018, Hall and his colleagues became the first scientists to test – in randomised controlled conditions – whether diets high in ultra-processed foods could actually cause overeating and weight gain. For four weeks, 10 men and 10 women agreed to be confined to a clinic under Hall's care and to eat only what they were given, wearing loose clothes so that they would not notice so much if their weight changed.

For two weeks, Hall's participants ate mostly ultra-processed meals such as turkey sandwiches with crisps, and for another two weeks they ate mostly unprocessed food such as spinach omelette with sweet potato hash. The researchers worked hard to design both sets of meals to be tasty and familiar to all participants. Day one on the ultra-processed diet included a breakfast of Cheerios with whole milk and a blueberry muffin, a lunch of canned beef ravioli followed by cookies and a pre-cooked TV dinner of steak and mashed potatoes with canned corn and low-fat chocolate milk. Day one on the unprocessed diet started with a breakfast of Greek yoghurt with walnuts, strawberries and bananas, a lunch of spinach, chicken and bulgur salad with grapes to follow, and dinner of roast beef, rice pilaf and vegetables, with peeled oranges to finish. The subjects were told to eat as much or as little as they liked.

Hall set up the study to match the two diets as closely as possible for calories, sugar, protein, fibre and fat. This wasn't easy, because most ultra-processed foods are low in fibre and protein and higher in sugar. To compensate for the lack of fibre, the participants were given diet lemonade laced with soluble fibre to go with their meals during the two weeks on the ultra-processed diet.

It turned out that, during the weeks of the ultra-processed diet, the volunteers ate an extra 500 calories a day, equivalent to a whole quarter pounder with cheese. Blood tests showed that the hormones in the body responsible for hunger remained elevated on the ultra-processed diet compared to the unprocessed diet. Hall's study provided evidence that an ultra-processed diet really does cause overeating and weight gain, regardless of the sugar content. Over just two weeks, the subjects gained an average of 1kg. This is a far more dramatic result than you would expect to see over such a short space of time (especially since the volunteers rated both types of food as equally pleasant).

Now that we have evidence of a link between diets high in UPFs and obesity, it seems clear that a healthy diet should be based on fresh, home-cooked food. But modern patterns of work do not make it easy to find the time to cook every day. For households who have learned to rely on ultra-processed convenience foods, returning to home cooking can seem daunting – and expensive. Hall's researchers in Maryland spent 40 per cent more money purchasing the food for the unprocessed diet.

In Britain and the US, our relationship with ultra-processed food is so extensive and goes back so many decades that these products have become our soul food, a beloved repertoire of dishes. It's what our mothers fed us. If you want to bond with someone who was a child in 1970s Britain, mention that you have childhood memories of being given Findus Crispy Pancakes and spaghetti hoops followed by Angel Delight for tea. I have noticed that American friends have similar conversations about the childhood joys of Nutter Butters. In the curious coding of the British class system, a taste for industrial branded foods is a way to reassure others that you are OK. What kind of snob would disparage a Creme Egg or fail to recognise the joy of licking cheesy Wotsit dust from your fingers?

I am as much of a sucker for this branded food nostalgia as anyone. There is a part of my brain – the part that is still an eight-year-old at a birthday party – that will always feel that Iced Gems are pure magic. But I've started to feel a creeping unease that our ardent affection for these foods has been mostly manufactured by the food corporations who profit from selling them. For the thousands of people trapped in binge-eating disorder – as I once was – UPFs are false friends.

In Australia, Canada, the US or the UK, to be told to avoid ultra-processed food – as the Brazilian guidelines do – would mean rejecting half or more of what is for sale as food, including many staples that people depend on, such as bread. Earlier this year, Monteiro and his colleagues published a paper titled 'Ultra-processed foods: what they are and how to identify them', offering some rules of thumb. The paper explains that 'the practical way to identify if a product is ultra-processed is to check to see if its list of ingredients contains at least one food substance never or rarely used in kitchens, or classes of additives whose function is to make the final product palatable or more appealing ("cosmetic additives")'.

Tell-tale ingredients include 'invert sugar, malto-dextrin, dextrose, lactose, soluble or insoluble fibre, hydrogenated or interesterified oil'. Or it may contain additives such as 'flavour enhancers, colours, emulsifiers, emulsifying salts, sweeteners, thickeners and anti-foaming, bulking, carbonating, foaming, gelling and glazing agents'.

For most modern eaters, avoiding all ultra-processed foods is unsettling and unrealistic, particularly if you are on a low income or vegan or frail or disabled, or someone who really loves the occasional cheese-and-ham toastie made from sliced white bread. In his early papers, Monteiro wrote of reducing ultra-pro-cessed items as a proportion of the total diet rather than cutting them out altogether. Likewise, the French Ministry of Health has announced that it wants to reduce consumption of Nova 4 prod-ucts by 20 per cent over the next three years.

We still don't really know what it is about ultra-processed food that generates weight gain. The rate of chewing may be a factor. In Hall's study, during the weeks on the ultra-processed diet people ate their meals faster, maybe because the foods tended to be softer and easier to chew. On the unprocessed diet, a hormone called PYY, which reduces appetite, was elevated, suggesting that homemade food keeps us fuller for longer. The effect of additives such as artificial sweeteners on the gut microbiome is another theory. Later this year, new research from physicist Albert-László

Barabási will reveal more about the way that ultra-processing actually alters food at a molecular level.

Even if scientists do succeed in pinning down the mechanisms by which ultra-processed foods make us gain weight, it's not clear what policymakers should do about UPFs, except for giving people the support and resources they need to cook more fresh meals at home. To follow the Brazilian advice entails a total rethink of the food system.

For as long as we believed that single nutrients were the main cause of poor diets, industrial foods could be endlessly tweaked to fit with the theory of the day. When fat was seen as the devil, the food industry gave us a panoply of low-fat products. The result of the sugar taxes around the world has been a raft of new artificially sweetened drinks. But if you accept the argument that processing is itself part of the problem, all of this tweaking and reformulation becomes so much meaningless window-dressing.

An ultra-processed food can be reformulated in countless ways, but the one thing it can't be transformed into is an unprocessed food. Hall remains hopeful that there may turn out to be some way to adjust the manufacture of ultra-processed foods to make them less harmful to health. A huge number of people on low incomes, he notes, are relying on these 'relatively inexpensive tasty things' for daily sustenance. But he is keenly aware that the problems of nutrition cannot be cured by ever more sophisticated processing. 'How do you take an Oreo and make it non-ultra-processed?' he asks. 'You can't!'

25 FEBRUARY

Harvey Weinstein tried to silence and blame victims. At trial it no longer worked

ED PILKINGTON

When the end came, there was no walking frame to lean on for Harvey Weinstein. As he was led away to spend the first of what promises to be many nights in a jail cell, he had to hobble along unaided with his arms handcuffed before him.

For the seven long weeks of his trial, the disgraced movie mogul had begun every day trundling into court behind his faithful trademark walker, with its incongruous fittings of two yellow tennis balls glued to its legs. There was much speculation among court reporters about what it all meant – was this a classic cinematic touch by the master producer of *Pulp Fiction* and *The English Patient* designed to stir sympathy among the jurors? Or was it, more prosaically, a genuine expression of physical anguish from a man who recently underwent back surgery?

Either way, as soon as Weinstein, 67, entered court and seated himself at the defence table, any signs of vulnerability vanished in the chilly courtroom air. Day after day, he was surrounded by his luxuriously apparelled and no doubt equally lavishly paid team of defence lawyers attending to his every whim. It was as though he was not in court, so much as holding court, in an outpost of his once legendary (and now sold) Tribeca film offices.

Much attention has been paid in the course of these weeks to the figure of Donna Rotunno, the defendant's larger-than-life and vastly outspoken chief defence lawyer. She spent the trial strutting in front of the jury as though she were in a throwback to the 1970s, berating the two main accusers for the choices they made in their dealings with the movie boss.

The clear implication of her cross-examinations was that when they accepted Weinstein's invitation to come up to his SoHo apartment, or to his midtown Manhattan hotel room, it was at least partially their fault that he then went on to sexually attack them. 'You were manipulating Mr Weinstein so you'd get invited to fancy parties, correct? You wanted to use his power, correct?' Rotunno said as she pummelled a key witness.

But the many huddles that she and her colleagues held around the defendant at his table suggested that if Rotunno were the messenger, Weinstein firmly dictated the message. When she grilled one of the two main accusers – a woman the *Guardian* has not named because her wishes over identification are not clear – so harshly over so many hours that the witness burst into uncontrollable sobbing, that was the product of a strategy that Weinstein had laid down personally years ago.

Silence the women – that was the strategy. Accuse them of being serial liars, as the defence lawyers did with the *Sopranos* actor Annabella Sciorra, make out that they were only in it for the money as they did with the other main witness, Miriam Haley, suggesting to the jury that Haley planned to sue Weinstein the minute the trial was done.

Initially, this old-style attack machine of a defence appeared to be effective. It may have been blunt, it may have been outdated in the #MeToo era, but it landed several punches on the six accusers. But then the women started speaking. One after another, they took to the witness stand.

When they pointed out Weinstein at his table their fingers were shaking and their voices faltering. But there was no mistaking the determination to have their day in court. And then they began to tell their stories, or rather their story. Like a celluloid movie wheel stuck on a scene that repeats over and over, they recounted an identical chronology as though they were speaking as one.

First came the social introduction to Weinstein, a towering presence in the industry that they loved; then the promise of an acting part or audition; then the request for a massage, followed by the flash of anger when it was declined; and then the woman's contrition and her fateful acceptance to come up to the apartment or the hotel room to continue the discussion. He was a Jekyll and Hyde, the woman who was raped said about the defendant. 'If he heard the word "no", it was like a trigger for him.'

It was the Jekyll and Hyde moments that will stay in the mind, lingering long after the trial is over. The terrifying accounts of violence. The rape victim describing how he blocked the door of his hotel room in March 2013, dragged her to his bed, injected himself with erectile dysfunction medicine and then attacked her. 'I kind of shut down a little bit,' she said. Haley relating how he held her down on his bed in July 2006, pushing her back when she tried to get up, yanking a tampon out of her before assaulting her.

Weinstein and his defence lawyers made much of the fact that his accusers stayed in touch with him after the attacks. Rotunno and co dwelt on the rape victim, teasing out every detail of how she sustained a relationship with the movie producer – degrading though it may have been – over several years.

The jury listened attentively, diligently took notes, then began their deliberations. Five days later they emerged on a blazingly sunny New York day to deliver a verdict that showed that the world has moved on. #MeToo has happened. A woman can lead her life in all its complexity, all its messiness and still expect a rape to be called a rape.

'I know the history of my relationship with him,' she had said under brutal cross-examination. 'I know it was complicated and difficult. But that doesn't change the fact that he raped me.'

29 FEBRUARY

I adored Caroline Flack, contradictions and all. She deserved even more than kindness

LENA DUNHAM

My adoration for Caroline Flack bordered on teenage. As an American abroad in the UK last summer, managing the vague, inchoate loneliness of time spent in a country not my own, the hours I watched her, six nights a week from roughly 9pm to 10.30pm, became a benchmark of cosy normalcy, a point of connection in an often cruel and unfamiliar world. She was, in the way that is specific to pop figures we engage with daily, a friend, albeit one I had never met. That raspy voice, her surprised guffaw, her dresses (pretty, bordering on wacky, like early Cher) and the empathy she brought to a bloodless and occasionally unkind television format lent her an air of approachable glamour, a local-girl-done-good sheen, aspirational but earthy.

Not since I saw Sarah Jessica Parker on Broadway in 1996, belting her heart out with a childlike vibrato, had I hungered so deeply for information about a star. I pored over Flack's Instagram, over dailymail.co.uk images of her pink-doored flat (I'm not proud of this), and histories of her love interests (most of whom were only figures of note to me because they had been pictured holding her hand outside a nightclub). I read her deceptively sunny memoir, *Storm in a C Cup*, and took comfort in her durable, bounce-back brand of vulnerability. Her quotes about heartbreak ('I feel at my most calm, in control and happiest when I'm single, so at the minute that's what I'm doing') reassured me, yet still I cheered 'Good for her!' when she was pictured on the beach in Ibiza with her latest athlete beau. Despite being on fairly intimate terms with the mechanics of celebrity, I felt sure we were connected. Caroline would like me. She would get *it*. I *got* her. I am clearly far from the only person who felt this way, which is why her every move, hairstyle and misstep were clocked and noted by the country at large.

This adoration, this childish sense of connection, is only a small part of why her death hit me with a sickening power. While I am not often at a loss for words, I felt that weighing in – especially with a Twitter micro-tribute – would be useless and borderline disrespectful. I am fairly allergic to the culture around celebrity death announcements. When the latest loss hits the timeline, we pile in with broken-heart emojis and prayers for the families, a kind of wan language of loss. And when a death is as tragic as Flack's, we stand even further on careful tippy-toes, offering soft-pedalled wishes that she had felt less alone, or footnoting our praise with terms like 'she had her demons'. We remind our followers that there's always someone to reach out to, even if we privately have often believed there is not. In our efforts to avoid saying the wrong thing, we resort to vagaries. I'm not suggesting I know of a better way.

But I do know of a better way to treat the living. And I am – with both gratitude and some bitter aftertaste – able to describe the inner state of a person who has placed their self-image in the hands of the public; a public that has made a sport of building up, then tearing down, the people we elect to entertain us. The deepest rage is reserved for women.

There are a few caveats to apply here: I do not claim to know what Caroline Flack felt when she took her own life. I know that obsessively following her holiday outfits and 'love rivals' does not make me an authority on her inner life, which was as rich, varied and insular as anyone's. I also do not claim to know why some people take their lives when their circumstances nosedive, and others do not.

What I can say, with the authority of someone who has been on a decade-long journey through the funhouse of public life, is that none of us benefit from a culture in which young women are told that being revered by people who do not really know them, in any forum from secondary school to the *X Factor* stage, is the answer to ancient feelings of low self-worth, or a salve for the pain and powerlessness that accompany so many forms of female identity. When we tell our daughters, both through what we value and what we imitate, that their truth lies in what others reflect back at them, we set a standard that no amount of self-love Instagram quotes can undo. And so young women continue to chase the holy trifecta of beauty, productivity and likability, hoping that hitting their marks and saying their lines will lift from their backs the load they have carried since birth. To quote Kate Bush: 'Oh, darling, make it go away.'

It is in this quest for their own culturally specific version of perfection and adulation that nearly every woman I've met, no matter their differences, is united. The equally evil twin of these desires is to simply coast and camouflage. To be adored for qualities that are not really yours is very close to disappearing. Caroline Flack was adored and attacked for many of the same reasons: her brassiness, autonomy when it came to personal decision-making, a sense of fight that kept her from taking criticism lying down. At the same time, she spoke (in an unpublished Instagram post shared by her family) of having repressed the stresses of trying to go along to get along: 'I've accepted shame and toxic opinions on my life for over 10 years and yet told myself it's all part of my job. No complaining. The problem with brushing things under the carpet is ... they are still there and one day someone is going to lift that carpet up and all you are going to feel is shame and embarrassment.'

History's habit of erecting monuments to women, and then dismantling them just as quickly, is well known to us: from Cleopatra to Hillary Clinton, Queen Esther to Whitney Houston. I used to think women got it worse if they didn't conform to the current standard of beauty, but being pretty is no picnic, either. (It seems we must always destroy our fantasy women; no wonder Farrah Fawcett took a side turn into the art world later in life, where at least some fun and identity play are permitted.) Any woman engaged in public life is used to a kind of constant temperature check, trying to gauge whether or not there is blood in the water around them that day – but then again, so are women in abusive relationships, or girls at dog-eat-dog middle schools. As is often the case, female celebrities represent a sort of canary in the coal mine for wider attitudes towards women.

Since Flack's death, there has been a lot of finger-pointing, as well as meta-discussions about the impact of both social and tabloid media on mental health. One of her final Instagram posts has been much quoted: 'In a world where you can be absolutely anything, be kind.' And, of course, kindness is a worthy, and necessary, goal. But I would ask that we also consider our ability to accept contradiction, complexity and grey areas in the women we idolise, and consider the violence of suspending them in mid-air above us and then cutting the harness. Our ability to forgive men in power, to celebrate their contradictory aspects, is well-documented. But the people who have lately been speaking to Flack's inner beauty, work ethic and vivaciously engaging presence were mostly too afraid to do so in the weeks after her arrest in December. Their willingness to say, 'A woman I admire may have done something that I don't' could have gone a long way to lessen her shame and expand her sense of possibility.

I am not dismissing the seriousness of the charges against her. But nor do I want my own attempts to stay on the right side of people's opinion to prevent me from saying what I really mean – which is that public vilification, especially as it follows public celebration, is almost too painful to bear for most, and a trauma like any other.

I know what it feels like to be adored – to be hailed as refreshing, delightful, necessary, approachably stylish and fun. I also know what it feels like to be cast out and away, for some valid reasons and other arbitrary ones or, more accurately, for valid reasons that then make the arbitrary ones seem pretty damn good, too. I know what it feels like to be so dependent on an influx of praise that the loss of it feels like the removal of a vital organ. I know what it feels like to fully believe the hatred that is being directed at you by strangers, and to stop believing the people who love you when they tell you there is more to your story. I know what it feels like to be sure you've failed your family, and to be isolated from them because you cannot forgive yourself that failure.

It was a long and lonely process, searching for another set of metrics by which to measure my own worth, to see myself as a human divorced from the echo chamber of fickle fandom and female perfection. It didn't change until I started asking myself: was I kind today? Was I honest? Did I do my best to be accountable to the people I love, and when I was wrong did I promptly admit it? These are the truths about a person that cannot be determined by a Reddit thread or a *Sun* article. And these are the units of measurement we so often forget to remind our daughters of – not because we have bad values, but because we have inherited a culture that does not believe in our essential right to be as messy and confounding as the men it celebrates. For me, getting to this place involved a combination of factors, an enormous amount of therapy and personal reflection, and, most of all, time. Time I wish Caroline had. There is no simple way to explain why she doesn't.

I imagine – with the stress on imagine – that Flack was reeling from several kinds of heartbreak, not least that which comes from being cast out of the golden circle of validation that celebrity has come to imply. I wish I could have told her that it changes. That it may not go back to the way it was, to life before you received death threats. Or dissections of your appearance by people who refuse to reveal their own. Or wittily constructed puns about what a total waste of lungs and a heart you are. But it can, with the right support and reconstruction, become something better – more self-reliant and therefore more peaceful, no matter how the boat may rock. I wish I could have told her all of this, but I also wish we could have showed her a more hopeful reality: that women who err and fail are just as worthy of love as the men who do the same.

To honour her complexity, to name and celebrate it, will go a long way towards changing the narrative for the women who watched her. After all, she was an example. She still is.

3 March

Holocaust survivor to Olympic gold: the remarkable life of Éva Székely

ANDY BULL

The fascists came for Éva Székely in the winter of 1944, when she was 17. 'I was told to lie down and say I was sick,' she remembered. '"Come on! Get going!" their leader shouted. Then my dad told him: "She is sick, can't you see, she cannot walk!" and he said back: "She doesn't have to walk far."' Only to the nearby banks of the Danube, where they were doing the killing.

'And then from some heavenly influence my dad said: "Don't take her, she is the swimming champion of Hungary, and one day you will be happy you saved her life. Tell him your name." And he looked at me, and I looked at him,' he had one grey eye and one brown eye, 'and I said my name. This is how I stayed alive, that Dad told him I was a swimming champion and he would still remember me.'

Székely died last Saturday. She was 92. She broke six world records, won 44 national titles, a gold in the 200m breaststroke at the Helsinki Olympics in 1952 and a silver in the same event at Melbourne in 1956. 'Despite my successes I was regularly defeated on one point,' she wrote later. 'No community ever embraced me fully; although I felt in my heart and soul I was part of my community it was always made known to me that I was an outsider.'

Székely decided she wanted to be a swimmer in 1936, while she was listening to the coverage of the Berlin Olympics. She heard Ferenc Csik win the 100m freestyle. 'Then and there I made a resolution – I, too, would be an Olympic champion.' She joined her local sports club, and soon after was part of the team who won a national open water title. Two months later she was kicked out for being 'an undesirable'. She was 14 but already used to antisemitism. At school she had fought with a boy who had drawn a cartoon, 'Erger, Berger, Schossberger – every Jew is a scoundrel! Get out!'

Her father told her it was only temporary. 'I was a Hungarian and when all the madness was over one's religion would make no difference.' But for the next five years 'the madness reigned'. She was banned from competing. Still, she grew more obsessed with her childhood dream. It became her reason to live. When the Germans came 'they decided we should be exterminated – I decided I should win the Olympics'. She was recruited into a labour battalion but escaped by leaping on to a passing streetcar during a forced march through the city. She returned to her family, who were now living in a two-room safe house.

Székely kept fit by running the stairs, five storeys up, five storeys down, 100 times a day. They called it a safe house; it wasn't. There were 42 people living in those two rooms. By the time they were liberated there were only 10 left alive. When Székely won her gold in 1952 she wasn't just swimming for herself but for those 32, the thousands more who were shot on the banks of the Danube and the millions more who died in the camps.

She married the great water polo player Dezső Gyarmati, who led Hungary to victory in three Olympics, in 1952, 1956 and 1964. For the second of those Games, in Melbourne, the couple left their baby daughter Andrea behind in Budapest. The revolution broke out while they were away. Székely was so sick with worry she lost five kilos fretting. She still won silver. Next year the family defected to the US but they didn't stay. They returned home to look after her parents. And after that the authorities said only one of them would be allowed to travel to the 1960 Olympics in Rome.

So Székely quit swimming, and became a coach. Her philosophy was that 'sport was a gift and a reward, not a job'. Her daughter grew up to be an Olympic medallist herself. She won silver in the 100m backstroke and bronze in the 100m fly at Munich in 1972. Eva was there with her during the Black September massacre. She had even had coffee with one of the victims, the wrestling coach Moshe Weinberg, the morning before he was killed trying to fight off the terrorists. He had told her he had not wanted to go to Germany but 'the boys had begged him to come'. He died trying to protect them.

In the years afterwards, Székely made a point of speaking out about her experiences. According to the *Encyclopedia of Jewish Women*, 'while few, if any, active or retired Hungarian Jewish athletes were open about their religious identity, Székely had the courage and determination to go public with her Jewishness'. In one TV interview she spoke about the anti-Jewish laws of the 1940s and referred to 'those who could document non-Jewish origin as far back as their grandparents. That was no problem for me, I did not have to go back as far as my grandparents. Unequivocally, I was a Jew.'

In 2004 Székely was named as one of Hungary's Athletes of the Nation. In 2011 she received a prestigious Prima Primissima award. Did that make her finally feel embraced? In 2017 she was alive to see Viktor Orbán's antisemitic attacks on George Soros, part of a rising tide of antisemitism across Europe and in Hungary in particular.

One last story. In 1950 Székely took part in an international meet on Margaret Island in Budapest. 'I swam very, very well there. When they announced the winners of the 100m freestyle I stood up. They said the gold medal would be given to me by the chairman of the swimming association and a special prize would be given to me by the major of the communist political police.

'And imagine, there I was standing on the top of the dais with a vase in my hands and the man looks at me ...' She realised she had seen him before when she looked into his eyes, one grey and one brown.

7 MARCH

I love the UK and would like to stay (please). But you need a few lessons on being Danish

SOFIE HAGEN

I'm from Denmark, but have lived in the UK for almost eight years. I'd love to stay. Fingers crossed. I call both countries home, but still find myself caught between the two because while there are Briticisms I have embraced, there are other things I can't. For as long as there is an ocean between us, or two hours on a low-budget aeroplane, there will always be some fundamental differences between our two kingdoms. Here are my five biggest.

YOU DON'T GET TO THE POINT

The Danes are direct. If you want to send a professional email to someone, asking for some files, regardless of how little you know them, your email will read: 'Hey, send the files.' That's it. It took me a while to learn the British way of making every request sound as if you are asking a person for their first-born's hand in marriage. 'Dearest Cliff, I hope you are well. I do apologise for getting in touch on this godless Tuesday, but I hope you might consider even the slightest possibility of perhaps finding the time ...' And so on. My emails now take 20 times longer to write. Often, I forget the pleasantries and simply send a Danish-style four-word message. Then I am filled with British shame. For this reason, I have considered adding an email signature that reads: 'I'm not rude, I'm Danish.'

YOU ARE FILTHY AS HELL, BUT ONLY SECRETLY

Put on any Danish film and you will see genitals. I am not talking about porn (which Denmark was the first country in the world to legalise, in 1967). I'm talking regular primetime television and mainstream movies. In the opening scene of *Nattevagten*, a 1994 thriller, we see Nikolaj Coster-Waldau's flaccid penis swinging back and forth as he gets out of bed. In the incredibly funny sitcom *Ditte & Louise* (2015–16), a scene where Ditte is having wild sex up against a desk cuts with another in which Louise is masturbating furiously while drinking wine. Again, primetime. I worked in a sex shop in Denmark when I was 16, which sold porn. It was my job to pack the parcels and send them out. I can reveal that the most hardcore porn was ordered by people in the UK. You're all filthy as hell, so start standing by it, OK?

YOU DO NOT NEED A HYGGE BLANKET

While I'm here, I'd like to blow the whistle on hygge. You must have heard the word a million times, because I've seen it a million times in bookshops all over the UK: *How to Hygge the Danish Way*, *Have a Hygge*, and other horrible misuses of my language. Hygge is a common word in Denmark. Instead of 'Take care!' we might say, 'Hygge!' Instead of 'This is nice!' we might say, 'This is hyggeligt.'

Instead of 'Ah, OK' we might say, 'Hyggeligt.' It covers almost anything, and means cosy or chill. It's not a Danish activity. You guys hygge all the time. You go to the pub, you watch TV, you drink tea to an almost psychopathic degree. The difference is, in Denmark there aren't £35 books on how to hygge. You cannot (and need not) buy a £50 hygge-blanket. If Danes are more relaxed than Brits, it's to do with our excellent infrastructure, our social security safety net, the fact that we are paid a salary to attend university and have 52 weeks of parental leave – all because we happily pay about 50 per cent in taxes. Socialism is the real hygge. You heard it here first.

You do Christmas once a week

I miss Danish food on a daily basis. But I have discovered the British Sunday roast. In Denmark, we eat Christmas food once a year, but you people have cleverly decided to do it *once a week*. And don't think I don't know about those special high-end restaurants next to the motorway that do a roast buffet every single day. Yes, I've eaten three in one week. No, I am not ashamed – I am British now.

Our queen is better than your queen

I've binge-watched *The Crown*, and I like your queen. She seems nice. She does that cool thing where she wears a provocative brooch if she wants to send a hidden signal. But have you met the Danish queen? Margrethe II of Denmark, 79, is regularly seen chain-smoking and shoving food into her mouth in public. Every New Year's Eve, she addresses the nation on live TV. Last year, she had a cold and we got to see the queen take a crumpled tissue from her drawer and blow her nose. Did I mention that our queen is also an artist? Her illustrations, sent to JRR Tolkien under a pseudonym in the 1970s, were used in Danish and English editions of *The Lord of the Rings*. She works part-time as a costume designer for the Danish Royal Ballet. What did your queen do? C'mon. Step it up.

One last thing, before my settled status is forcibly taken from me for blowing the whistle on hygge: you can't pronounce it, no matter how hard you try. You can't pronounce my name, either. I'm talking specifically to the British man who corrected my pronunciation of it. Don't do that. Also, I love living here. Please let me stay.

10 MARCH

How to work from home: an expert's guide

RHIANNON LUCY COSSLETT

There's a way of answering the phone that sounds as though you weren't just asleep, and after nearly eight years of working from home, I've mastered it. The affected tone in question is one imbued with a sort of casual brightness. Timing is key. When the phone goes, you're OK to leave it for a few rings to foster the impression that you were too busy concentrating on your work to answer immediately; snatch it up too soon and your voice will sound as though it is still steeped in half-sleep, which tends to prompt the dreaded question: 'I'm sorry, did I wake you?' This question is impossible to answer in a way that is not defensive.

Since the coronavirus outbreak has led more companies to bring in home-working, some – admittedly strange – people appear to be panicking about how they are going to cope away from the office. Social media abounds with well-meaning threads that sound as though they were written by head girls trapped in a Kafka novella. Get dressed as though you're going to work, they say. Try not to take naps. Make sure you go for a walk. In the absence of a boss, they have actually made themselves a schedule. These people are amateurs who have been indoctrinated by advanced capitalism, and most of them are also American (when it comes to skiving off, continental Europe must always be your model). Do not listen to them. They have internalised their own oppression.

Listen to me: I'm very good at working from home. This is always put down to my natural temperament. 'Oooh, I could never do that,' people invariably comment. 'I'd get too bored/ distracted/stir-crazy/lonely.' I try not to judge these people, but I do. You'd rather work in an office with a boss breathing down your neck, really? Your preferred environment is an open-plan hellscape devoid of quiet places to read or think over the din of people making small talk about biscuits, rather than your own kitchen? Clearly you have Stockholm syndrome.

Tedious bores will tell you that you need a designated workspace in order to work from home, but this shows a tragic lack of imagination. Why not take advantage of your entire living space? Answer some emails on the toilet, do some spreadsheets in bed, then hop over to the sofa for a bit of a change of scene. Regular trips to the kitchen for hot drinks and snacks help to mix it up a bit. If you're lucky enough to be home-working in hot weather, invest in a wifi connection that reaches to the back garden or balcony. That way you can sunbathe while occasionally refreshing your email.

As for workwear: forget getting dressed properly, wear whatever feels good. Some veterans will advocate a full pyjama; that is their right. Personally, I prefer leggings, slipper socks, some form of T-shirt, and a cardigan. It just about passes as daywear when you venture to the shop or answer the door to accept your neighbours' Amazon packages. If you absolutely must, because you have a Skype meeting or something, you may get dressed from the waist up.

Working from home provides an excellent opportunity to spend time on your hobbies, whether that is making your own chutney, practising guitar, or creating your own oatmeal face-masks. Remember that if you're at the point where you are googling the weather, it's probably time to go outside. You have to leave the house sooner or later, if only to note that the world basically has nothing to offer, before you retreat again indoors. Welcome to a brave new world, my friends. All you need to do now is work out an acceptable time at which to start drinking.

15 MARCH

I'm an epidemiologist. When I heard about Britain's 'herd immunity' coronavirus plan, I thought it was satire

WILLIAM HANAGE

Your house is on fire, and the people whom you trust with your care are not trying to put it out. Even though they knew it was coming, and could see what happened to the neighbours as they were overwhelmed, the UK government has chosen to encourage the flames, in the misguided notion that somehow they will be able to control them.

When I first heard about this, I could not believe it. My colleagues assumed that reports of the UK policy were satire – an example of the wry humour for which the country is famed. But they are all too real.

Let me take the arguments on their merits. The stated aim has been to achieve 'herd immunity' in order to manage the outbreak and prevent a catastrophic 'second wave' next winter – even if Matt Hancock has tried to put that particular genie back in the bottle this weekend. A large proportion of the population is at lower risk of developing severe disease: roughly speaking, anyone up to the age of 40. So, the reasoning goes that even though in a perfect world we'd not want anyone to take the risk of infection, generating immunity in younger people is a way of protecting the population as a whole.

We talk about vaccines generating herd immunity, so why is this different? Because this is not a vaccine. This is an actual pandemic that will make a very large number of people sick, and some of them will die. And the mortality rate will climb when the NHS is overwhelmed. This would be expected to happen, even if we make the generous assumption that the government were entirely successful in restricting the virus to the low-risk population: at the peak of the outbreak the numbers requiring critical care would be greater than the number of beds available.

And, of course, you can't restrict it to this age group. Think of all the people aged between 20 and 40 who work in healthcare, or old people's homes. You don't need many introductions into settings like these for what we might coyly call 'severe outcomes'. In Washington State, nearly all the deaths reported so far have been associated with nursing homes. Is everyone in a high-risk group supposed to withdraw themselves from society for six months until a second wave has been averted?

About that second wave: let me be clear. Second waves are real things, and we have seen them in flu pandemics. This is not a flu pandemic. Flu rules do not apply. There might well be a second wave, I honestly don't know. But vulnerable people should not be exposed to a virus right now in the service of a hypothetical future.

Keeping people safe means self-isolation if you develop symptoms, but the official advice here is also misleading. While it is of paramount importance that sick people stay at home to avoid infecting others, it is increasingly clear that transmission can occur before symptoms develop. We know this is true from modelling and observational studies. I have seen it happen myself. We do not know how often it occurs or how important it is in the epidemiology, but it definitely does happen.

However, arguments about the case fatality rate, the transmission parameters and presymptomatic transmission all miss the point. This virus is capable of shutting down countries. You should not want to be the next after China, Iran, Italy or Spain. In Italy, the choices of whom to save and whom to allow to die are real. You should instead look to the example of South Korea, which, through a combination of intense surveillance and social distancing, appears to have gained some semblance of control. We can learn from Singapore, Hong Kong and Taiwan, all of which have so far done a good job mitigating the worst outcomes despite having reported cases early in the pandemic.

The UK should not be trying to create herd immunity, that will take care of itself. Policy should be directed at slowing the outbreak to a (more) manageable rate. What this looks like is strong social distancing. Anyone who can work from home, should. People who do not yet work from home should be encouraged to do so. Employers should guarantee sick pay, including for contacts of known cases, and do everything they can to discourage the practice of 'presenteeism'. You should not shake hands. Not with anyone. You should wash your hands for 20 seconds several times a day and whenever you enter your home (or someone else's home). Call a halt to large gatherings. Educate people about masks and how they should be reserved for the medical professionals who need them. All this and more should have started weeks ago.

Deciding whether to close schools is hard; they do so much more than just education. But this is a pandemic, and so you should expect they will be shut sooner or later. In Hong Kong, they have been shut for weeks. If you hear any talking head on TV explain that kids don't get sick, remember that doesn't mean kids cannot be infected and transmit. It's probably a good idea to hold off on visits to Nana and Grandpa.

The most fundamental function of a government is to keep its people safe. It is from this that it derives its authority, the confidence of the people and its legitimacy. Nobody should be under the illusion that this is something that can be dodged through somehow manipulating a virus that we are only beginning to understand. This will not pass you by; this is not a tornado, it is a hurricane. Don't panic, but do prepare. If your government won't help you, do it yourself.

Dr William Hanage is a professor of the evolution and epidemiology of infectious disease at Harvard.

15 March

Belgravia review – Julian Fellowes is caught in an uptown funk

LUCY MANGAN

Julian Fellowes has been typing again. It is the year flimpty plomp, the pasteenth century in days of yore. There are worried English people in Brussels and a French war person, Napoleon Bonaparte – 'Boney', as people would period-specifically call him; you can check in books! – is making them worry Englishly. But the Lady Duke of Richmond is holding a ball, to show that she has a period-specific ballroom and won't be intimidated by French war people, no she will not!

Philip Glenister is James Trenchard, a trenchant trencherman and victualler – which is pronounced 'vittler' –- to the English soldiers who are stationed in Brussels in case Boney tries any of his French warring. To the chagrin ('shame and embarrass-ment' across La Manche) of his slightly better-born wife, Anne (Tamsin Greig), James has wangled invitations to the lady duke's ball, despite being born to a family of tubers in Covent Garden before he became a successful merchant potato in Frenchland. He is also ignorant-potatoly encouraging his daughter Sophia in her flirtation with the duchess's nephew, Edmund, Lord Bellasis (Jeremy Neumark Jones), even though she is, of course, half-po-tato and he cannot marry for love, no matter how much he wants a plate of chips.

All clear so far? Frenchies! Englisheses! Balls! Great! The ball begins, even though Anne 'Maris Piper' Trenchard has said: 'How strange that we should be having a ball when we are on the brink of war!' Anyone who is anyone is there, especially if they are the Duke of Wellington or the Prince of Orange ('Top Dutchman! Feel m'clogs!'). The Lady Duke of Richmond is enchanting, Anne is mortified and everyone manages to keep a straight face during the sword-dancing display.

Everything is going swimmingly, although Sophia professes to Edmund that she is a bit worried about the Wikipedia entry she read before the director shouted 'action' about Boney's advance, and the possibility of this becoming the most famous ball in history. At that exact moment, Wellington is notified by a messenger that Boney has arrived unexpectedly at the nearby strategic crossroads of Quatre Bras (French for Four Somethings). But Edmund tells her: 'Don't be silly, my little Jersey Royal! Nothing can happen to us! We're the luckiest couple alive!' Sophia is relieved. 'And the most in love!' she replies. No, she really does.

Alas, alack, a message *is* delivered to Wellington. It *does* say that the Bonester is at the strategic crossroads of Quatre Bras. Sacré bleu – or, more patriotically, crumbs! Everyone who has a penis, is wearing a red jacket and is not one of the sword dancers gathers in the Man Duke of Richmond's study to pore over a parchment map and note that, if they don't stop French war man at Four Somethings, they may have to do battle nearby at ... Where-a-loo? What-a-loo? Waterloo!

Crikey. I hope we win. Off they go – Wellers, Orangey and, I am sad to say, young Edmund. Sophia is distraught. Also, they need a victualler, pronounced 'vittler', so James heads off, too. He comes back from his first battlefield a broken man – and no wonder. 'A very awful sight it was, too,' he tells Anne while staring into the middle distance, possibly at his agent, whom I imagine is standing with everyone else's in the wings urging them to think of Maggie Smith's pension and stagger on. 'Bodies everywhere,' he says. 'Groans from the wounded. Scavengers' – you can practically see the beads of sweat that must have formed on Fellowes' brow as he dug deep to recreate the scene for viewers – 'picking at the corpses!'

Not only that, but Edmund was killed. James breaks the news to his baby new potato that her bit of fancy steak has had his frites. She is distraught again.

SMASH CUT to 26 years later. Afternoon tea has been invented, Sophia is dead, the titular London district of Belgravia has been built (by James, in partnership with Thomas Cubitt, dontcha know) and the script is even worse. Once we are ensconced with the Trenchards in their townhouse, we are introduced to the servants and all pretence that this is not *Downton Abbey* – in, uh, Belgravia – collapses. On the upside, Harriet Walter has arrived as Lady Brockenhurst and Alice Eve is an early Victorian meany of the first water.

So: something to pass the time as the coronavirus curfew descends, or something to send you screaming into the streets and licking the first handrail you can find? The decision is yours. The agents, at least, are happy either way.

21 MARCH

Social distancing?
That comes naturally to me

TIM DOWLING

I never go anywhere, and I wash my hands a lot. Social distancing is a guiding principle of my existence. When it comes to adjusting my behaviour in line with the latest medical advice, I haven't left myself much room. I was already doing all I could.

Because it comes naturally to me, I also find it hard to give advice about self-isolation. People say: how do you cope with the loneliness of working from home? I think: what are you talking about? They ask: do I have to get dressed, or what? I say: you're missing the point; your whole day is one long, disgusting secret. Nobody has to know.

'Well, that was a shit-show,' my wife says, coming into the kitchen with two bags of shopping.

'Was it?' I say.

'There were huge queues at Morrisons,' she says. 'People pushing and shoving. I had to abandon my trolley and walk out.'

'Wow!' I say. I think: I walked out of Morrisons three months ago, when it wasn't even that crowded.

'I had to go to another supermarket,' she says. 'It's like the *End of Days* out there.'

'Did you get celeriac?' I say.

'Yes,' she says. 'Nobody was panic-buying celeriac.'

After lunch, the sky darkens and it begins to rain. My wife decides she wants to close the curtains and watch a film on TV. Halfway through, the youngest one walks in.

'You're watching *Contagion*?' he says. 'Why are you doing that to yourselves?'

'It's meant to be prescient,' my wife says.

'I know,' he says. 'I've seen it.'

'It's spot-on,' I say. 'Although "starring Gwyneth Paltrow" is a bit of an exaggeration.'

'It's making me paranoid,' my wife says.

'She turns blue eight minutes in,' I say.

My phone rings: a FaceTime call from the United States. I hold the phone at arm's length. My brother appears in the middle of the screen. Next to him is the middle one, who went to America a month ago. One of my brother's four-year-old twins is sitting on his lap. The other one's head looms hugely into the frame sideways.

'I'm John,' the head says.

'Hi John,' I say.

'So, yeah, we're just here,' my brother says.

'We're watching *Contagion*!' my wife shouts.

'Timely,' my brother says.

'Yeah,' I say, 'but if you were a massive Gwyneth Paltrow fan, you'd be like ...'

'Hello,' the youngest one says, appearing at my side.

'Hey,' the middle one says.

'I was out with people from your old work last week,' the youngest one says.

'Which people?' the middle one says.

'I took these guys out of school on Monday,' my brother says.

'Really?' I say.

'Some red-haired dude,' the youngest one says.

'Then on Friday, they closed the school,' my brother says. My 99-year-old father walks into the room. The camera lens swivels to his crotch.

'Pan up!' I shout.

'Who's that?' my father says.

'It's your son,' my brother says. A twin's face appears, upside down, then vanishes.

'Are you panic-buying?' I say. His answer is drowned out by laughter, and crying, and the sound of bodies hitting the floor. It's clear that the action is happening off-screen.

'What's going on?' I say. The camera spins to face the middle one.

'Fighting,' he says.

'There's no football,' I say.

'I know,' the middle one says. My brother reappears at his side.

'So it turns out they can't even do the test at the local hospital,' he says. 'They don't have the facilities.'

'Huh,' I say.

'No licking!' my brother shouts. 'Licking gets sent upstairs!'

When the call ends, I return my attention to the TV. A flashback sequence shows people in a nightspot at intervals, the camera zooms to emphasise the handling of glassware and cutlery. I think: this is what we'll remember. People going out and touching stuff and getting ill. And deserving it, the celeriac-eating bastards.

'You'd be like, she's barely in it! I want my money back!' I say.

'Shut up,' my wife says.

22 MARCH

The coronavirus crisis may lead to a new way of economic thinking

LARRY ELLIOTT

Rishi Sunak says the measures he has announced to support the economy are without precedent in peacetime – and he's right. Never before has the British state agreed to pay the wages of those at risk of losing their jobs. Never before has the government ordered pubs and restaurants to shut.

The chancellor is not the only one to compare the struggle against the coronavirus pandemic to a military operation. Boris Johnson sees this as the summer of 1940, with himself as Churchill. Harking back to the second world war is inevitable given how strongly influenced Britain is by an event that ended 75 years ago, but there are some key differences. The main one is that between 1939 and 1945 the economy was running at full tilt. It took the fight against Hitler finally to eradicate the high unemployment of the 1920s and 1930s. Britain had full employment and would have had rising inflation had it not been for rationing and price controls.

Contrast that with today. As yet, there are only estimates of the likely hit to the economy from Covid-19, but they range from very bad to catastrophic. The consultancy Capital Economics has estimated a 15 per cent drop in output in the second quarter of 2020, but says it could be 20 per cent.

Instead of production being scaled up, it is being scaled back. There are a few sectors where activity is rising – food production and healthcare – but those increases will be dwarfed by the lost output elsewhere. About one-third of workers in the UK have jobs in the sectors most affected by the pandemic: retail, restaurants, bars, clubs, hotels, cinemas, theatres, gyms, sport – and they are all closed for business for months to come. This is not 1940, with factories working round the clock: it is more like a neutron-bomb attack that targets the people but leaves the buildings unscathed.

Another big difference is that unlike in 1940 it is not just a question of holding on until the Americans get involved. The US was never under threat of being invaded and was able to put its enormous economy on a war footing. But the US is not immune to the coronavirus. On the contrary, it is going to suffer grievously: in part because Donald Trump was in denial about the risks, in part because the public healthcare system is so poor and in part because the social safety net is so weak.

America, because of its size and its place at the heart of the global financial system, will still have a vital role to play in any recovery. But the number of people losing their jobs as large parts of the economy go into hibernation is going to be colossal. The US is where it was in 1930, when the dole queues were lengthening after the Wall Street crash, rather than in its much more robust state a decade later.

Those seeking parallels with the second world war need to broaden their perspective. One way of looking at today's events is to see the 15 years before the financial crisis of 2007–08 as the equivalent of the years leading up to the first world war. Although this seemed a peaceful, prosperous period – the so-called long Edwardian summer – things were not quite as benign as they appeared. The global balance of power was changing. There was political unrest and growing class conflict. The first few years of the 21st century – marked by debt-fuelled growth and financial market anarchy – were just as delusional.

The mood of complacency was shattered by the financial crisis, just as it had been by the outbreak of war in 1914. In both cases, winning the struggle proved harder than expected and, in both cases, there was an attempt once victory had been declared to go back to business as usual: balanced budgets and a return to the gold standard in the 1920s; balanced budgets, debt-driven growth and financial speculation in the 2010s.

But turning back the clock proved impossible. Political discontent and anger grew as economies struggled. Trust in the democratic process frayed. There was little international cooperation.

Then, around a decade and a half later in both cases, there was a second shock: the collapse of the financial bubble in 1929 and the Covid-19 pandemic in 2020. If history is any guide, it is the second shock that makes fundamental change possible.

Four big things happened in the 1930s and 1940s. First, the old style of economics was abandoned. Countries came off the gold standard and states began to pump-prime growth, albeit timidly in most cases. John Maynard Keynes' general theory inspired an entire generation of economists and policymakers. Second, there was an attempt to inject equity into economies through enhanced power for trade unions, more progressive taxation and the expansion of welfare states. Third, work began early on this progressive agenda. In Britain, the Beveridge Report, Butler's Education Act of 1944 and the white paper on employment policy all emerged while the second world war was still raging. Finally, there were serious attempts to build a new international architecture – through the creation of the United Nations, the International Monetary Fund and the World Bank – that would avoid the global policy fragmentation of the 1930s.

How close are we to a repeat of all this? Just consider, a model that has failed not once but twice has been ditched. Governments recognise they have to support their citizens through the crisis. New ideas – such as universal basic income – are being championed. And without multilateral cooperation there will be no victory against Covid-19. Sunak is right. This is different, perhaps even more fundamentally so than he thinks.

26 MARCH

Social media bragging is over – coronavirus has made it redundant

YOMI ADEGOKE

The biggest threat to celebrities during the battle against coronavirus doesn't appear to be the disease, but the threat of being 'cancelled' thanks to their horrifying displays of disconnectedness with reality on social media. Take Madonna, the world-famous multimillionaire who declared Covid-19 'the great equaliser' on Twitter and Instagram in since-deleted posts.

'We are all in the same boat,' she said, sitting surrounded by rose petals in a bath that, were it to be sold, the funds raised could probably see me through the looming recession. 'And if the ship goes down, we're all going down together,' she added.

And yet, coronavirus is still in some small ways a leveller. Only weeks ago, I wrote of the burden of 'thrilled to announce' culture – the growing pressure to publicly declare every and any work win online. The universe has since intervened, ridding us of opportunities. With vast postponements and cancellations because of social distancing, there is little for most of us to be thrilled about and even less to announce.

At first, many coped by mournfully listing the lost opportunities they would have announced but for the pandemic. Now, as several days have passed and lockdown is official, our social media accounts are catching up with this sudden change. We are pivoting to sharing news about our personal hobbies – knitting, bread baking and gardening – instead of side hustling. I have discovered that people I followed for years have a passion for singing that they've never had time to share; I am watching ex-colleagues learning to play instruments. And I've been able to pursue my dream of learning to sculpt.

Instagram has aided this shift, releasing a 'Stay Home' sticker to add to your posts, encouraging users to share what they are doing while isolated, such as showing followers how they are passing the time, and vice versa. These updates are less about professional point-scoring and more: 'PERSONAL NEWS: I've just made and eaten my third banana cake of the week!'

Of course, that isn't to say that home living will remain whole-some and uncompetitive: there are tangible gains to be made during this strange period. The stock market may have plunged, but coronavirus has seen the clout economy boom: three days ago, American DJ D-Nice jumped from having 200,000 followers to 1.3 million on Instagram after a livestreamed dance set that even Michelle Obama tuned in to. 'The Body Coach' Joe Wicks has become a household name, after conducting daily PE lessons from his living room for schoolchildren. For most of us, however, social media right now is like a low-stakes year 6 talent show, where everyone wins simply by taking part. Perhaps that is something worth taking back with us into the real world when all of this is over.

26 MARCH

'My heartthrob days are over': Joe Wicks on health, happiness – and training the nation

ZOE WILLIAMS

It is not these extraordinary times that have made Joe Wicks. He was already huge, initially from Instagram cooking videos that lasted just 15 seconds. Rudimentary but engagingly zany, they attracted a substantial if hodgepodge fanbase from body-conscious Zoomers to middle-aged mums. So, when he brought out the cookbook *Lean in 15*, five years ago, his publisher said she would be delighted to sell 70,000 copies. Instead he sold 700,000, to become the second biggest seller in the cookery hall of fame, behind Jamie Oliver.

This week, though, his live workouts on YouTube have put him in a different league. Every morning at 9am, he is running a 'PE lesson': an exercise class for kids that you can do in your living room. It sounds like a simple idea, but now every child in the country (and their mum) is talking about it, his name forming a compound noun with his chosen title: 'Yes, I've done my PE homework, I've done JoeWicksBodyCoach.' Kids love the kangaroo hops and parents love the fact it gets their children burning off excess energy when they are trapped inside.

Wicks runs the numbers: 'On day number one, we had 806,000 households streaming it. Today it was 954,000 livestreams; 3.7 million people have watched the first video since yesterday. It's just growing, I'm over the moon. I feel quite overwhelmed by it.' He has been up since seven, and so busy he has only had time for a piece of toast. This is a salient detail from the nation's ultimate dietary role model, whose MO is to show not tell; normally his lunch is way more balanced.

It was in 2016 that he started visiting schools, up and down the country, trying to embed a passion for physical jerks. He wanted to teach the world to star jump; he wanted a TV show, like Jamie Oliver's *School Dinners* but for exercise. He could not get any takers. But that was then. Yesterday, he was in discussions with Channel 4 about streaming his online workouts, while the *Sun* was poring over his videos, trying to spot evidence of a lavish lifestyle from the shots of his living room in Richmond, Surrey.

I do not think Wicks has a particular fitness secret: his workouts are successful because people love him. This is the mystery of the man – why is it that people, across generations, like him so much? It is not a question that you can ask directly. You have to go back to the beginning.

A disruptive and naughty kid, 'a bit of a clown', he says, Wicks was always into sport, football, cross-country, anything where he

The UK flag is taken down in Brussels on 31 January, as Britain formally exits the European Union after 47 years. ANADOLU AGENCY/GETTY IMAGES

Factory workers in Wuhan, China, where the coronavirus outbreak began, strictly distanced during lunch after returning to work in March. YI XIN/EPA

Goats take advantage of deserted streets in Llandudno during the UK's national lockdown. Animals and birds became more visible in many urban areas as humans retreated. PETER BYRNE/PA WIRE

Dancers from the Bolshoi use their kitchen in Moscow for ballet practice in April as Russia's lockdown shuts the theatre. KIRILL KUDRYAVTSEV/AFP/GETTY IMAGES

Children in Nairobi pass a street mural warning 'corona is real'. Kenya introduced a curfew and shut schools but reported death rates in Africa have been low, the WHO says, because of younger populations. BRIAN INGANGA/AP

Hospital staff in Barcelona take a Covid-19 patient to the sea front for fresh air after six weeks in intensive care. Spain had one of the highest infection rates in Europe. DAVID RAMOS/GETTY IMAGES

Parts of the UK were repeatedly flooded between November and March. This house in East Cowick, Yorkshire, was one of many that had to be evacuated.
IAN FORSYTH/GETTY IMAGES

Silhouettes of people in Manchester during the weekly UK 'clap for our carers' when NHS staff were applauded from balconies, doorsteps or windows. CHRISTOPHER THOMOND/GUARDIAN

Dominic Cummings greeted by protesters outside his home amid a public outcry after the *Guardian* revealed he'd broken lockdown guidelines.

A-level students whose exams were cancelled protested in August, after grades calculated by algorithm left many missing out on university places.

A protester in San Jose, California, takes a knee in front of a line of riot police after the killing of George Floyd in Minnesota sparked global Black Lives Matter demonstrations. THE MERCURY NEWS/GETTY IMAGES

Donald Trump returns after posing with a Bible outside St John's Episcopal Church in Washington, amid growing unrest across the US. SHAWN THEW/EPA

A statue of Bristol slave trader Edward Colston being thrown into the city's harbour in June. Anti-racism protesters said it was a symbol of colonial crimes. NURPHOTO/GETTY IMAGES

Anti-racism demonstrator Patrick Hutchinson carries an injured counter-protester at a march in London. Hutchinson said, 'His life was under threat so I scooped him up.' DYLAN MARTINEZ/REUTERS

Joe Biden and his vice-presidential nominee Kamala Harris at the
Democratic National Convention, held online in August because of the
coronavirus pandemic. OLIVIER DOULIERY/AFP/GETTY IMAGES

Belarusians march through Minsk on 29 September demanding the
resignation of president Alexander Lukashenko, who has ruled for 26 years.
ARTEM DUBIK/GETTY IMAGES

could blow off a bit of steam. The defining moment of his teenage years was when, at 15, a group of his schoolmates was taken on an immersion day at St Mary's University, in Twickenham, London. 'I remember looking round the bus, and it was all the naughtiest kids, the ones who were always in detention. I think they must have wanted us to see how it could be different.'

On the way home, he rang his mum and announced that he wanted to be a PE teacher – and he did start as a teaching assistant, before becoming a personal trainer. It was not an obvious trajectory, he says. 'I had quite a chaotic home life, it wasn't stable, my diet wasn't great. I was never an overweight child, but I had behavioural issues. I think that was linked to my upbringing and not having a great start with my nutrition.'

His mother was 17 when she had his brother, 19 when she had Joe; his father was in and out of rehab for drug addiction. 'There was a lot of shouting, a lot of doors slammed, we didn't sit down and have dinner together.' And yet, he says: 'One thing I had more than anything, I had love and support from my mum and dad. My mum used to say: "I don't care if you become a dustman or a doctor, you can be who you want."' It is a powerful and unusual stance, and it means he really gets imperfection – human frailty, too much sugar, not enough lunges – he gets that you can make poor choices without being a bad human being, he is palpably non-judgmental, without ever saying: 'I'm not here to judge you.' I think viewers can smell that, at any age, even through their smartphones.

There is also, of course, the impossible to ignore eye-candy element, which meant in his early career he was often seen on the covers of fitness magazines displaying his washboard torso. He is quite uncomfortable about that now. 'The heartthrob days are over,' he says. 'I'm 34 now, receding hairline, I'm not as lean as I was.' Which is stretching things a bit, since to the untrained eye, he looks the same, only more famous. But he is certainly serious about his family. 'It's a nice calm feeling, since I got married and had kids [a daughter of two, a three-month-old son]. I'm not chasing anything, I'm not rushing to get anywhere, I'm really content with what I've got. There isn't much more that will ever make you happier than that.' If you have to pretend to be going bald to damp down the passions of a whole nation who refer to you as 'Juicy Joe', I guess that's a price worth paying.

Anyway, back to the fitness; there is a good reason to start with younger kids. Before coronavirus hit, when he was still touring the country, 'I went to a secondary school, and they were already a little bit too cool: "I'm not training with him, who is this dude?" My whole philosophy is to get kids exercising at a young age, which you can really create with role modelling. "My mum's sweating, she's out of breath, she's laughing."'

Take a sedentary teen, who is into their devices, and good luck training them, he says. This might be disheartening news if you already have a house full of sedentary teens, but he continues persuasively, and by the end of it I'm convinced that you probably could persuade even older kids, so long as you directed them his way and didn't try to role model it by sweating yourself. 'It's just about happiness,' he says. 'True motivation comes from how exercise makes you feel. If you're very demotivated, you've got to remember that the sense of achievement comes at the end of the workout, not at the start.'

As much as Wicks proselytises fitness, he is careful to show his flaws. 'You can put on a front, but people see through that very quickly, and they disengage.' He never sounds censorious, even while he is describing his meal plans for the day – oats and berries, omelettes and salad, vegetable curries in the evening – and sketching out the unutterable wholesomeness of his mood management. 'There are days when I wake up feeling flat, I don't know why. I'm not unhappy but I'm not happy. I know, if I feel like that, I'll go and do a workout and it will lift my mood.' His workouts sail forth on this tide of infinite enthusiasm, which it is hard not to get swept up in. 'I don't know if you believe in the energy and the secret?' he says at one point. I have no idea what this means, so I say that, yes, I most definitely do. 'I do believe,' he elaborates, 'that the more you put out into the universe, the more that comes back.'

If the positivity is a bit relentless, it is definitely not unthinking. He allows in anxieties: small, medium-sized, vast. Since he had children, 'I have days when I start thinking about the Earth, about pollution, about the sea, about the economic stuff. I've started to think about what it's going to be like in 50 years, and I didn't used to think like that at all.' It has made him more driven, he says, but not for money. 'I'm proud of what I've achieved, yes. You have to understand I grew up on a council estate, and back in the day you had tokens for your lunch at school. I didn't come from a background of wealth, but it wasn't something I talked about, I still had a good life. And I'm still not motivated to be financially successful. I don't think about financial gain. What makes me feel good is reaching people, trying to change the culture so that parents want to exercise with their kids.'

I think back to how stung he was when the *Sun* picked over his living room for signs of poshness. It actually doesn't look posh at all. He has just moved all the furniture out so there's room for press-ups, and there is a map above the mantelpiece. 'It's a plastic map!' he says, mock-scandalised.

He asked me at the start of the interview whether I was Zoe Williams the media doctor, and I said no, but I was once invited to give a keynote to the Royal College of GPs, and because of my weird ego, I exchanged loads of emails on my thoughts about general practice, before my Mr said: 'It's possible they don't mean you.' He has a version of that story, and it's much better. 'My brother got invited to do a speech at an event at YouTube for the Who. He's a massive fan of the Who, he's been listening to their music for years. The day before, he thought: 'Why do they want me there?' And it was only the World Health Organization.' It's a signal of how big Joe Wicks was, even before the online workouts, that the WHO wanted his brother, Nikki, who is also his social-media strategist, to talk through how best to improve the world's health.

Even while he is in no way blase about the lockdown, he is constitutionally oriented towards the bright side. 'I think the real value that people get from my YouTube videos are these questions. Are you going to feel good today? Are you going to sleep better tonight? Do you want to give yourself the opportunity to feel the best you can?'

Well, OK then. If you put it like that ...

27 MARCH

I remember the wartime evacuation. Eventually the isolation gets to you

NANCY BANKS-SMITH

'Alone, alone. All, all alone' – Samuel Taylor Coleridge

PG Wodehouse, interned in a lunatic asylum in Upper Silesia, rose buoyantly to the situation and wrote *Joy in the Morning*. 'Weeping may endure for a night but joy cometh in the morning.' He was well versed in the psalms and hardened to privation having been to a public school. No one who has been to Eton, they say, need fear prison. Which in Jonathan Aitken's case was just as well. Recently, forced to enjoy my own company, I have been remembering Roedean. As the school song said: 'Visions of schooldays will float now before us.' It added, bafflingly, that the field would ring again and again with the tramp of the 22 men. For years I had no idea what the hell was going on.

Dame Emmeline, the headmistress, had one of those undivided bosoms popularised by Queen Mary. More a shelf for resting stuff on. She had evacuated the school overnight from Brighton to Keswick with, I like to think, a Bible in one hand and a *Baedeker* in the other.

The Lake District, full of leech gatherers and idiot boys, seems to have suited Wordsworth down to the ground. He quite liked wandering lonely as a cloud, though, in fact, his sister was always with him taking shorthand notes. Plucked from the boozy roar of my parents' pub, I hated it. I was soaking wet and hungry for four years nonstop. In the grounds of the Keswick Hotel was a lonely white parakeet, a gay prewar survivor, wind-tossed and evil-natured. I knew how it felt. I also thought it looked edible.

Did I tell you about the vanishing pork pie? I will hold you with my glittering eye and tell you again. Every half-holiday we had to climb a mountain. Suck on that thought for a second. I was very small and stout and the backs of my legs were on fire but in my lunchbox was, unspeakable joy, a pork pie. Helvellyn is chamfered to a fine point in case you feel inclined to hang about and enjoy yourself.

I perched gingerly and opened my lunch. The pie leaped out and raced to the bottom of the mountain in increasingly joyous bounds. Never was a pie so full of beans; so happy in its liberty. Much like David Attenborough when he shook off the shackles of being a BBC boss and, it is said, skipped down Wood Lane singing: 'Free at last! Free at last! Thank God Almighty, free at last!'

Standing by Sainsbury's empty shelves today, I see it still. Boing … boing … gone.

Eventually the isolation gets to you. Rosalie and I went stir-crazy. Having just noticed we had bosoms, we cut a couple of bras from a blackout blind, dazzling titillation for a passing Dornier. Dame Emmeline was exceeding wroth. She summoned the school and ordered the culprits to confess.

I do so now. With a bit of luck there is only me left and, perhaps, the parakeet.

27 MARCH

A letter to the UK from Italy: this is what we know about your future

FRANCESCA MELANDRI

I am writing to you from Italy, which means I am writing from your future. We are now where you will be in a few days. The epidemic's charts show us all entwined in a parallel dance.

We are but a few steps ahead of you in the path of time, just like Wuhan was a few weeks ahead of us. We watch you as you behave just as we did. You hold the same arguments we did until a short time ago, between those who still say: 'It's only a flu, why all the fuss?' and those who have already understood.

As we watch you from here, from your future, we know that many of you, as you were told to lock yourselves up into your homes, quoted Orwell, some even Hobbes. But soon you'll be too busy for that.

First of all, you'll eat. Not just because it will be one of the few last things that you can still do.

You'll find dozens of social networking groups with tutorials on how to spend your free time in fruitful ways. You will join them all, then ignore them completely after a few days. You'll pull apocalyptic literature out of your bookshelves, but will soon find you don't really feel like reading any of it.

You'll eat again. You will not sleep well. You will ask yourselves what is happening to democracy.

You'll have an unstoppable online social life – on Messenger, WhatsApp, Skype, Zoom ...

You will miss your adult children like you never have before; the realisation that you have no idea when you will ever see them again will hit you like a punch in the chest.

Old resentments and falling-outs will seem irrelevant. You will call people you had sworn never to talk to ever again, so as to ask them: 'How are you doing?'

Many women will be beaten in their homes.

You will wonder what is happening to all those who can't stay home because they don't have one. You will feel vulnerable when going out shopping in the deserted streets, especially if you are a woman.

You will ask yourselves if this is how societies collapse. Does it really happen so fast? You'll block out these thoughts and when you get back home you'll eat again.

You will put on weight. You'll look for online fitness training.

You'll laugh. You'll laugh a lot. You'll flaunt a gallows humour you never had before. Even people who've always taken everything dead seriously will contemplate the absurdity of life, of the universe and of it all.

You will make appointments in the supermarket queues with your friends and lovers, so as to briefly see them in person, all the while abiding by the social distancing rules.

You will count all the things you do not need.

The true nature of the people around you will be revealed with total clarity. You will have confirmations and surprises.

Literati who had been omnipresent in the news will disappear, their opinions suddenly irrelevant; some will take refuge in rationalisations which will be so totally lacking in empathy that people will stop listening to them. People whom you had overlooked, instead, will turn out to be reassuring, generous, reliable, pragmatic and clairvoyant.

Those who invite you to see all this mess as an opportunity for planetary renewal will help you to put things in a larger perspective. You will also find them terribly annoying: nice, the planet is breathing better because of the halved CO_2 emissions, but how will you pay your bills next month?

You will not understand if witnessing the birth of a new world is more a grandiose or a miserable affair.

You will play music from your windows and lawns. When you saw us singing opera from our balconies you thought: 'Ah, those Italians.' But we know you will sing uplifting songs to each other too.

And when you blast 'I Will Survive' from your windows, we'll watch you and nod just like the people of Wuhan, who sang from their windows in February, nodded while watching us.

Many of you will fall asleep vowing that the very first thing you'll do as soon as lockdown is over is file for divorce.

Many children will be conceived.

Your children will be schooled online. They'll be horrible nuisances; they'll give you joy.

The elderly will disobey you like teenagers: you'll have to fight with them in order to forbid them from going out, to get infected and die.

You will try not to think about the lonely deaths inside the ICUs.

You'll want to cover with rose petals all medical workers' steps.

You will be told that society is united in a communal effort, that you are all in the same boat. It will be true. This experience will change for good how you perceive yourself as an individual part of a larger whole.

Class, however, will make all the difference. Being locked up in a house with a pretty garden, or in an overcrowded housing estate, will not be the same. Nor is being able to keep on working from home, or seeing your job disappear. That boat in which you'll be sailing in order to defeat the epidemic will not look the same to everyone, nor is it actually the same for everyone: it never was.

At some point, you will realise it's tough. You will be afraid. You will share your fear with your dear ones, or you will keep it to yourselves so as not to burden them with it too.

You will eat again.

We're in Italy, and this is what we know about your future. But it's just small-scale fortune-telling. We are very low-key seers.

If we turn our gaze to the more distant future, the future which is unknown both to you and to us too, we can only tell you this: when all of this is over, the world won't be the same.

27 March

'Dropping like flies': Spain's health care workers run ragged by the pandemic

SAM JONES

For Sara Gayoso, and tens of thousands of other medical staff across Spain, the last few weeks have been an unprecedented blur, an indistinct, urgent succession of days that drain into each other as healthcare workers struggle to do what they can with what they have. But, even by recent standards, the past few days have been bleak, as the death toll soared to new heights, doctors announced legal action to secure proper protection and an ice rink was turned into a mortuary.

Gayoso's own moment of coronavirus clarity came a few weeks ago when an older woman was brought into the El Escorial hospital outside Madrid where she works as a doctor in the A&E department. It turned out the patient had pneumonia. 'The hardest thing for me so far,' says Gayoso, 'was having to stand two metres away and tell her daughter that she wouldn't be able to see her.

'Her daughter's face just dropped and she said to me: "So, I won't get to see my mother again?" I couldn't tell her that she'd definitely get to see her mother again, because I had no way of knowing if she would.'

Even though human contact soon became one of the earliest casualties of the pandemic, almost 15 per cent of Spain's 64,059 cases are among healthcare workers. In Madrid and other regions, stocks of basic protective equipment such as face masks are running dangerously low. 'The material we have is being very strictly rationed so we don't run out,' says Gayoso. 'You're careful not to get your gown dirty because you know you'll have to reuse it, which ups the risk of contagion. We're having to take very good care of the high-quality material.'

Her colleague Pablo Cereceda, a surgeon and representative for the AMYTS medical association, is currently off in precautionary quarantine and has had more time to reflect – and to seethe. 'The reality is that this is an epidemic that's getting the better of us and we need to ask why,' he says. 'The only thing you can really compare this with is the situation we saw with the terrorist bombings in Madrid in March 2004. Yes, it was days of furious activity, especially for surgeons and in intensive-care units, but it was nothing like this.'

Cereceda and many other doctors and nurses argue that the coronavirus has shown what happens when you make unprecedented demands of a health service that, in many areas, is still struggling to recover from the 2008 economic crisis and the deep cuts that followed.

'We've been warning for years that we don't have enough nurses to look after patients even in normal circumstances, let alone in a pandemic like the one we're in,' says María José García, a spokeswoman for the Satse nursing union. If the number of infected nurses continues to increase, wonders García, 'who's going to look after all the patients?'

Cereceda is especially angry that huge public events three weeks ago – including the International Women's Day marches, a 9,000-person meeting in Madrid of the far-right Vox party and countless sporting fixtures – were allowed to go ahead despite what was going on elsewhere in the world. 'We failed to listen to the alarm bells that were ringing in our sister country, Italy, and that's led to a huge, exponential growth in cases,' he says.

'There was a tsunami warning that they ignored. Now the wave's hit and we're all underwater.'

But it isn't just hospital workers who are finding themselves on the coronavirus frontline. Three residential-home workers, who are members of the Aetesys nursing association, are in hospital themselves after they tended to infected residents. 'Healthcare workers are dropping like flies at the moment,' says the association's president, Elvira González Santos.

'And we're the ones who are being told to do the job that some nurses don't have to do; we're the ones who look after all a resident's hygiene needs.'

And then there are the funeral companies. On a normal March day, says Alfredo Gosálvez of the National Association of Funeral Services (Panasef), undertakers would deal with 80 deaths in Madrid. They are now dealing with about 300 a day. Gosálvez says his members also lack the protective equipment they need 'as the last link in the public health chain' and are struggling to keep up with the demand. 'Funeral workers are used to difficult situations and they're giving it all they've got, working double shifts, 18-hour days and running themselves ragged. Hundreds of them haven't rested for days.'

Juan Camilo Meza is a 'very, very tired but still healthy' anaesthetist at Mataró hospital near Barcelona. 'Everyone's putting in the same hours: you can see it in the bags under their eyes and in the fact that they're not making jokes like they used to,' he says. 'You can feel the tension and the fear in the air. No one was ready for anything like this.'

Spring

Who stockpiled all the yeast? Don't worry, bread-lovers, I have a solution

ADRIAN CHILES

There is so much I don't understand about all this ghastly business. But one question torments me above all others: where has all the bloody yeast gone?

First, they came for the toilet roll. And then for the flour. The strong white bread flour was first to go, followed by the plain white, the wholemeal, the self-raising and then, in no particular order, the rye, the spelt, the khorasan and all the other mysterious varieties that no one normally buys. Soon there was none.

I was livid. I thought I was the only clever dick clever enough to bake his own bread. Who were these flour thieves? I know we are all in this together blah blah, but this was beyond the pale. I bet these arrivistes watched a couple of *Bake Offs* and bought Paul Hollywood's book, which I dare say has remained unopened. Well, good luck to you.

The first flour to make it back on to the shelves in my supermarket was strong white bread flour, in big 3kg bags. I had a standoff with a bloke who had the last one clutched to his chest like a rugby player going into a maul. I would happily have fought him, as he was much smaller than me, but couldn't have done so without breaching social distancing guidelines. We were nose-to-nose, resembling fighters at a weigh-in, except these floury fighters' noses were 200cm apart. He flicked his eyes upwards to the top shelf. There were three more bags up there. So I forgave him and the matter was closed.

When this crisis first broke, I felt I knew for the first time what really mattered: the health of loved ones, and not much else. Big things I had previously worried about suddenly seemed so small. But then the small things, such as bread flour, themselves became big things.

I have flour now but nowhere, anywhere, can I get yeast. Where has it all gone? There must be so much out there that if a biblical flood were added to our woes, all this unused yeast would dissolve in it and rise up, frothing, to bake us in a giant crusty loaf of calamity.

Luckily, I don't need yeast. Since I was a student, I have been fascinated by Irish soda bread. When I was revising for my finals in 1990, I tore a recipe out of a newspaper and, seeing a fine excuse not to read any more stupid Henry James, I got busy. I have been fiddling away trying to perfect this recipe for 30 years, to the extent that it's now no more authentically Irish than I am. But it is, if I may say so, perfect. This is my gift to the yeastless:

Combine 15g of bicarbonate of soda, 10g of salt, 5g of caraway seeds, a handful of porridge oats or any other random seeds. Then mix that with 400g of a combination of any flours. Stir in half a litre of milk, soured with the juice of one lemon. Then melt together a generous tablespoon of black treacle and an equally generous teaspoon of Marmite in a small pan and stir that in, too. Lick the Marmitey/treacly pan clean; it's a taste sensation. You should now have either a sloppy dough or stiff batter, depending on how you look at it. Bake at 190°C (fan-assisted) for an hour in a one-litre loaf tin.

The yeast-rich can try it when they finally run out in five years or so.

6 April

For the EU to emerge stronger, Merkel must seize the moment

TIMOTHY GARTON ASH

'Europe will be forged in crises,' said Jean Monnet, one of the founding fathers of the European Union, 'and will be the sum of the solutions adopted for those crises.' What kind of Europe emerges from the coronavirus crisis will depend on the answers given to three tests.

First, the Hungarian test: can a dictatorship be a member of the EU? Even before this year, Viktor Orbán and his Fidesz party had so far eroded democracy in Hungary that the country would not qualify for admission to the EU if it were a candidate for membership. He has now used the coronavirus pandemic as justification to take sweeping emergency powers, allowing him to rule by decree for an unlimited period. Hungary is – for the duration of these powers – a dictatorship. Monnet also said a dictatorship cannot be a member of the European Community (which subsequently became the EU). Today, one is.

The sanctions available to EU institutions are slow and complex, but there is one organisation that can and should act decisively now: the European People's party (EPP), the hugely influential centre-right grouping to which Fidesz still effectively belongs. (Although the party is notionally suspended, Fidesz MEPs still operate as part of the EPP group in the European parliament.) The EPP should have kicked Fidesz out long ago. Instead, it has pursued a policy of appeasement. If it does not expel the Hungarian dictator's party now, it will lose any last shreds of credibility. When

EPP politicians make fine speeches about democracy, the rule of law and European values, young Europeans will be more than justified in shouting: you utter hypocrites!

Next, the Italian test. Is there solidarity in the heart of Europe? Will the eurozone enable its hardest-hit member states to recover? Last month we watched with horror as one of the most highly developed parts of our continent, with one of the best health services, was overwhelmed by the pandemic. When Italy emerges from this Gehenna, it will face a huge challenge of economic recovery, handicapped by the fact it already has one of the eurozone's heaviest burdens of national debt. Its ability to borrow the large sums needed will depend on the credibility of mutual support inside the eurozone.

Even before the pandemic, Italy had gone from being one of the most Europhile countries in the EU to one of the most Eurosceptic. The crisis has exacerbated these feelings. In one poll conducted early last month, 88 per cent of Italians said they felt that Europe was not supporting Italy, and a staggering 67 per cent said they saw EU membership as a disadvantage. There is a European Union without Britain. There is no European Union without Italy.

And finally, there is the test facing Germany: can it save the day? Will Europe's central power finally face up to the logic of a monetary union from which it has very significantly benefited? Germany has produced the most impressive national response to the pandemic of any democracy outside Asia. Its provision of large-scale testing, ventilators and critical care beds shows the advantages of having both good public services and a strong medical industry. Angela Merkel gave an outstanding television address to the nation – a lecture on democracy, solidarity and individual responsibility, delivered with the brain of a scientist and the heart of a pastor's daughter. Only one thing was missing. The word 'Europe' was not mentioned.

In the meantime, Germany has shown solidarity with its hard-pressed European neighbours, sending consignments of face masks to Lombardy and transporting critically ill Italian and French patients to German hospitals. But it is in responding to the economic and political crisis that German leadership is really called for.

Germany can help Europe pass the Hungarian test, not least because Merkel's Christian Democrats are the most powerful party in the EPP. Now they must surely come out for the expulsion of Fidesz. All the candidates to succeed Merkel as leader of the Christian Democrats should be asked where they stand on this.

It is in meeting the Italian test, however, that Germany's contribution will be decisive. As one recent headline put it, Italy's future is in German hands. If the eurozone – and therefore Europe – is to recover economic health, the Italian government and other southern European governments must be able to borrow money using the financial credibility of Germany and other northern European states. In the dry jargon, there would be 'debt mutuali-sation'. Next to Italy, Spain has been hardest hit by the crisis. The Spanish prime minister, Pedro Sánchez, has talked of the need for Europe to build a 'wartime economy' and appealed for a new intra-European Marshall plan.

Seven leading German economists have cogently argued that this recovery plan should include the issuance of €1 trillion of community bonds, jointly guaranteed by all eurozone govern-ments. Unlike the eurobonds discussed after the financial crisis, this would be new money, dedicated to addressing the results of a disaster for which no southern European government could possibly be held responsible. To ask how precisely this support is best given would take us into the acronymic weeds of ECB, EIB, ESM and even EFSM (don't ask). But the basic question is simple: having cast aside its own fiscal taboos ('debt brake', 'black zero') to help itself out, to the tune of what may well turn out to be close to €1 trillion, is Germany prepared to do a fraction of that to help other countries in the same boat? In the case of a monetary union, 'the same boat' is not just a loose metaphor. Whatever package European leaders agree upon this week, it must be big, and be seen to be big.

Germany's leading tabloid, *Bild*, recently published an open letter to Italy headed: 'We are with you!' It praised Italy for having brought 'good food' to Germany and concluded: '*Ciao, Italia*. We'll see you again shortly. Here's to an espresso, a *vino rosso*, whether on holiday or in the pizzeria.' An interesting idea of solidarity. A few days earlier, the same paper published an article headlined: 'What will become of the euro? Debt mutualisation is threatened.' Dear *Bild* reader, what Italy needs is not your custom over a holiday espresso in Tuscany, charming though that would doubtless be, but the mutualisation of debt, as a necessary consequence of a European monetary union from which you, dear *Bild* reader, have benefited greatly.

There is one person in Europe who can both take and defend the necessary actions: Chancellor Merkel. Last year, I argued that Germany needed a change of government, because the grand coalition was exhausted and was strengthening the political extremes in opposition to it. That is out of the question now, in the middle of a force-10 storm. Instead, Merkel has an unexpected last chance to go down in history as a major architect of a stronger European Union. Bismarck said a politician's task is to hear God's footsteps advancing through history, and then jump to hang on to his coattails. That coat is passing now.

6 April

The *Guardian* view on Keir Starmer: a serious politician

GUARDIAN EDITORIAL

Sir Keir Starmer's arrival as Labour leader is an important moment for British politics. He offers diligence and expertise, not bellowing and finger-pointing. In a crisis this seriousness will be an asset. Sir Keir has unified the party by retaining a tax-and-spend agenda. He also represents a break with the past. There is no resonant phrase, or signature policy, that one can decode to understand the incipient Starmer project. This makes it hard to define what Sir Keir stands for politically. But it is clear what he is not: a populist.

Sir Keir's victory does signal a more competent and less sectarian approach. Labour's shadow cabinet has room for defeated rivals, with the leftwing Rebecca Long-Bailey getting education. His apology to the Jewish community is heartfelt and overdue. The symbolism of the three top Labour jobs, the leader aside, being occupied by politicians from the north, Wales and Scotland sends a powerful message that the party aims to represent the whole country. Making a welcome return to the frontline is Ed Miliband, a former party leader and an articulate proponent of the Green New Deal, who will become shadow business, energy and industrial secretary.

Labour's frontbench is powered by some prominent members of the People's Vote campaign. It might have helped to keep a Labour leaver, such as Jon Trickett, on for balance. Although the 2020 Labour leadership contest stretched out over three long months, the Covid-19 pandemic has meant that the hiatus did not give the Conservatives an opportunity to frame Labour as an irrelevance. The Tories have retained a substantial lead in recent opinion polls. This advantage will probably evaporate as the sloppy response from government ministers sinks in.

In an encouraging sign of his professionalism, Sir Keir attacked the government's shambolic handling of the crisis at the weekend, while offering constructive suggestions for ministers to set out an exit strategy from the lockdown. In the longer run, the Labour leader cannot let coronavirus define his opposition to the government. He will need to respond to the current crises of our age, which have been thrown into sharp relief by the Covid-19 outbreak. A decade of cuts has shredded the welfare safety net and left health and social care systems woefully under-resourced, while the fissuring of the workplace makes it difficult for governments to send help to workers with insecure employment. Sir Keir is right to say that the wealthy must pay a fair share to rebuild a post-coronavirus society.

Corbynism rose as a response to the living standards crisis, a concentration of corporate power and years of austerity. Sir Keir's project will have to define the question it is the answer to. There is no shortage of pressing issues beyond the pathogen: dealing with growing wealth inequality; a climate emergency; how to bring a fractured United Kingdom back together.

Sir Keir has remade the shadow cabinet. He will want to change the party. His ability to exude Blairite competence and Corbynite idealism will only take him so far. There are precious few clues as to the direction in which he will head. We live in an era when political ambiguity is subject to a level of scrutiny that can brutally punish those who deploy it ineffectually. Sir Keir's embrace of a programme to transform society and tame capitalism means that his party's supporters won't swallow timid policies. The next election is scheduled to be four years away. The country may be very different to the one we live in now. Sir Keir's job is to make sure that his party's progressive and radical policies inspire hope, not fear.

7 APRIL

Boris Johnson's illness is a message to us all about the true nature of coronavirus

MARTIN KETTLE

Boris Johnson's move last night into intensive care in London's St Thomas' hospital marks a turning point in Britain's national Covid-19 crisis. On one level it is just one more personal crisis for another of the more than 1.3 million human victims of the virus around the world. But on another level it is much more than that, and its full significance for Britain has not yet been properly understood.

The incapacity of any prime minister at any time always throws a government machine into confusion. That's no different in the case of Johnson's sickness than in the many previous cases in British history in which other prime ministers have been afflicted by illness or the need for surgery. But the machine will adapt. It's what government machines do.

What is different this time, and much more important, is the wider potential resonance across the country of Johnson's worsening condition and his hospitalisation. The prime minister has been struck down by something that threatens every person in the land directly every day. Most of us are dutifully following the lockdown advice in our hidden away anonymity to defy it. Only a minority of us have caught the coronavirus. Many of us know no one in our close circle who has had to go to hospital because of it.

But we all know Johnson. We all know what and who he is. Even my three-year-old granddaughter knows that it is Boris Johnson who has said she can't go outside. Johnson's medical crisis is not just his own. It speaks more widely to the nation. It conveys an unexpected, brutal and disturbing message. Whether we voted for him or not, Johnson is this country's elected leader. He's in charge. In a crisis, the buck stops with him. But in this crisis, our prime minister is receiving oxygen in an intensive care unit and is not in a fit state to govern.

The words 'Boris Johnson' and 'seriousness' are not often encountered together. He has spent much of his life breaking rules and behaving self-indulgently. But his hospitalisation over- leaps all that. I suspect it also takes this country into a more serious place than it has previously reached in the battle with Covid-19. The thought of a prone Johnson surrounded by the doctors, nurses and equipment that were so powerfully glimpsed in the intensive care department of another London hospital on Monday night's BBC news bulletins will come as a shock to supporters and opponents of the prime minister alike. Millions will have discovered a deep well of compassion towards Johnson that they never suspected they could possess.

The leader who is struck down amid the fight for survival is a potent archetype in art and literature. The wounded chieftain is a deep point of reference in the history of many cultures of every tradition, and in every part of these islands from at least Arthu- rian times onwards. Johnson may never acquire the legendary status of an Arthur, but the shock of the news of his hospitalisa- tion reaches out nevertheless into every corner of the country.

There will, glumly, be some who respond to Johnson's distress without compassion of any kind. Some will simply not care. For most, though, the effect is likely to be more sobering and stiff-ening. Nothing that has yet happened in this outbreak brings home more clearly that we are in a collective struggle. Nothing is more likely to supply a voice in people's heads when they ask themselves whether they should stick to the state's advice to self-isolate and maintain distance from others. Nothing is more likely to nudge our behaviour in a more responsible and sensibly cautious direction.

Boris Johnson's political career has often been divisive. But his vulnerability to the virus and his current distress tell a different and ultimately more important story. We are living through a time when the shadow of death is passing across the land more fatefully than normal. Perhaps the most improbable thing in Johnson's life is that in this dark hour he has surprised us into the need to be serious.

12 APRIL

10,000 UK coronavirus deaths: don't forget that this was preventable

NESRINE MALIK

Cast your mind back four weeks. Coronavirus deaths in the UK were in the tens, and the disease was ravaging Italy. The daily death tolls from Italy and then Spain were reported every 24 hours and the numbers were staggering, unfathomable and rising. Italy was 'overwhelmed', succumbing to a tragic scenario because of quarantine enforcement failures, and an inability to predict how quickly the disease would be transmitted. The highest daily death toll recorded in Italy was on 28 March, with 971 deaths. Spain's highest came five days later with 950. On Friday, the death toll in UK hospitals was 980.

The UK is now surpassing the apocalyptic tolls we fixated on just two weeks ago. The same tragedies are unfolding across our country. Doctors and nurses are dying, exposed to heavy viral loads and often without adequate protective equipment. Covid-19 wards are saturated, echoing the calls of distress from Italian medical staff, as the specific shifts of doctors and nurses disappear and blend into one long rota. But the sense of distress with which the Italian scenario was reported and received in the UK is strangely absent. Missing, too, is the urgent need to understand why this is happening.

It is as if those who should be asking the questions, from the media to opposition politicians, have been subjected to a mass memory-erasing exercise. Every report showing the scale of the crisis should be framed in the language of accountability and anchored in the premise of preventability. With all the benefits of hindsight, the government dragged its feet, wasted precious time and infused the issue with a sense of British exceptionalism: drastic measures need not be taken because in the UK things will somehow be different.

If there was any chance of the interrogation happening, it was made even less likely by Boris Johnson's illness. It was folded into a larger, editorialised narrative about his martyrdom and indefatigability, turning his sickness and recovery into a virtue. And as that hagiography was being enthusiastically written, the stories of thousands of dead and grieving were buried under daily updates of the prime minister's 'high spirits' from his ICU bed. Questions over his responsibility for the national carnage –

his complacent messaging over shaking hands with the afflicted, his delay in shutting down the country, his 'herd immunity' policy, the ongoing lack of testing, of equipment and of ventilators – were not asked. The organisers of Cheltenham festival, which attracted more than 250,000 people between 10 and 13 March, justified going ahead by citing the presence of Johnson at an international rugby match a few days before.

The terminology of war did much of the work. The virus was framed in the context of an enemy to be fought in the trenches, rather than a series of public health policy failures. The death toll became not a daily count of individual devastation, but a cold sterile ticker of battle casualties. The Queen's message, a call for noble resolve, further generalised the crisis into an act of God that we must weather by mobilising the powers of the British national character. It's now a matter of grit, of reaching into our reserves to see us through until we meet again.

Despite the extent of the crisis, many doctors and nurses fear speaking on the record. I have received WhatsApp messages from NHS staff too afraid even to email them in case the paper trail leads to disciplinary action – detailing horrors of an NHS stretched thin, of ill-protected staff doing 36-hour shifts. They will be clapped every week, as the government claims to champion the NHS, yet gagged if they dare raise concerns. There is an effort to silence voices such as that of Abdul Mabud Chowdhury, a consultant who appealed publicly for protective equipment, only to perish from coronavirus days later. The official line last Tuesday was that we could be 'moving in the right direction'. That day, the daily death toll almost doubled to 786.

The contrast between the numbers and the jadedness with which we meet them is down to some daily numbing effect, no doubt. This is made worse by the fact there are other exceptional circumstances to reckon with as we deal with self-isolation, loss of income and disruption to work and personal lives. And then there's the time lag. It's hard, as we lock down, to nurture an outrage when the loss of life is happening today – more so when the government has shifted the responsibility entirely on to the public by robotically repeating the mantra: 'Stay home, protect the NHS, save lives'. So, as lives are extinguished in their hundreds every day, we become busied with questions of policing, of social distancing, of shutting down parks, rather than on the government's failed policymaking.

So, again, cast your mind back four weeks. Remember how it felt to see those numbers from Italy, how our hearts sank every time they went up by the hundreds, how we envisioned those numbers as terrorised citizens facing the end of their lives. Remember how we reeled at the thought that they all had families and friends whom they could not contact in their final moments, and who are now devastated by their loss. Relocate the pain and recall that this need not have happened. Ten thousand people, in UK hospitals alone, have now died.

16 APRIL

Corbyn and Sanders may have gone, but they have radically altered our politics

OWEN JONES

With compelling symmetry, four days after Jeremy Corbyn's tenure as Labour leader ended, Bernie Sanders suspended his presidential campaign. The insurgencies they led first gathered pace in a political galaxy far, far away, back in 2015, before the era of Brexit or Trump. Both were implausible figureheads: little known outside left milieus, used to addressing sparsely attended meetings on rainy Thursday nights rather than mass rallies, men of a certain age who were largely rejected by their own generations leading movements disproportionately powered by those born after they had reached adulthood. And now their often bitter critics – whether on the right or centre – celebrate their defeats as something more profound: as a rout of the ideas and political vision they had come to represent.

They are likely to be disappointed. Yes, the British and US new left have failed to achieve lasting political leadership in their own parties, let alone assume state power; their activists are currently demoralised and exhausted. Both found a mass reception for their ideas after the left had spent a generation in the wilderness, meaning they lacked personnel with political experience, all while being undermined by entrenched hostility from their own parties. But on neither side of the Atlantic is the left going anywhere.

Their opponents saw the Corbyn and Sanders phenomena as mass irrationality and delusion, as flight from reality and an indulgence of impossible dreams. In truth, both emerged because of material conditions for millions of people that, far from improving, are about to plumb new depths. There was a reason why Sanders enjoyed the overwhelming support of Democrats under 35, or why more voters under 40 opted for Labour in 2017 than polling has ever recorded. This isn't a story of the supposed naive idealism of youth, slowly eroded by the experience of adulthood. If this cliche were true, then several polls in the 1980s wouldn't have suggested Ronald Reagan was most popular among the young, while Margaret Thatcher would not have won the youth vote so decisively in 1983.

The answer is straightforward. The free-market revolution promised to liberate the individual from the supposedly oppressive confines of the state and collectivism, to allow them to achieve their full potential unhindered. Instead, that 'freedom' was experienced as insecurity, which was only heightened by the aftermath of the financial crash. While nearly half of American baby boomers were homeowners by the age of 30, only just over a third of millennials have acquired a home by the time they hit their thirties. The number of middle-income young adults in Britain who own a home has halved in two decades, while getting a council house – stocks of which have been drastically depleted during the same period – isn't an option, and the privately rented sector devours their pay packets.

Those who went to university are clobbered with student debt, and even then an often low-paid, insecure job beckons. In no high-income country other than Greece have the under-30s suffered such a fall in income as in Britain. From cuts to social security to the shredding of youth services, so much that gave people a sense of security and the sense that things will get better has been stripped away. It is this that drove the Sanders movement, Corbynism and Podemos in Spain; and although all failed to convince enough of the older generation, proving a fatal roadblock to victory, does anyone think the material conditions that led so many young people to seek radical answers will suddenly evaporate?

The opposite, of course, is true. When lockdown finally ends, the vaccine is injected into our veins and commuters pack again into buses and trains, the question of who foots the bill for economic calamity will beckon. 'No one wants to hear it,' says George Osborne, singing from his only hymn sheet, 'but we're going to have to make uncomfortable choices about how we pay for this.' Those who spent most of their adulthoods in the shadow of Lehman Brothers' collapse may find their wallets are going to be inspected again by Tory politicians. Unprecedented peacetime state interventionism has shifted what is deemed to be politically possible, while grand social injustices – how badly paid 'essential workers' are, the economic insecurity of millions, the underfunding of the NHS, our shredded welfare state – have been painfully exposed. If now isn't the time for radicalism, then when?

Here's how the story usually goes when the left is defeated. Disheartened and directionless, it is enveloped by infighting and bitterness, by the internal spats its critics love to caricature as *Monty Python*-esque. This would be a grave error. While the likely Democratic nominee, Joe Biden, is politically closer to a 'one-nation' British Tory than a Labour politician, the US left has unquestionably radically repositioned the Democratic party's political centre of gravity. Keir Starmer's mandate is rooted in promising to abide by the core tenets of Corbyn's political prospectus. The British and US left must defend their political gains, resist sectarianism and strike broad political alliances.

After its colossal defeats in the 1980s, Britain's left retreated into being a grumpy, isolated fringe; it fell into political opposition to its previous allies on the so-called soft left, many of whom then entered into alliance with the party's right. A repetition of history must be resisted. A coalition should be built between those who voted for Rebecca Long-Bailey or Starmer to defend the '10 pledges' of the victor, from raising taxes on the rich to common ownership to extending the welfare state. The new left was an alliance between survivors of past political struggles and a youth politicised by movements against war, tuition fees, tax avoidance, austerity and climate emergency. It is the latter group that must now assume its leadership.

When the financial system crashed in 2008, the left had few ideas of its own in the bank, and was instead defined by slogans expressing what it was opposed to rather than any coherent vision of what a new society could look like. Now the left brims with policies and ideas that are not just appropriated by mainstream centre-left politicians but even raided by the political right. Those who were inspired by 'For the many not the few' in Britain, by 'Not me. Us' in the US, by '*¡Sí, se puede!*' ('Yes, we can!') chanted in the squares of Spain have not gone anywhere. The age of corona and looming climate emergency demands an even more ambitious vision. The left has not triumphed, but it hasn't died either: and it may well be today's disappointed youth who will find vindication in a new world free of injustice that they may yet one day build.

17 APRIL

Who needs a middle-aged woman screaming: 'I am scared to go to Morrisons' via video link?

GRACE DENT

It struck me, during week four, as I made yet another freezer inventory and mail-ordered herbs to avoid my once-weekly shop, that I have become a little too good at obeying the government's orders. Much is made of the rule-flouters – the Frisbee-chuckers and park pond-paddlers; we hear lots, too, about the ramblers and picnickers. My favourite 'Covidiot' pictures, which I search out daily for light relief, are the Stasi-style pap shots of shoppers coming out of The Range. Among all the death and dystopian headlines, I grimly enjoy these people, sheepishly trundling trolleys to their Volvos filled with ceramic garden Buddhas, 15 litres of Daffodil White paint and signs that say, 'It's Prosecco O'Clock'.

I may tut and cluck at this wilful dissent, but part of me is just jealous. These people are still rushing out the moment a 'reason' allows them to. Meanwhile, I stand in my kitchen, re-wiping surfaces with pine forest disinfectant and batch-freezing *mirepoix* (a fancy name for diced carrot, onion and celery) so as not to waste some sad-looking veg. It's not sunbathers the government should fret over; it's the millions of us it will need to convince, once this is over, to come out, blinking into the light.

I'm already teetering on the brink of agoraphobia; let's call it agoraphobia-lite. I'm not strictly qualified to self-diagnose anxiety disorders, or allot them cute names, but I'm guessing the NHS is a bit snowed under right now. They do not need a middle-aged woman with a Mallen streak and rough hands like Skeksis from *The Dark Crystal* screaming: 'I am scared to go to Morrisons' via video link.

Lockdown is disastrous for the economy, it has riven families apart and imprisoned others with their tormentors. So why do I fear it ending? Perhaps it's because, I, like millions of others, may be treading water in a difficult place, but at least it's the known unknown. I fear fresh, frightening unknowns to come to terms with all over again. I should probably pop a recipe idea or something in here, because this is ostensibly a food column. How about, when the existential angst comes, open your cupboards, smear peanut butter and mashed ripe banana on white bread, and fry it in butter? Elvis lived on these, apparently, during his last difficult years at Graceland. He found them a positive boon, until he, well, didn't.

My mother, classed as highly vulnerable by Matt Hancock, is talking much less now about a normal life after Covid-19 in our daily phone calls. Cream teas in crowded tea-rooms, fish and chips on the Northumbrian coast and Sunday pub lunches at the Drunken Duck in Ambleside feel impossible. 'I can't imagine me going out after this,' she says, before reading out more deaths from the local paper.

My mother appears not to be remotely scared of dying. What's more, the lack of fuss around any funeral suits her down to the ground.

'Don't even bother coming,' she says, casually.

'No, I won't,' I say, drily.

'And no flowers – they're just a waste of money,' she says.

'How about a coffin?' I ask. 'Or shall we just wrap you in tea towels?'

'Suits me,' she says. 'I won't know.'

How will the world look when I can finally visit her again? Will I travel on the train in a mask and gloves surrounded by 100 other faceless travellers, clutching paperwork? Will I be met with suspicion when I arrive, as an outsider bringing germs? Will I walk into her lounge and hug her or will I stand 12 feet away in a hazmat suit, shouting muffled platitudes?

And if all this happens soon, forgive me if I stay a shut-in for a little bit longer. The future is an uncharted country. At least I know what weird is now.

21 APRIL

Doubt is essential for science – but for politicians, it's a sign of weakness

JIM AL-KHALILI

During the coronavirus crisis, everyone seems to have a 'scientific' opinion. We are all discussing modelling, exponential curves, infection rates and antibody tests; suddenly, we're all experts on epidemiology, immunology and virology. When the public hears that new scientific evidence has informed a sudden change in government policy, the tendency is to conclude that the scientists don't know what they're doing, and therefore can't be trusted. It doesn't help that politicians are remarkably bad at communicating scientific information clearly and transparently, while journalists are often more adept at asking questions of politicians than they are of scientists.

It has never been more important to communicate the way science works. In politics, admitting a mistake is seen as a form of weakness. It's quite the opposite in science, where making mistakes is a cornerstone of knowledge. Replacing old theories and hypotheses with newer, more accurate ones allows us to gain a deeper understanding of a subject. In the meantime, we develop mathematical models and make predictions based on data and available evidence. With something as new as this coronavirus, we started with a low baseline of knowledge. As we accumulate new data, our models and predictions will continue to evolve and improve.

A second important feature of the scientific method is valuing doubt over certainty. The notion of doubt is one worth exploring. We can trace its origins to a medieval intellectual movement, and to two individuals in particular, the Arab scholar Ibn al-Haytham (Alhazen) and the Persian scholar Razi (Rhazes). The movement was called *al-shukuk* in Arabic ('the doubts'), and it refuted the wisdom inherited from ancient Greek scholars more than 1,000 years earlier in subjects such as astronomy and medicine. Al-Haytham, an early advocate of the scientific method, cast doubts on the writing of the Hellenic astronomer Ptolemy, and suggested that one should question not only existing knowledge but also one's own ideas – and be prepared to modify or overturn them in light of contradictory evidence. He overthrew the millennium-old idea that we can see things because our eyes shine light on objects, and gave the first correct explanation of vision.

This approach still informs how we do science today. Indeed, this is how the scientific method differs from the stance of conspiracy theorists. Conspiracists will argue that, like scientists, they too are sceptics who question everything and value the importance of evidence. But in science, while we can be confident that our theories and descriptions of the world are correct, we can never be completely certain. After all, if an observation or new experimental result comes along and conflicts with an existing theory, we have to abandon our old presuppositions. In a very real sense, conspiracy theorists are the polar opposite of scientists; they assimilate evidence that contradicts their core beliefs, and interpret this evidence in a way that confirms, rather than repudiates, these beliefs.

Often, in the case of such ideological beliefs, we hear the term 'cognitive dissonance', whereby someone feels genuine mental discomfort when confronted with evidence that contradicts a view they hold. This can work to reinforce pre-existing beliefs. Ask a conspiracy theorist this: what would it take for them to change their minds? Their answer, because they are so utterly committed to their view, is likely to be that nothing would. In science, however, we learn to admit our mistakes and to change our minds to account for new evidence about the world.

This is crucial in the current pandemic. Stubborn adherence to a particular strategy despite new evidence to the contrary can be catastrophic. We must be prepared to shift our approach as more data is accumulated and our model predictions become more reliable. That is a strength, not a weakness, of the scientific method.

I have spent my career stressing the importance of having a scientifically literate society. I don't mean that everyone should be well versed in cosmology or quantum physics, or understand the difference between RNA and DNA. But we should certainly all know the difference between bacteria and viruses. Even more importantly, if we are to get through this pandemic, we must all have a basic understanding of how science works – and an acknowledgment that during a crisis of this kind, admitting doubt rather than pretending certainty can be a source of strength.

27 APRIL

'The bliss of a quiet period': lockdown is a unique chance to study the nature of cities

PHOEBE WESTON

Peregrine falcons have swapped sea cliffs for the UK parliament and red-crowned parrots have left tropical forests in Mexico for the leafy neighbourhoods of Pasadena. Cities all over the world have their own unique ecological concoctions created by mixing human settlements with wildlife. Coronavirus-induced lockdown is changing the daily rhythm of urban life, shining a light on emboldened animals that usually prefer to remain hidden. Biologists and ecologists normally feel more at home studying remote jungles or inaccessible mountain tops, where 'real' nature is. But as our planet gets covered with cities, more and more environments are being run by humans, who have become a super keystone species.

Cities are not mausoleums for nature but modern-day versions of the Galapagos archipelago, according to Menno Schilthuizen, author of *Darwin Comes to Town*, a book about contemporary evolution in cities where rapid changes can be observed within a human lifetime. 'Only in our flights of fancy can we still keep nature divorced from the human environment. Out in the real world, our tentacles entwine nature's fabric,' Schilthuizen writes. 'While we have been trying to save the world's crumbling pre-urban ecosystems, we have been ignoring the fact that nature has already been putting up the scaffolds to build novel, urban ecosystems for the future.'

Haunting images of wolves, bison and bears living in deserted towns following the 1986 Chernobyl disaster indicate what happens when humans leave a place for good. The coronavirus lockdown shows how quickly wildlife closes in. 'It is interesting to consider how fragile our urban environment is. If we're not constantly present, it's being taken over by nature very quickly,' says Schilthuizen, who is professor of evolutionary biology at Leiden University in the Netherlands.

The unique thing about coronavirus is that it is causing multiple cities across the globe to simultaneously go into hibernation. This gives ecologists an insight into how humans change urban biodiversity in multiple locations. 'Animals are nearby, constantly watching us from the outskirts and the forests, and as soon as our presence seems to be abating they start exploring where new terrain could be won ... It makes you aware of how we're constantly competing with many species,' says Schilthuizen.

Historically, urban environments have been seen as too contaminated by humans to teach us anything important about biodiversity. In the past few decades this has started to change but we still know little about the urban wildlife we live alongside, says Rana El-Sabaawi, associate professor of biology at Canada's University of Victoria. 'If you look in the literature, the field of urban ecology doesn't really come into its own until the last decade or two. Before that there were a smattering of papers and reports, mostly descriptions of biodiversity trends in and around specific cities. In recent years there has been a growing appreciation of the ecological mechanisms that explain biodiversity in the city,' she says.

Urban environments are messy places (full of lights, pollution and people pursuing their own interests), which makes studying them difficult. It's all very well to observe animals and plants in urban places, but understanding how these different processes fit together is more problematic.

At the same time, there is increasing recognition that few places on Earth are free from human influence – there is a plastic bag at the bottom of the Mariana Trench, and Antarctica's remote glaciers are flecked with microplastics. Understanding places where humans interact with nature most should help planners and developers create cities that hold as much wildlife as possible.

Broadly speaking, 'sensitive' species, whose habitat is destroyed by urban developments, are unlikely to venture into urban areas. 'Opportunists', which have a much broader diet and high tolerance for noise and pollution, are more at home. Coronavirus means species that might lie in the grey area between these categories are now more likely to venture into previously unexplored urban areas.

Racoons, pigeons, foxes, gulls and crows are opportunists and considered a nuisance by many humans who live alongside them. Animals such as these, which scavenge human rubbish to get food, are likely to be struggling during lockdown. Ring-necked parakeets might disperse away from urban parks and forage on agricultural land instead. Residents of the East Riding in Yorkshire have been warned seagulls could be more aggressive because there are fewer seaside day-trippers feeding them leftover chips. In Amsterdam, even coots – which sometimes line their nests with plastic – may have a tough time finding replacement materials.

'Often what happens when food supply runs short is increased competition and aggression between animals,' says El-Sabaawi. 'There have already been fascinating reports from Asia about monkey "brawls" caused by food shortages. If the food shortages are really severe and extended, then populations might decline.'

Other animals seem to be doing well with fewer people on the street. Urban songbirds, for example, can communicate more easily when the din of background traffic is reduced. Deer, badgers and wild boar might be emboldened to start pinching food from suburban gardens or roadsides. A herd of goats has been running riot through the Welsh town of Llandudno, munching on people's gardens as they go.

Most researchers are agreed these species' corona-related behavioural changes are temporary and the luxury of living in town will stop when humans re-emerge. Lockdown will probably have a similar effect on wildlife populations as an exceptionally wet or hot year – provided things return to how they were.

In terms of wildlife sightings during this period, it's hard to separate fact, fiction and wishful thinking – it's a complex picture and new research is starting to try to make sense of what is happening.

Scientists have launched a Silent Cities project to look at the diversity of sounds in places normally masked by anthropogenic noise. People are being encouraged to record sounds in 'ordinary' suburban/urban spaces such as in a backyard or on a balcony during lockdown, and compare it to noises when things are back to normal.

Cities are also powerhouses for permanent changes. For example, there are distinct subspecies of mosquitoes found on the London underground that no longer hibernate and feed on human blood as opposed to bird blood, according to research published in *Nature* in 1999. Even more remarkable, mosquitoes living on different tube lines do not mix so the population living on the Circle line is genetically different to those living on the Piccadilly line. This change happened over 100 generations or so – significantly faster than Charles Darwin thought possible.

Urban blackbirds are also morphing into a new species, according to Schilthuizen. Across European and north African cities, blackbirds living in urban areas have developed shorter bills (probably thanks to an abundance of bird feeders and easier pickings in cities). Traffic noise has caused urban blackbirds to sing in the night when it's quieter, and they also breed around a month earlier than their countryside cousins.

Scientists think the urban blackbird, *Turdus urbanicus*, could be the first of many species to adapt to life in the city. Schilthuizen writes: 'The pace of evolution is set by ecological opportunities that emerge from human interactions … In those pressure cookers of environmental change, species will need to speed up their evolution or become extinct.'

Changes in botany have been massive in the past decade, with huge shifts in wild plants living in urban areas, according to London-based botanist Dr Mark Spencer. 'Plants have lived with us in our cities for thousands of years and they move along with us and they tell stories about us,' he says.

London is an important focal point for the arrival of non-native species in the UK, either arriving accidentally by international trade (via wool, for example) or escapees from domestic horticulture. Cities are the first pitstop for species that could later spread around the whole country. For example, loquat (a common cousin of plums, cherries and apricots) is becoming established in London where Greek and Turkish communities typically live because people spit out the pips on the ground after they've eaten the fruit. And now it's starting to sprout in the wild.

Will lockdown change how people interact with nature? Probably not, says Schilthuizen. 'I'm enjoying the quiet. I keep thinking to myself, this is the way things should be, without constant air traffic overhead and without constant noise of traffic and throngs of people spending money on the streets ... But I think we have a short memory. The bliss of a quiet period – or the memory of that period – will disappear quite quickly.'

30 APRIL

What my mother's glorious life taught me about Britain today

ADITYA CHAKRABORTTY

My darling mother died early this month. Her death was peaceful and painless – and it was not due to the coronavirus. Yet it was shaped by the pandemic, as is its aftermath. The register office, the undertakers, the crematorium: the usual institutions of death are now inundated. The administrative and social rituals that busy your mind have practically disappeared. The friends dropping by, the swell of a funeral, the hugs: all are statutorily absent.

It began with a urinary tract infection, of all things: a bothersome visitor but hardly unknown to my mother. If her body could not fight it off, then ordinarily an ambulance would whisk her off to hospital for stronger drugs and a bag of fluids. Not this time. The hospitals are almost overwhelmed, I was told, and parts are rife with contagion. And already she was so weak. On my mother's last afternoon, I sat by her bedside, on the phone to the community matron, who told me that another nursing home had that day sent a resident to A&E – just for the medics to call and say they were returning her to the home to die.

As her only child, I took what I hope was the best decision. Whether it really was is still a question that wakes me up in the dark.

Another question ought to be asked, this one in public. Amid the focus on pulling the NHS through this plague, how many people have had their lives cut short because they couldn't get hospital treatment for illnesses other than coronavirus? The leading statistician David Spiegelhalter, at Cambridge University, told me he sees a 'large transfer' in the number of non-Covid-19 deaths from hospitals to homes and care homes. Some have been misrecorded, while others have died in their bed rather than under the stark lights of a strange ward. But, as he observes, 'many could have had their lives extended had they gone to hospital'. The Office for National Statistics says it is now examining that gulf, but there is a high chance that those people are the collateral damage of a health system that has been starved of cash for years.

When the undertakers came to take my mother's body, three of the staff at the nursing home where she spent her last few weeks ushered me away. All were black and, on my reckoning, first-generation migrants: from Cameroon, Ghana and the Caribbean.

I would also guess that at least one earns less than the £30,000 baseline for non-EU citizens to get work visas. But for now they are carers to be applauded on Downing Street.

A primary school teacher in Hackney for decades, Arati Chakrabortty would today be termed a 'key worker'. And as I looked at the carers in their protective gear, too flimsy to deter any virus, I knew my mother would have recognised something of their world.

In the 1980s her staffroom was a whistle-stop tour of the British empire: Nigeria, Trinidad, Ireland, India, Pakistan. All women, quick on their feet and with their wits, and on pay far below their qualifications. Every day she went in wearing a sari far too lovely for the litter-strewn streets. During my holidays she would drag me along: as we trundled down the road in our rickety hatchback, van drivers would cut her up and shout that she was a 'Paki' who should fuck off back home.

She was more than they could ever know. In the 1940s, when she was little, her family fled the Japanese bombing of Burma on the last ship out of Rangoon. All except her father, who, along with other Indian men, was stripped of his ticket by the British and had to walk through the mountains to get to India. The trek broke his health and he died not long after, leaving my mother and her brother and sister to be raised by a young widow – in a time where jobs and money were men's business. They were plunged close to poverty, then saw their family land in East Bengal disappear after partition. Even now, as our world is turned upside down, it is worth remembering that some among us have lived through far worse.

When she arrived in London in the late 1960s to do postgraduate study, my mother hunted for a bedsit among signs reading 'No Irish, No Blacks, No Dogs'. But she hardly dwelled on bad memories, preferring to talk about how Sarat Chandra Chatterjee's novels of Bengali peasant life reminded her of Thomas Hardy.

Then came the era of Margaret Thatcher and her alien hordes. In those days the right viewed my mother as they now see Polish builders and Somali carers: outsiders here to take from Britain. The left retorted, as they still do, by counting how much they give Britain. Even today, neither side sees them as people with their own memories, dreams, worlds. Who might have something to teach Britain.

My mother's love of William Shakespeare and William Hazlitt was not an attempt to fit in. She claimed them as she claimed all of world culture. Nothing was off limits. That liberty was what she wanted for everybody – especially for the generations of children who passed through her classroom.

After retirement, she volunteered to teach Turkish and Kurdish migrant families who were moving into the streets where I'd been brought up – and when poor health meant she couldn't take the bus, she got my father to drive her. When he died, she asked me to lobby the school opposite her house for the use of a classroom in the evenings so she could carry on.

Towards the end, my mother's faculties were corroded by dementia. I wheeled her up to the hospital for a memory test. The questions were childishly simple – what is the date, who is the prime minister – but my mother's responses were faltering, which exasperated her. It was not pleasant to see. Then, right at the end, the doctor asked her to write her name. For the briefest moment, a look I knew well passed over my mother's face. Carefully she wielded the pen. The doctor looked down, then in confusion showed me the pad.

She had written her name, all right – in Bengali. Although silent, her message was clear: she would not fit someone else's categories.

Now she has left me, us. She will not see our toddler grow up, or meet her second granddaughter, who arrives next month.

But if both girls learn not to be defined by others, to stay instead sharp and mischievous and free, then Mrs Chakrabortty will have delivered a most valuable lesson.

30 APRIL

'Utter disaster': Manaus fills mass graves as Covid-19 hits the Amazon

TOM PHILLIPS AND
FABIANO MAISONNAVE

Day and night the dead are delivered into the tawny Amazonian soil, the latest victims of a devastating pandemic now reaching deep into the heart of the Brazilian rainforest. On Sunday 140 bodies were laid to rest in Manaus, the jungle-flanked capital of Amazonas state. On Saturday, 98. Normally the figure would be closer to 30.

'It's madness, just madness,' said Gilson de Freitas, a 30-year-old maintenance man whose mother, Rosemeire Rodrigues Silva, was one of 136 people buried there last Tuesday as local morticians set yet another grim daily record. Freitas, who believes his mother got Covid-19 after being admitted to hospital following a stroke, recalled watching in despair as her remains were lowered into a muddy trench alongside perhaps 20 other coffins. 'They were just dumped there like dogs,' he said. 'What are our lives worth now? Nothing.'

Arthur Virgílio, the mayor of Manaus, a city reached by a four-hour flight from São Paulo, pleaded for urgent international help. 'We aren't in a state of emergency – we're well beyond that. We are in a state of utter disaster. Like a country that is at war – and has lost,' he said.

The coronavirus appears to have reached this riverside metropolis of more than 2 million people on 11 March, imported by a 49-year-old woman who flew in from London. Six weeks later it is taking a terrible toll, with gravediggers so overworked that two men this week had to bury their own father. 'Manaus is in a race against time to avoid becoming the Brazilian version of Guayaquil,' the local newspaper *A Crítica* warned last week in reference to the Ecuadorian city where bodies have been left rotting in the streets and thousands are feared to have died.

Freitas said he knew little of the ailment that had robbed him of his mother, aged 58. 'It comes from China, doesn't it?' he said this week on the day Jair Bolsonaro, Brazil's president, prompted outrage by shrugging his shoulders at the country's dead. 'All of us are afraid ... Today we're alive. Tomorrow we just don't know,' Freitas said.

With more than 100 people dying daily and Manaus's authorities performing night-time burials, many fear any response will be too late. City officials say they expect to bury up to 4,500 people in May. Funeral homes say they will run out of wooden coffins this weekend. In Parque Tarumã, the city's biggest cemetery, excavators carved out mass graves called '*trincheiras*' (trenches) in which the dead were being stacked in three-high piles until the practice was halted after a revolt by mourning families. Edmar Barros, a photographer documenting the burials, said: 'It's absurd what is happening here. It's a situation of devastating sadness.'

Emergency and health services in Manaus are buckling under the strain, with ambulances roaming for up to three hours in search of hospitals able to admit the patients they have collected. Gruesome video footage has emerged from hospitals showing corridors lined with corpses. Another video shows an unconscious patient with his head inside a ventilator hood improvised from a large plastic bag. 'There's a shortage of mechanical ventilators, of oxygen, of staff, of stretchers. Everything is lacking,' said Dr Domício Magalhães Filho, the technical director of the ambulance service, Samu.

Experts and officials say several factors explain the intensity of the catastrophe. One is that the epidemic struck at the end of the rainy season when respiratory illnesses are rife and hospitals stretched. Another is that Manaus's chronically underfunded health service was poorly equipped and understaffed even before medical workers began contracting Covid-19.

But many also blame corruption and the government's failure to effectively implement containment measures once Covid-19 was detected. Only on 23 March – 10 days after the first case was confirmed – did the state governor declare a state of emergency, ordering all non-essential businesses to close. Even now, with the death toll soaring, social distancing is being flouted in parts of the outskirts, with huge queues outside banks and people refusing to wear masks.

Virgílio, the mayor, said he had failed to keep people indoors but said Bolsonaro should shoulder much of the blame for undermining such measures. 'It saddens me to know these lives ... weren't saved, in part because Brazil's main leader ... said it was OK to go out.'

Marcia Castro, a Harvard University demographer specialising in public health in the Brazilian Amazon, said it was unrealistic to expect people to follow ministry advice when 43 per cent of residents did not even have access to water for handwashing. 'What this pandemic is doing is throwing wide open the inequalities that have existed for so long.'

Additional reporting by Daylla Kobosque.

14 MAY

Office life is not over – but the way we work must surely change

GABY HINSLIFF

'Don't bother coming back to the office.' It's the kind of message everyone dreads receiving, but for Twitter's employees it was benign. The tech company announced this week that home-working arrangements made for the pandemic would stay for good: nobody need ever commute in again, unless they particularly wanted to. In Britain, the telecoms giant BT also declared that staff could choose whether to come back to call centres or just carry on from home.

The idea that office life is over is almost certainly overdone. Not everyone loves typing away on the sofa day after day, panicking about being out of the corporate loop. But for those lucky enough to have the choice to work from home, the collective near-death experience we've endured as a nation may be prompting a re-evaluation of what matters.

Commuter dads who once rarely saw their children awake have got used to the casual intimacy of being around them all day long. In the privacy of their personal Facebook feeds, more than one hard-hitting Westminster type has melted into a puddle of baby pictures. For the less sentimental, savings from weeks of raiding the fridge for lunch and not filling the car are adding up; the environmental benefits of keeping traffic off the roads are a happy bonus. But if the shift to home-working has been relatively painless, that's merely the beginning.

Modern working hours are in part a legacy of the Great Depression of the 1930s, when collapsing demand for labour encouraged companies to share around what work there was: what had been a six-day week for many shrank to five. Now it may be shrinking again.

The world's largest law firm, Dentons, is among companies asking staff to work a four-day week for 80 per cent of salary due to falling demand. The Adam Smith Institute, one of the more bracingly rightwing thinktanks, is pushing its 'four days on, 10 days off' model designed by an epidemiologist for a safer return to work: companies would split staff into groups, each doing four days in the office or factory followed by 10 days off, with the groups rotated in order to limit numbers and help social distancing. (If you do get infected, the idea is that symptoms would be more likely to emerge during the days off, allowing people to self-isolate.)

It sounds hell to match with childcare, but at least it's evidence of right as well as left accepting that we cannot simply return to business as usual. The next step, however, is working out how to make any of this fair on people who can't afford a pay cut. Rishi Sunak made a big leap of imagination, for a Conservative chancellor, to embrace furloughing – but to get us out of it will require another one.

This week it emerged that from August, employers must start picking up some of the bill for furloughing their own people, currently met by the Treasury. The risk is that redundancies will follow, but the best hope of avoiding them is for the Treasury to allow part-time furloughing. People could be paid conventionally to work, say, three or four days a week, with the furlough scheme topping up their salaries. An enlightened government could effectively turn furloughing into a mechanism for spreading work around in lean times, while buying time to reimagine working hours for the long-term.

Around the world, people are already grappling with the question of how to shorten the working week. The organisation 4 Day

Week Global has been experimenting for years in New Zealand with reorganising companies so that five days' work can be done in four, giving employees a longer weekend for the same pay. (The reward for their bosses is better productivity, happier people and lower staff turnover.) Now it's looking at adapting that model through the current crisis.

In Scotland, the Post-Covid-19 Futures Commission, created by the Royal Society of Edinburgh, is examining four-day weeks; Labour too could dust off its report on them, commissioned by John McDonnell long before the pandemic. But is the current government up to such bold thinking? This week's clumsy stab at thawing a frozen economy hardly inspires confidence.

In England, the treatment of teachers has been a model of how not to encourage anxious people back, with unions accused of sabotage for daring to express concerns about the risk of infection spreading and people dying. Social distancing on public transport visibly isn't working, and mixed messages about what is now allowed have eroded trust. Why can an estate agent visit your home, but not your grandchildren? True, you're less likely to hug the former. That doesn't, however, explain why you can carshare with colleagues if going to work, but not sit next to them in the park. It looks horribly as if rules can be bent for anything that makes a profit.

But there is still just about time to go back to the drawing board. When, and only when, it's safe to go back to the workplace, the return should be framed much as lockdown was seven weeks ago: as an act of social solidarity that helps others, while also benefiting individuals. It should come with encouragement for anyone who has dreamed of cutting their hours, focusing on working fathers who constantly tell surveys they'd like to work less but feel they can't actually do it.

But, most of all, it should come with a promise of living better, and sharing the pain of slumping economic demand. Theresa

May was once mocked for insisting nothing had changed. Her successor must acknowledge that something profoundly has.

16 MAY

I flew to Greece and began solo IVF. Then the world shut down

LAURA BARTON

It is 7.53am, the last Wednesday in March, and at a courier depot in Athens, the sperm of a Bermudian mechanical engineering student arrives, carried in a nitrogen tank. For the last three days, I have followed the tank's journey across Europe, loading and reloading the courier website as it made its way from a cryobank in Denmark through Germany to mainland Greece.

It has one final leg, a short hop from Athens to the island of Crete. But today is Greek Independence Day, a national holiday, and so all through Wednesday and long into Thursday the sperm waits at the depot. I call the courier company. All planes being grounded, it will travel to its destination by boat, the handler says brightly. 'It is very urgent,' I tell her. 'It's for a *medical procedure*.' She is reassuring but noncommittal. What I do not tell her is that, on Friday, I will have my eggs collected at a fertility clinic on Crete, and it is crucial that the sperm of the engineering student be there to meet them.

Undergoing IVF at any time is a peculiar experience. In the midst of a pandemic, it becomes surreal. In early March, as the world shut down, I imagined my scheduled treatment would be postponed, but to my amazement the clinic said it would proceed. And so, one Saturday afternoon, as the virus gathered pace and airports acquired a new and fearful mood, I took one of the last flights from London to Heraklion. I was making this trip alone; my local health authority does not treat single women.

With its own health system buckled by years of austerity, the Greek government had moved quickly to prevent a coronavirus outbreak of the magnitude of those in Italy or Spain. The evening I arrived, 14 March, Greece was on its way to lockdown, and Heraklion's shops, bars and restaurants stood newly shuttered. I let myself into my rental apartment, ate the kalitsounia left by my host, and wondered what on earth I was doing.

For some reason it is always taxi drivers who ask the question, though I imagine they are only voicing what others wonder: 'Why don't you have children?' I suspect many assume I didn't want to be a mother, that I was too caught up in my career, that I left it too late. None of this is true. Having multiple miscarriages over many years, for which no medical investigation could find a cause, has been an exhausting, distressing and intensely lonely experience. And though my life has been rich and rewarding in many ways, the absence of a child is a sadness that has gnawed the edges of all other joys.

When I wake, it is to the sound of wood pigeons, and piano practice, and Sunday church bells. The day is bright and warm, and for some time I wander the city's empty, sunlit streets. The supermarket is closed, but I find a minimarket to buy a few groceries. Bread, feta, tomatoes. The owner regards me darkly across the counter, locking eyes as he sanitises his hands.

The clinic is a large, grey, modern building not far from the port. It takes 20 minutes to walk there in the rain, a fierce wind whipping in off the water. At the reception desk, I am told to stand behind a line as they fire a thermometer gun at my head, then permit me to ring the fertility centre doorbell. I fold the sleeve of my jumper over my thumb to press the buzzer.

A foreign clinic is disorienting when you are accustomed to another medical system: the rhythms are subtly different, the smells, the light all wrong. I notice the cigarette smoke on the senior nurse's breath, the junior who chews gum behind her mask as she draws my blood. Even the tourniquet strapped around my arm feels flimsier than back home. 'Take a breath,' the nurse says solemnly, as she inserts the needle. She leaves a small trail of blood along my skin, then dispenses the contents of the large syringe into several containers; a spring-like gurgling sound that I find oddly hopeful.

I walk home along the backstreets, past ageing stucco apartments and the sound of a couple arguing through an open window. When you are not familiar with a culture or a language, your senses become heightened – the colours louder, the sounds and scents more pronounced. I try to notice the details: the hover of wasps over the bowls of water left out for street cats. A snail on a bright blue wall. The firebug on an orange tree. It stops my mind from spiralling. I stop by the supermarket, where they are already limiting the number of customers, and plastic gloves are mandatory. But the shelves are full and no one is stockpiling.

The following day, I return to the clinic. My blood test results have proved heartening and my consultant tells me he hopes for 15 or 16 eggs. He chatters warmly as he performs my ultrasound: about his time living in London in the days of disco, the fact that English women never cook. 'I like to cook,' I tell him. 'What do you cook? Sandwiches?' he asks, then reels off the measurements of my ovaries to his assistant. When I leave, the senior nurse gives me a face mask, ties it tightly so that it covers my nose, and rubs my back with a kind of tenderness. 'It's for you,' she says. 'Make sure you wear it.'

There is little new I can tell you about IVF medication. The basic protocol is to stimulate the ovaries to produce eggs, which are then removed, fertilised and returned; a further array of drugs help make the pregnancy sustainable. And so for the weeks to come my days are measured out in injections, pills and pessaries, in the fiddliness of mixing powders and solutions, of needles and small glass vials. Soon my stomach is puffy and bruised; my body feels distorted and misshapen.

Meanwhile, I follow news of the pandemic on my laptop. When my flight home is cancelled, I feel something like relief. I feel safe here.

On 23 March, Greece grounds all flights to the UK and docks all boats to the islands. I can now only leave the house for an hour each day: to buy groceries, seek medical treatment or take exercise, and must first text the government for permission. A strange serenity settles over these days of confinement: I sleep well and long, read, work, take afternoon walks down to the waterfront. I do not return phone calls from well-meaning friends; texts and emails go unanswered. I feel beholden to nothing besides my own body, feed it yoghurt and oranges and sesame snaps. One day I read that IVF clinics around the world are closing, that treatments are being postponed indefinitely, and am filled with a great swell of gratefulness.

When I return to the clinic for my second ultrasound, my consultant is in a less jovial mood. He scowls slightly, as if I have disappointed him, tells me the ovarian stimulation has not been as successful as expected; he now hopes for five eggs.

I am accustomed to sitting in doctors' offices receiving bad news. To be told repeatedly that you have lost your baby, that there is nothing they can do, that your identical twins have no heartbeat, develops a kind of composure. I have learned how to imperceptibly bite my lip, and close my eyes, and know that the grief will come later, far from here, when it will be solitary and wild and flailing.

That I have done all of this alone is testament to what my friends call my terrible taste in men. I have a particular talent for choosing unsupportive partners, men who will ask you to choose between your baby and them, who will miss hospital appointments, and find commitments more pressing than helping you through a miscarriage.

Last summer, I sat in my GP's surgery and told her I wanted to pursue solo IVF. I pressed my fingernails into my palm to steady myself as I spoke. She was supportive and kind, and made a referral to the fertility department at the local hospital.

I was not technically single at the time, but two weeks later I left my boyfriend of four years. Some months earlier I had learned that he had cheated on me, constantly, for the entirety of our relationship, including while I was pregnant. I had loved him more than I had loved anybody, and perhaps this was the reason I had tried to make things work, but the days had soon settled into a kind of mute despair.

It was liberating to feel in charge of my own destiny again, and for the three months while I waited for my first appointment with the fertility clinic, I felt thrillingly alive. When it came, that appointment was dispiriting: the nurse explained my local health authority's policy on treating single women. She was sympathetic, ordered a range of fertility tests, cautioned against using a donor I knew, and suggested I look at clinics abroad. 'Greece,' she said. 'They have some good clinics there.'

There followed several months of waiting – for test results, for a round of MMR vaccinations (my GP had no record of my ever having had them). The new year turned and it was almost spring. I told the clinic in Heraklion, chosen for its impressive success rates and peaceful location, that I would come in March.

I had not heard of coronavirus then, though already in China the disease was spreading. It seemed very far away. I focused instead on the small, steady world I had created, of fertility acupuncture, sobriety and sperm selection.

It is easy to get lost in the process of choosing a sperm donor, to dwell upon academic qualifications, professions, favourite pastimes. The more you pay, the more you know: baby photos, adult photos, voice notes, family medical histories. Some cryo-banks will supply handwriting samples and outline drawings of your donor's face in profile; this can have the strange effect of making everyone look like a criminal.

Above all, I decided, let him be kind. From hundreds of donors, I whittled it down to two: the mechanical engineering student whose profile was somewhat restrained, but about whom the staff appraisal spoke glowingly; and a Danish musician with wavy hair who talked about his love of nature and art. 'He sounds like the kind of man I would date,' I told my friends. This was not necessarily a good thing, they pointed out. That night I lay in bed and imagined their profiles being read in the voices of my very worst boyfriends. I chose the engineer.

Friday morning, the day of my egg retrieval, and the donor sperm has not arrived. The courier office can tell me only that it has left Athens. I take the coast road to the clinic, walk slowly through the uncertain morning, and try not to think about the catastrophe before me. The air is sweet and soft, the sea a searing blue. I am watching the light play on the waves when, just beyond the port, I see the daily cargo boat approaching the shore, bringing supplies from the mainland: food and medicine and a nitrogen tank of donor sperm.

In the days that follow, I like to think of my eggs in the labora-tory, cells dividing, happily gathering into blastocysts. It makes me feel less alone. I await news from the embryologist, sleeping, eating, taking long walks. One morning, I wake to a ruffling sound beyond my bedroom curtains. It is a bird, I think, that has flown into my courtyard. But when I look I find it is rain: heavy, plump drops on the corrugated iron roof and the broad leaves of the potted plants. That day the embryologist calls: transfer will be in two days' time.

Another flight is cancelled. Getting home will now take some 42 hours, several changes of plane, and hundreds of pounds. 'Do I need to come and rescue you?' an ex-boyfriend emails. I tell him he should know by now that I am not someone who takes well to rescuing. Perhaps if I did, I would not be here doing IVF alone in a foreign country in the first place.

I am the only patient at the clinic on the morning of my embryo transfer. The number of treatments is dwindling as no one can travel and there is too much uncertainty. My consultant, the junior nurse, the embryologist and I gather in the operating theatre. The embryologist plays Mozart through her phone to drown out the whirr of the generator. It is a simple procedure – the embryo being transferred to the womb via a catheter. 'There!' the consultant says. On the screen I watch a small dot make its way across the darkness and then settle.

For the next two weeks it will become the pale white dot upon which I live. I think about my tiny speck of hope as I follow the growing bleakness of the world: nurses in London wearing bin bags and scuba masks, the want of ventilators in New York City, the death toll in Italy that rises and rises. I try not to think about how I will get home, about the potential dangers of travelling across a continent, newly pregnant, in a pandemic.

In my isolation chamber I feel like a Russian doll, inside me another smaller me, confined in her own small isolation. I have been pregnant enough times that this state feels familiar: all-engulfing, electric. And yet I have miscarried enough to know that nothing is certain. I have often thought that the two-week wait between conception and pregnancy test is like being alone in a strange house: every sound, every shadow, can convince you that someone is there.

For a week I feel truly pregnant. And then suddenly I do not. One day I wake to feel a tangible distance between the synthetic hormones and my own body. I do not tell anyone. Instead I walk down to the water, stay out far beyond the mandated hour. I marvel at the flicker of tiny fish moving between the boats in the harbour. I look at the bright yellow tangle of fishing nets, the deep pink of wooden shutters, the distant mountains, snow-peaked against the bluest sky.

I walk on beside the sea, past young couples, hands entwined, and think of how clinical and lustless the IVF process is. Of how a week ago I sat in a room that smelled of disinfectant, wearing a thin blue gown and a surgical mask. How there was no one's hand to hold, no love in the room. In the streets outside, spring had begun. There was the smell of orange blossom, and violet carpenter bees danced between branches. I stared up at the voluminous petals of bright red flowers, at stamen and pollen and anther and stalk, and thought that this was how reproduction ought to be: stickiness and scent, warmth and desire, all the senses colliding at once.

On the day I get a negative pregnancy test, 717 people die of coronavirus in the UK. For a long while, I sit on the edge of my bed and try to balance rationality and sorrow. I look at pictures from Italian hospitals, follow the upward curves of the latest graphs. Friends have lost loved ones, I tell myself; I have lost someone who barely ever existed. And yet I walk out into the cool sun of my courtyard and cry.

Some years ago, the writer India Knight published a self-help book, *In Your Prime*, in which she discussed the way that in adulthood our lives diverge into two camps: the have-children and the have-nots. For those caught up in the business of parenthood, she wrote, 'there is no especial pleasure to be had in a single and/or childless person banging on about the minutiae of their small, unpeopled little life'.

The phrase has stuck with me. As my friends have paired off and become parents, I have seen them less, travelled more, grown quieter. I cannot hope to understand the dramatic shifts and expansions in their lives, just as they are unlikely to understand the reduction of my own.

And as the weeks of lockdown rolled on, that phrase has returned to me anew; I came to think how all our lives have grown small and unpeopled. How we have come to find pleasure in the minutiae: the slow drift of days, the unfurling of blossom, a street filled with clapping on a warm spring evening. And sometimes, too, when all seems lost, a small patch of blue sky above a courtyard in Greece.

25 MAY

Regrets? St Dom had a few, but then again too few to mention

JOHN CRACE

Classic Dom: Downing Street's very own Prince Andrew. Show how much respect you have for the public and the media by turning up 30 minutes late for your own gig. There again, start as you mean to go on. Because Dominic Cummings' press conference in the Downing Street rose garden was all about his own exceptionalism. How the rules applied differently to him than to the little people.

On Sunday we had Boris Johnson, the understudy prime minister, fail to convince the country there had been nothing untoward about Cummings' trip to Durham. A midnight flit that had been so normal Downing Street had spent nearly six weeks trying to cover it up. Now we were to get the full story – or what approximated to it – from the person who is really running the country. And what we were treated to was an hour-long confused ramble that was disguised as the martyrdom of St Dom. A man who had only ever acted in the best interests of his family and the country. A man more sinned against than sinning.

'Hi there,' he said, when he turned up after a half-hour row with his wife over whether he really needed to change out of his hoodie and put on a shirt. 'Sorry I'm late.' He wasn't of course. Dom is never sorry, but that was the closest we were going to get to any form of apology for having driven 260 miles to Durham to self-isolate on his parents' estate, when the country was obeying the letter of the law he helped write.

Much of what Dom had to say made little sense. His wife had initially been ill but he had broken with his own health guidelines by going into work the following day. And no, he hadn't bothered to get any medical advice or tell Boris what he was planning on doing. Because he was the Special One so there was no need. His car had had a full tank of petrol – nice touch – and his son, who couldn't last a 30-minute drive to Barnard Castle without stopping for a pee, had proved iron-bladdered for the entire six-hour journey north.

Once in Durham, both Dom and his wife Mary had been ill with coronavirus – they had only broken lockdown once by nipping out to the local hospital because their son was unwell – and had self-isolated for the full 14 days. Then on the 15th day, St Dom had risen again. There was just one small problem. His vision was playing up. So the obvious way to see if he was safe to drive was to pack his family into the car and take a 30-mile journey to Barnard Castle.

All this was said in a state of barely repressed anger. This statement was costing Dom dear. Classic Dom never explains and never apologises. Everything was totally above board, which is why he and his wife had written stories in the *Spectator* that they knew to be completely misleading. Then he went full-on Trump. Everything that had been written about him was completely Fake News. Apart from everything in the *Guardian* and the *Mirror* which he had as good as corroborated.

There was to be no redemption for Laughing Boy. The majority of the country could only see a man who had chosen to break the rules and had – worse still – put the nation's health at risk by effectively telling everyone they could interpret the rules however they wanted. Not that Dom would have cared. What would have hurt most was that he had been seen for who he really was. A man who can turn any hint of regret into a giant 'fuck you'.

30 MAY

'This man knows he's dying as surely as I do': a doctor's dispatches from the NHS frontline

RACHEL CLARKE

Death has been headline news for so long now, I am beginning to feel like a plague doctor. My next patient, an 89-year-old from a care home, is perilously ill. Despite the highest flow of oxygen we can deliver through his face mask, he is gasping for air at a rate of 40 breaths per minute, two or three times the norm. Swiftly, I search his hospital record for a glimpse of the man he used to be before coronavirus so violently reduced him.

In my mind, the voices from this morning's car radio linger. Listening to the politicians and journalists talk – loftily, from afar, an Olympian perspective – coronavirus can feel like a mathematical abstraction, an intellectual exercise played out in curves and peaks and troughs and modelling. But here in the hospital, the pandemic is a matter of flesh and blood. It unfolds one human being at a time. And when the statistics threaten to throw me off balance – the unprecedented number of deaths for peacetime – I try to keep things as small as I can. Winston used to work in the local glass factory. His wife died three years ago. He has two sons called Michael and Robert.

Usually I work in a hospice as a palliative care doctor. But now, with the wards of my local hospital filling with patients dying from coronavirus, the need is there instead. I'm already wearing my mask. I've pressed the metal strip down hard on to my nose and cheekbones, endeavouring to make it airtight. Now I layer on more protection. Apron, gloves and visor, the minimum with which we approach our patients these days.

In PPE, everything is sticky and stifling. Voices are muffled and smiles obscured. Sweat starts trickling into your underwear. Even breathing takes more effort. Behind our masks, we strain to hear each other speak and are forced to second-guess our colleagues' expressions. Being protected entails being dehumanised.

Entering the antechamber to Winston's side room, I'm dismayed to discover his sons are here. Someone has helped them into their own protection, but one mask, I can see, is on inside out and both men look limp and bewildered. 'We don't know how close we're allowed to get to him,' says one. 'Can you tell us how long he has?' asks the other, in a voice made hard by fear.

I fight for a second to maintain my composure. The sons have been permitted to visit only because their father is dying. I am a doctor with neither a name nor a face. My hospital badge is hidden from view and my eyes – the only part of my face still visible – are obscured by a layer of Perspex. So much for the healing presence of the bedside physician. I scarcely look human.

Six feet away, a father, a man I am yet to lay eyes on, is dying of a disease only named a month ago. 'Hello Michael, Robert,' I say warmly, though doubtful any warmth will carry. 'My name is Rachel. I'm one of the doctors caring for your father. Forgive me for not knowing which of you is which.'

'I'm Michael,' says the brother with the stony edge to his voice. 'No one's told us anything. Can he even hear us?' Everything about this is wrong. The physical barriers between us. The harsh and jarring words that conceal rising panic. The glaring need – that can't be met – to rip off the masks and gloves and shake hands, sit down, read each other's expressions and begin, inch by inch, to cross the gulf that divides us.

The sons step aside to allow me in closer. And there, palms turned upwards, chest heaving and trembling, is their father, spreadeagled in tangled cotton. Winston's mask clamps down on skin slick with sweat. His lips are grey, fingertips the colour of bruises. An intravenous line drips antibiotics into one arm. A catheter drains urine the colour of mud into a bag left lying on the bedclothes. His arms and legs, barely more than bones, are twitching and scything. The only part of his body not in motion, I realise, are his eyes, white-rimmed and fixed on the ceiling.

The radio programme crosses my mind again. The language of war has been rife during the pandemic but never more so than when the prime minister was rushed to intensive care.

Since then, battle tropes have dominated the national conversation. Cabinet members assured us Boris Johnson would beat the disease because he's a fighter, as though survival is somehow a test of character, a matter primarily of valour. The reality, of course, is more banal. People do not die from this illness – or from any other – because they lack grit. Nor do they live by sheer pugnaciousness.

I look down at the bedsheets, stained with sweat, and the coil of limbs squirming in fear. It could not be plainer to anyone here that Winston is no participant in a battle. He is, instead, merely the battlefield. His body, worn out to begin with, is being methodically disposed of by a virus so primitive it scarcely qualifies as life. Character has precisely nothing to do with it. It never does in the real world of the hospital where the good, the bad, the brave and the timid all kneel alike before cancers and microbes.

I move closer. Speaking sufficiently loudly to be audible above the thrum of the oxygen, I say his name. Nothing. No flicker of response. Still closer. Again, almost shouting: 'Winston.' His eyes remain locked on the ceiling. I can feel those of his sons fixed on mine.

In this alien time when even breathing the same air as your patient is heavy with risk, physical contact is permitted only when strictly necessary. I observe the muscles on Winston's neck bulging to drag a little more air into his waterlogged lungs, and reach forwards, inching nearer.

Gently, I take his hand in both of mine. His pulse flutters so faintly, it is barely there. No warmth from his flesh creeps through my gloves. I am holding the hand of a man who is dying and who knows it as surely as I do. Behind closed doors, with neither fanfare nor drama, he has been quietly drowning all night.

I squeeze Winston's fingers, repeat his name once again, and now, at last, his eyelids flicker. Our gazes meet for the first time.

'Are you in any pain?' I ask. A barely perceptible shake of his head. But when I ask if his breathing is distressing, he manages to nod. 'In just a moment, we'll help your breathing,' I promise.

I go on, a vital question. 'Are you afraid?' He nods a second time and in turn I make a second promise. 'I'm going to ask the nurses now to bring you an injection which will help you relax and help your breathing.' A final nod and then, just before turning to his sons, I lean closer still: 'Winston, Michael and Robert are here. They're going to sit with you now until the nurse comes.' I straighten up from the bedside. I note the glint of tears beneath the brothers' visors. 'Would you like to pull up these chairs?' I ask them. 'You can sit as close as you want, you can hold hands, you can say anything.'

Later, when Winston has all the medications he needs and has finally lost that look of undisguised horror, his sons and I converse in low voices. I explain that, yes, time is short, yes, he is probably in the last few hours of his life. Suddenly Michael interjects, his voice abrasive. 'I don't want him to be a statistic.' He knows full well – each of us in the room does – that tomorrow's death toll and its televised dissection will include, in all likelihood, his father. I see through his eyes the colossal affront of someone you love – of all that your beloved has been and meant to the world – being reduced to a numerical bit part in tomorrow's headlines. 'He is not a statistic,' Michael repeats. Then he pauses. And in the bleakness and tenderness of the next four words, I think I understand for the first time the true cost of a pandemic. 'He's my best friend.'

In March we knew full well – because the data from China had already told us – that those most at risk from coronavirus were elderly patients, such as Winston, plus those with underlying comorbidities. But far from being cocooned, he and the other 400,000 residents of UK care homes were being quietly incarcerated. No testing. No contact tracing. No proper PPE, even, for care-home staff. Worse, care-home residents were being sent to homes from hospitals without knowing they were not infected.

When, therefore, at the end of April I watched the prime minister declare our coronavirus strategy a 'success', I felt physically sick. We had 'avoided the tragedy that engulfed other parts of the world', he insisted, 'because at no stage has our NHS been overwhelmed'. How very cheap – how spectacularly expendable – one human life must be, I thought, if the avoidance of tragedy is consistent with the deaths of 27,000 people, as the toll then stood.

Does it matter that 400,000 of our most vulnerable citizens were promised shielding while being effectively abandoned? That for them, even the most basic measures of protection were at best overlooked, at worst deliberately ignored? That the alleged 'success' of April came at such stupendous cost to those too elderly, frail or disabled to live in their own homes? You could argue – indeed, some commentators have essentially done so – that there was little point to a man like Winston. He was 89 years old, after all, and probably hadn't been economically productive for three decades. He was lucky, frankly, to have had an innings like that. Of course the young must come first. You might even champion another old man's exploits – the charm, determination and ebullience of Captain Tom – while being secretly at peace with the expendability of certain parts of the 'herd'.

But to those of us up close with this dreadful disease – who see, as we do, the way it suffocates the life from you – such judgments are grotesque. The moment we rank life according to who most 'deserves' it, we have crossed into a realm I don't want to be a part of – and I struggle to believe many other Britons do either. The way out of this pandemic cannot, surely, entail the sacrifice of those deemed less worth saving? Like many in the NHS just now, I keep my head by looking down – at one patient and then another. I am lucky in this respect: I have focus. Sometimes I fret that most people don't know how very close the NHS came to being overwhelmed this Easter – how we avoided the hellishness of Lombardy or New York City only by superhuman efforts. I fear, too, that most people are unaware of how exhausted, stunned – shellshocked, even – some NHS staff and carers are. How daunted we feel as we watch lockdown being relaxed before proper testing, tracing and isolation infrastructure are in place. How incredulous we are as we see government figures breaking the rules they wrote, that so many others have lived and died by.

In my darkest moments, I worry that the televised coronavirus press conferences are increasingly being used to distract us from what is really at stake. That the flood of pseudoscientific statistics is intended to bamboozle – to leave the population dazed and bemused. When you are invited daily to celebrate supersized statistics – 100,000 tests a day, no, make that 250,000 – it is easy to lose sight of what matters.

Sir David Spiegelhalter, professor of the public understanding of risk at Cambridge University, suggested earlier this month that Downing Street is using 'number theatre' to manipulate the message rather than actually inform people. The chair of the UK Statistics Authority, Sir David Norgrove, has even been forced to write to the health secretary, Matt Hancock, urging him to improve the 'trustworthiness' of the way he presents data on coronavirus testing.

The true metric of success in a pandemic is simple: the overall number of deaths prevented. The point of our response to coronavirus is not to flatten curves, ramp up headlines, protect the NHS or invent mathematically nonsensical equations: it is the prevention of unnecessary dying.

As we reel, punch drunk, from press conference to press conference, we must not allow those standing at their lecterns on the podium to gloss over recent history. It is a fact that a whole swath of our most vulnerable citizens, those residing in care homes, have already been abandoned once to coronavirus. And no matter what any government figure implies – no matter how distracting or persuasive their abstractions – this is entirely and inexcusably wrong. Our society may be endemically unequal, but no one in Britain is expendable. Winston, though vulnerable, was loved and cherished. His death was not inevitable, his time hadn't come. He was no more disposable than any of us.

31 MAY

'Not my friends any more': Minneapolis residents redirect their anger in George Floyd protests

CHRIS McGREAL

The governor had promised that Saturday night would be different, and it was. As the clock ticked towards the 8pm curfew, hundreds of protesters gathered outside the fifth precinct police station in a particular show of defiance. The previous evening, they had refused to obey the lockdown and, when push came to shove, it was the police who retreated.

What followed that night – looting and burning along a two-mile stretch of Lake Street, a busy thoroughfare of shops often owned by minorities – led the governor, Tim Walz, to mobilise the National Guard, saying there would be no repeat.

Outside the fifth precinct station on Saturday, some protesters were certain that if they kept it peaceful, even while breaking the curfew, they would be allowed to make their point. They still wanted to see the three other sacked police officers implicated in the killing of George Floyd arrested alongside Derek Chauvin, who is facing murder and manslaughter charges.

But not long after the curfew kicked in, any such illusions were quickly dispelled. A line of state police in riot gear appeared from a side street. A call for the protesters to disperse was swiftly followed by teargas, flash bombs and baton rounds. As the crowd surged away, the police line moved forwards, driving people back with more gas and rounds. It quickly became clear that after the politically damaging humiliation of the previous night, Walz had no intention of being embarrassed again.

The governor had laid the ground earlier in the day when he claimed the protests had been hijacked by 'elements' of domestic terrorism, ideological extremism and international destabilisa-tion. He specifically blamed the arson and looting on a group of agitators from outside the city, easing the way to escalate the use of force.

Just who the protesters are, and their motives, has become an increasingly sharp debate in Minneapolis. It has suited both politicians and some community leaders to blame the violence on politically motivated outsiders.

Minnesota's lieutenant governor, Peggy Flanagan, accused those she said did not have the community's interests at heart. 'There are white supremacists there. There are anarchists. There are people who are burning down institutions that are core to our identity,' she said.

The narrative of outside agitators stirring up trouble was not without some truth. Young white people dressed in black, who at times did not seem to know their way around the city, were among the most aggressive in their confrontations with the police. But residents of the area and callers to local radio stations quickly undermined the claim that the people stripping bare shops on Lake Street, and hauling their contents home in shopping trolleys or cars, were not people from Minneapolis.

Whoever the protesters were, sympathy for their cause among people living around Lake Street was tempered by anger over the destruction of locally owned businesses and fear that violence might spread to the residential areas. Residents of the surrounding blocks organised their own security, throwing up makeshift barriers with bollards, roadworks signs and metal posts. Some carried guns.

As the protesters fled the fifth precinct station, the police kept up pursuit. Some demonstrators tried to build barriers and make a stand but were swiftly overwhelmed. Eventually the scattered crowd regrouped on Lake Street and several hundred people began to march its length, chanting Floyd's name.

But within 15 minutes, the police and National Guard descended again, coming at the marchers from both ends of the street with waves of teargas and baton rounds. That sent the protesters scattering into residential areas, to the alarm of people living there. As the police pursued them, officers also at times fired on residents guarding their streets or people standing in their gardens.

One Latino homeowner cursed the police and the demonstrators. 'I don't like the police and I don't like the protesters. The police abandoned us for days and now they're here they're shooting at us defending ourselves,' he said.

Outside a house on a neighbouring block, Jeff Schibilla had armed himself. 'I'm OK with freedom of speech. I'm not OK with you ruining my neighbourhood. I've got elderly neighbours on both sides of me and across the street who need protecting,' he said. 'I've lost my job because of coronavirus after 22 years. But I'm not out here pillaging and looting.'

Schibilla said that while he had no doubt that people from outside the city were involved in the trouble, he also knew people who had taken part in the looting. 'They came around here trying to sell stuff, electronics and stuff, at pennies on the dollar. I'm not going to turn them in but they're not my friends any more,' he said.

A few minutes later, and about three hours after the first clashes, the police and National Guard came down his street. Schibilla stood in his garden and cheered them.

1 JUNE

The ghosts of the care-home dead will come back to haunt this government

POLLY TOYNBEE

The pandemic firestorm still burns in care homes. Untested residents and unprotected staff in this neglected private archipelago used to be out of sight and out of mind. But no longer. The government will not escape the ghosts of needless care-home deaths.

The *Guardian*'s Robert Booth last week revealed that the government rejected a radical plan by Public Health England to lock down care homes, move staff in and use empty Nightingale hospitals to isolate suspected Covid-19 cases. Research from the London School of Economics suggests that care homes have suffered 22,000 extra deaths. All staff and residents need persistent testing, but almost two-thirds of homes have had no staff tested yet, according to the Data Analysis Bureau.

Blame is cast in many directions: councils and care-home companies have turned up the volume of conflict with the NHS, though the sectors are supposed to be blending locally in integrated care systems. While many work well together, national representatives of the care industry are on the warpath.

Talk to Prof Martin Green, the spokesman for Care England's larger care companies, and his charge sheet against the government is blood-curdling. 'From the start the NHS was prioritised,' he says: the signs read 'Save the NHS' and that's what they did. 'PPE was redirected away from care homes. Managers were told by suppliers their orders were requisitioned by the NHS.' He claims some areas had 'blanket policies not to admit residents to hospital. I've seen the letters from GPs saying they will not admit residents, putting DNR [do not resuscitate] on their notes. Some refused to visit.' He says: 'There was a clear instruction to empty hospitals in March and send people to care homes despite no testing for infection. I've seen patient notes altered to disguise infection.' Local hospitals deny it, protesting that care homes are trying to blame the NHS for their own failings.

Green attacks the government with gusto for 'systematic ageism'. Indeed, at first the NHS was gripped by fear of the dying queuing outside, with no ventilators and overflowing morgues. There was whispered speculation about letting the over-65s go to save younger victims. That didn't happen. But the NHS was only saved, Green alleges, because hospitals dumped the crisis on care homes. Exaggerated or not, with so many deaths the government rightly fears his allegations will stick.

Hot denials come from the NHS, with Hancock's credulity-straining claim that he had tried to 'throw a protective ring around care homes'. Chris Hopson, the head of NHS Providers, sprang to the defence of his hospitals: 'Trusts invested consider-able time and effort into protecting care homes and deeply resent the suggestion that they would knowingly discharge a [Covid-19] or suspected [Covid-19] patient into a care-home setting.' The problem, he says, was the lack of tests until mid-April so hospitals couldn't know if they were sending the infected into care homes. Then he strikes right to the heart of the matter: 'The scandal here is the repeated failure of politicians to solve our long-running social-care crisis.'

The health select committee has been taking devastating evidence, eagerly chaired by Jeremy Hunt who fiercely challenged Boris Johnson over patients discharged to care homes at last week's liaison committee. Downing Street is plainly rattled and infuriated by Hunt, suspecting him of leadership manoeuvres, should Johnson fall. Aides are drafting attack lines on Hunt's six years as health secretary, highlighting his failure to prepare for a pandemic despite warnings, reports the *Mail on Sunday*. Many in the NHS are equally dumbfounded by Hunt's reinvention as NHS champion, after willingly implementing the most brutal budgets in NHS history.

At the heart of the care-homes scandal is the government's failure to reform social care's ramshackle finance. The attempt sank Theresa May's election campaign and there is no sign yet of Johnson's promised 'clear plan'. The NHS v care home row shows that both are utterly interdependent, yet can never meld while one is free, the other paid for by families or councils. Martin Green said to me revealingly: 'Imagine the row if NHS PPE had been diverted to private care homes!', unwittingly exposing the wicked issue: merging state and profit-making sectors is like oil and water.

In 1979 two-thirds of care was NHS- or council-run, but now 84 per cent is for-profit. You can watch this bizarre market of care-home sales and takeovers in the trade magazine *Health-Investor UK* or Knight Frank reports: the money and property enticed in private equity with funds in tax havens. But austerity has squeezed fees for state-paid residents, while family-run businesses are verging on bankruptcy as occupancy falls in this crisis: they protest that councils aren't passing on emergency funds, stricken councils say they can't pay.

After this, care needs to be renationalised, locally run with a single seamless NHS/care profession. Care beds are essential with the number of over-85s doubling over the next 25 years. But the service needs to be free for rich and poor alike by the time they use it, to stop this financial conflict. There is no better time for brave reform, with care newly valued by all who have stood and clapped. The former Tory pensions minister Ros Altmann has slammed big care companies, 'bought up by hedge-funders at knockdown prices, loaded with debt, tripling their money'. If they think they're too big to fail, she says, 'don't bail them out, take them over'.

Johnson is no nationaliser. But families will not forgive the scandal of care-home deaths on his watch, left with tragic images of grandparents dying alone, feared to be without morphine or tranquillisers. Divorced from the NHS, private ownership of social care is a key reason why this horror is happening.

3 JUNE

The racism that killed George Floyd was built in Britain

AFUA HIRSCH

The headlines are now describing the US as a nation in crisis. As the protests against the killing of African American George Floyd by a white police officer enter their second week, there is a far deeper, more important message. Because the US is not, if we are honest, 'in crisis'. That suggests something broken, unable to function as planned. What black people are experiencing the world over is a system that finds their bodies expendable, by design.

African Americans told us this when they lost Trayvon Martin, Sandra Bland, Ahmaud Arbery, Breonna Taylor, Eric Garner, Chinedu Okobi, Michael Brown, Aiyana Jones, Tamir Rice, Jordan Davis, Alton Sterling, Philando Castile, and so many more.

African Americans told us this after 9/11, when headlines described the US as being in a 'state of terror'. 'Living in a state of terror was new to many white people in America,' said Maya Angelou, 'but black people have been living in a state of terror in this country for more than 400 years.'

African Americans told us this during the civil rights movement, the last time the US knew protests on this scale. And if the world paid attention to black people, then it would know that this state of terror extends far beyond the US. The Ghanaian president, Nana Akufo-Addo, captured the trauma of so many Africans around the world when he said that black people everywhere were 'shocked and distraught'.

In Australia, protesters relived the death of David Dungay, a 26-year-old Indigenous Australian man who died while being restrained by five guards in 2015. He also cried the haunting phrase, 'I can't breathe.'

In the UK, black people and our allies are taking to the streets as I write, to wake British people up out of their fantasy that this crisis of race is a problem that is both uniquely American, and solvable by people returning to the status quo.

The foreign secretary, Dominic Raab, said on behalf of Britain: 'We want to see de-escalation of all of those tensions.' If he had bothered to listen to black British people, he might have discovered that many of us do not want de-escalation. We want protest, we want change, and we know it is something for which we must fight. Because many of us have been fighting for this all our lives.

The British government could have had the humility to use this moment to acknowledge Britain's experiences. It could have discussed how Britain helped invent anti-black racism, how today's US traces its racist heritage to British colonies in America, and how it was Britain that industrialised black enslavement in the Caribbean, initiated systems of apartheid all over the African continent, using the appropriation of black land, resources and labour to fight both world wars and using it again to reconstruct the peace.

And how, today, black people in Britain are still being dehumanised by the media, disproportionately imprisoned and dying in police custody, and now also dying disproportionately of Covid-19.

What the British government did instead is remarkable. First, it emerged that it may have used George Floyd's death as an excuse to delay a report into the disparity in ethnic minority deaths from Covid-19. Although the Department of Health officially denies it, there were reports that the Public Health England review was delayed because of concerns in Whitehall about the 'close proximity to the current situation in America'. The government needn't have worried, because instead of meeting the grief in our communities at so many deaths from Covid-19, its review fails to offer any new insight anyway.

The government's response has been to appoint Kemi Badenoch, the minister for equalities, and a black woman, to 'get to the bottom' of the problem. What do we know about Badenoch's approach to racism in Britain? On 'institutional racism' – a phenomenon that affects minorities in Britain – she has been reported as saying that she doesn't recognise it. On former mayoral candidate Zac Goldsmith's Islamophobic campaign? She helped run it. On the black community? She doesn't believe that it really exists.

On American racism? 'We don't have all the horrible stuff that's happened in America here,' Badenoch said in 2017.

For those of us who see racism for what it is, as a system that kills – both our bodies, and our humanity – this is traumatic. I listened to the health secretary, Matt Hancock, announce – as if it was his new discovery – that 'black lives matter', and offer someone as seemingly uninterested in anti-racism as Badenoch as a solution.

Meanwhile, that 'horrible stuff that's happened in America'? Our reaction to George Floyd's death as black British people is our expression of generations of lifelong, profound, unravelling pain. Some of us are speaking about this for the first time, in too many cases that I'm personally aware of, attracting reprimands and sanctions at work.

My own personal protest has been silence. Not silence at those protesting, with whom I am in full solidarity, and to whom I offer my support, my labour, my platform, my time and my resources. But a refusal to participate in the broadcast media, which – when racism becomes, for a few short days, a relevant part of the news cycle – call me in their dozens, inviting me to painstakingly explain how systems of race are constructed.

This time I'm watching other black people graciously, brilliantly, appear on these platforms to educate hosts and viewers alike. And I know next time they will be asked to come again and repeat the same wisdom.

We do this work all the time. We have taken what we inherited and had no choice but to make sense of it. We have studied, read, written and understood the destructive power of race. And we are telling you that race is a system that Britain built here.

We are also telling you that as long as you send all children out into the world to be actively educated into racism, taught a white supremacist version of history, literature and art, then you are setting up a future generation to perpetuate the same violence on which that system of power depends.

We are telling you that we need to dismantle, not to de-escalate. Pay attention.

Trump reaches for Nixon playbook after protests that have rocked America

DAVID SMITH

They were 48 minutes of mayhem that shook the republic. With a bizarre pageant of riot shields, a Bible and a designer handbag, they also represented what could be Donald Trump's last best chance of clinging to power.

Before sunset last Monday, the US president stood in the White House Rose Garden, threatened to turn the American military on the American people and declared: 'I am your president of law and order.'

Beyond the perimeter fence, park police and National Guard troops fired teargas and chased away peaceful protesters so Trump could cross the road to the fire-damaged St John's church. Trump was joined by officials including his daughter and senior adviser, Ivanka, clutching a $1,540 handbag. The self-anointed strongman posed for the cameras while awkwardly holding aloft a Bible – or was it the Richard Nixon playbook?

This was the moment that Trump finally found a re-election campaign strategy in his comfort zone. Like his idol Nixon during the turmoil of 1968, he promised to put out the fires in American cities and assuage the fears of white suburbs. It is a framing that portrays Democrats as soft on crime while selling Trump as the national security president – less 'Keep America Great' than 'Keep America Safe'.

'The Radical Left Democrats new theme is "Defund the Police",' the president tweeted. 'Remember that when you don't want Crime, especially against you and your family. This is where Sleepy Joe is being dragged by the socialists. I am the complete opposite, more money for Law Enforcement! #LAWANDORDER.'

In a year of extraordinary tumult, Trump has found the electoral battleground constantly shifting beneath his feet. Just a few months ago, he was painting the Democrats as radical socialists in thrall to Senator Bernie Sanders, but the party's nomination was secured by the moderate Joe Biden. He was also trumpeting the strength of the economy, but that narrative was shredded by the coronavirus pandemic – although there was some encouraging news at the end of last week to suggest that US jobs were returning after the lockdown was lifted in many states.

Trump pivoted to blaming China for the virus but polls suggested this gained little traction as voters scrutinised the president's own sluggish response. But then came the tragedy of George Floyd, an African American man killed when a white Minneapolis police officer pressed his neck with his knee. The subsequent social unrest, the most widespread in half a century, may now have thrown Trump a political lifeline.

The great majority of the protests, including that outside the White House on Monday, have been peaceful, highlighting the injustices of 400 years of slavery and segregation. Some have been met with vicious state-sanctioned force. However, incidents of violence, including ransacking stores and burning police cars, received outsized TV coverage and handed Trump a cultural wedge issue to exploit.

Like an autocrat in a teetering regime, Trump has staged a massive show of force in the humid capital, with General Mark Milley, the chairman of the joint chiefs of staff, strutting the streets in combat fatigues while military helicopters roared overhead. The White House was fenced off, unidentified law enforcement patrolled and troops stood guard at the Lincoln Memorial, a shrine to democracy.

On Wednesday, a Republican party press release was headlined: 'President Calls For Law & Order, As Democrats Turn Blind Eye To Violence.' Never likely to be accused of subtlety, the president himself repeatedly tweeted what may now be his three-word re-election manifesto: 'LAW & ORDER!'

The theme is calculated to inflame divisions rather than make new friends. But there are doubts over whether such a pitch can work in a country facing its biggest public health crisis since 1918, biggest economic crisis since 1933 and biggest race relations crisis since 1968. Michael Steele, former chairman of the Republican National Committee, said: 'It's not the smartest strategy in the world, given not just the complexity but the volatility of the nation's grappling with race and the death of this young man and the response by the police and now the response by the administration.

'So I think that cooler heads will ultimately try to prevail. I doubt they will be successful, at least completely, with Trump because he sees the law-and-order angle as his gate key to open up a new line of conversation. For example, we're not talking about Covid-19 and the failure of the administration to grapple with the enormity of that crisis.'

Some around Trump compare the moment to 1968, when Nixon ran as the law-and-order candidate after a summer of riots and won the White House. Unlike Nixon, Trump is an incumbent, but seeking to shift blame for the violence to Democratic state governors and city mayors in places such as Minneapolis, New York and Washington.

Nixon vowed to represent the 'silent majority', a phrase Trump tweeted during the past week. After the Watergate scandal, Nixon became the only US president in history to resign, yet it is his ghost with whom Trump is most likely to commune at dead of night. The 45th president told *Fox & Friends* on Fox News last month: 'I learned a lot from Richard Nixon.'

John Farrell, author of *Richard Nixon: The Life*, said of Trump: 'The best single analogy of Trump's behaviour and Nixon's comes from May 1971 when the justice department had a massive amount of protesters rounded up and deprived of their civil rights, huddled in stadiums, because Nixon had made the calculation that this would make him look strong to the country. If you are a liberal and you're worried about this working against Biden, then 71 and 72 are the years that give you nightmares.'

Recent polls show Biden leading Trump nationally and in swing states, and eating into his advantages among older voters. The president's law-and-order stance would seem calculated to win them back while setting a political trap for Biden, who must strike a delicate balance between validating anger over police brutality towards African Americans while condemning violence as a response.

John Zogby, a pollster and author, said: 'Trump has seen some serious slippage among white voters over 65. That was a bedrock of his base, so this could be a way: these are people that are far removed from the violence in the streets and fairly one-dimensional in their view of both protesting and violence in the streets, and the most conservative on matters of race.

'Now, will it work? It's risky and it's hard to see it working but then he has defied so many rules of engagement. It's really incumbent now on Joe Biden and the Democrats to win.'

8 JUNE

The toppling of Edward Colston's statue is not an attack on history. It is history

DAVID OLUSOGA

For people who don't know Bristol, the real shock when they heard that the statue of a 17th-century slave trader had been torn from its plinth and thrown into the harbour was that 21st-century Bristol still had a statue of a slave trader on public display. For many watching the events unfold on social media, that was the real WTF moment.

Edward Colston, the man in question, was a board member and ultimately the deputy governor of the Royal African Company. In those roles he helped to oversee the transportation into slavery of an estimated 84,000 Africans. Of them, it is believed around 19,000 died in the stagnant bellies of the company's slave ships during the infamous Middle Passage from the coast of Africa to the plantations of the new world. The bodies of the dead were cast into the water where they were devoured by the sharks that, over the centuries of the Atlantic slave trade, learned to seek out slave ships and follow the bloody paths of slave routes across the ocean. This is the man who, for 125 years, has been honoured by

Bristol. Put literally on a pedestal in the very heart of the city. But tonight Edward Colston sleeps with the fishes.

The historical symmetry of this moment is poetic. A bronze effigy of an infamous and prolific slave trader dragged through the streets of a city built on the wealth of that trade, and then dumped, like the victims of the Middle Passage, into the water. Colston lies at the bottom of a harbour in which the ships of the triangular slave trade once moored, by the dockside on to which their cargoes were unloaded.

Slave ship captains were often permitted to bring one or two enslaved people back to Britain and sell them privately for their own profit. The practice offered successful captains a bonus and the Africans enslaved in this manner were called 'privilege negroes'. Many were young boys who were sold as exotic servants: fashion accessories. They appear as commodities for sale in advertisements in 18th-century Bristol newspapers, publications which also carried notices offering rewards for the recapture of enslaved people who had absconded from the grand homes of the city's elite. Metres from where Colston's statue now rests runs Pero's Bridge, named after Pero Jones, one of those enslaved people who lived and died in Bristol. A man who may well have taken his first steps on British soil on the docks from which Colston's statue was hurled.

The crowd who saw to it that Colston fell were of all races, but some were the descendants of the enslaved black and brown Bristolians whose ancestors were chained to the decks of Colston's ships. Ripped from his pedestal, Colston seemed smaller: diminished in both size and potency. Lying flat, with his studied pensive pose, he looked suddenly preposterous. It was when the statue was in this position that one of the protesters made a grim but powerful gesture. By placing his knee over the bronze throat of Edward Colston, he reminded us of the unlikely catalyst for these remarkable events.

The fact that a man who died 299 years ago is today on the front pages of most of Britain's newspapers suggests that Bristol has not been brilliant at coming to terms with its history. Despite the valiant and persistent efforts of campaigners, all attempts to have the statue peacefully removed were thwarted by Colston's legion of defenders. In 2019, attempts to fix a plaque to the pedestal collapsed after Bristol's Society of Merchant Venturers, the high priests of the Colston cult, insisted on watering down the text, adding qualifications that, it was felt, had the effect of minimising his crimes. Yet what repelled many about the statue was not that it valorised Colston but that it was silent about his victims, those whose lives were destroyed to build the fortune he lavished upon the city.

The long defence of the figure and Colston's reputation was overt and shameless, but not unique. In other British cities other men who grew rich through the trafficking of human beings or who defended the 'respectable trade' are venerated in bronze and marble. In Edinburgh's St Andrew Square, on a pedestal 150 feet high, stands Viscount Melville, Henry Dundas, another of history's guilty men. His great contribution to civilisation was to water down and delay attempts to pass an act abolishing the slave trade. Historians struggle to estimate how many thousands died or were transported into slavery because of his actions. Already social media is ablaze with calls for Dundas to be thrown into the Forth.

Today is the first full day since 1895 on which the effigy of a mass murderer does not cast its shadow over Bristol's city centre. Those who lament the dawning of such a day, and who are appalled by what happened on Sunday, need to ask themselves some difficult questions. Do they honestly believe that Bristol was a better place when the figure of a slave trader stood at its centre? Are they genuinely unable to understand why those descended from Colston's victims have always regarded his statue as an outrage and for decades pleaded for its removal?

If they do not confront such questions they risk becoming lost in the same labyrinth of moral bewilderment in which some of Colston's defenders became entrapped in 2017. That year Colston Hall, Bristol's prime concert venue, and one of the many institutions named after the slave trader, announced that it was to change its name. In response, a number of otherwise reasonable decent people announced that they would be boycotting the hall. Think about that for a moment. Rational, educated, 21st-century people earnestly concluded that they were taking a moral stance by refusing to listen to music performed within the walls of a concert hall unless that venue was named after a man who bought, sold and killed human beings.

Now is not the time for those who for so long defended the indefensible to contort themselves into some new, supposedly moral stance, or play the victim. Their strategy of heel-dragging and obfuscation was predicated on one fundamental assumption: that what happened on Sunday would never happen. They were confident that black people and brown people who called Bristol their home would forever tolerate living under the shadow of a man who traded in human flesh, that the power to decide whether Colston stood or fell lay in their hands. They were wrong on every level. Whatever is said over the next few days, this was not an attack on history. This is history. It is one of those rare historic moments whose arrival means things can never go back to how they were.

'The data was there – so why did it take coronavirus to wake us up to racial health inequalities?'

ANGELA SAINI

One of the last things I did before lockdown was speak at the Royal College of Obstetricians and Gynaecologists at an event on race and maternal mortality. It has been known for a few years now that – incredibly – black women are five times more likely to die in pregnancy than white women, while Asian women are twice as likely to die. The atmosphere in the room was heavy with anger and disappointment. Black doctors, nurses and midwives were exasperated by the failure to protect women.

In the United States, too, black and Native American women suffer greater rates of maternal mortality than white women. This is just one of many examples of racial inequality in health. A US study found last year that black patients were 40 per cent less likely than white patients to get medication to relieve acute pain. A UK study published in January showed that Asian patients with dementia were 14 per cent less likely to be prescribed anti-dementia drugs than white patients were.

Many of us have been shouting for years about this into what has felt like a void, trying to get professional health bodies and politicians to act on what has always been apparent: that to be black or brown is to see your body suffer disproportionately to the point where you may die earlier than average. The problem is particularly pronounced in the US. According to research from the Centers for Disease Control and Prevention, the life expectancy gap between black and white Americans has narrowed, but still sits at more than three years.

Little did we know that it would take a pandemic to put minority-ethnic health at the top of the agenda. Within weeks, data began to show that ethnic minorities in both the US and the UK were bearing the brunt of the virus. As we began clapping for NHS workers, stories emerged in the press of Asian and black doctors dying in surprisingly high numbers: Ate Wilma Banaag, a nurse at Watford general hospital, in early April; Krishan Arora, a GP in Croydon, later that month; Cecilia Fashanu, a nurse at Cumberland infirmary, at the end of it.

The UK's Intensive Care National Audit and Research Centre found that a third of patients needing breathing support in intensive care who had tested positive for the virus were non-white. Data published by the Office for National Statistics (ONS) in early May suggested that black people in England and Wales were around four times more likely than white people to die from Covid-19.

The media attention on coronavirus meant these figures couldn't easily be ignored. But neither should we have been all that surprised. All the factors that have long impacted the health of minorities were inevitably going to play out in the event of a pandemic. When you factor in that London – which has a minority white British population – was hit first, and that many high-risk frontline jobs, particularly in hospitals, are held by BAME people, then the data pretty well matched expectations.

What was odd was all the head-scratching in the press. 'Mystery over high risk to black and Asian Britons', ran an online *Daily Mail* headline. It was as though people had forgotten that racial disparities in health have always existed. A hasty government review into minority-ethnic deaths due to Covid-19, published last week, scrambled to explain in a few weeks what researchers have been documenting for decades. The Public Health England report not only failed to tell us anything we didn't already know, but even fell short of telling us everything we did.

Meanwhile, in their desperation to solve the race puzzle they had invented for themselves, scientists have continued to ask whether there might be deeper genetic factors at play. Could BAME people have innate qualities that make them more likely to get sick, those horribly faulty black and brown genes? The UK Biobank, a repository of public DNA, is being mined for correlations as I write. Some medical researchers appear to have forgotten that the racial categories we use every day are socially, not genetically, defined. In the US, for instance, a person can have just one ancestor of African origin and still be categorised as black based on their appearance and society's perception of them.

But then, this is what the medical community has always done: pathologise blackness. In the US in the 19th century, as Harvard historian Evelynn Hammonds has documented, a medical condition known as 'drapetomania' was invented by the white physician Samuel Cartwright to describe black slaves fleeing their owners. How else to explain the errant behaviour of the naturally enslaved? From bone density and skin thickness to susceptibility to pain, doctors have long sought to isolate what is tangibly different about the oppressed. Despite their persistent failure to find any meaningful differences, they still do it now.

As the pandemic has rolled on, many experts have wondered whether vitamin D might be responsible: we know it's linked to immunity and is harder to get enough of when you've got darker skin and live in a colder climate. Voilà! A neat explanation that absolves society of all blame for social disparities in health. Those with darker skins are dying because they've forgotten to take their supplements!

A more likely explanation that people are slowly beginning to acknowledge following the killing of George Floyd in Minneapolis lies not in race, but racism. Racial health inequality has its roots in the same neck-crushing racism as a bigoted thug with a police badge, but it plays out in more subtle ways: in the white flight that creates ethnic ghettos, in the inhumanity shown to migrants and refugees, in the difficulties black and Asian people face getting good jobs, in ethnicity pay gaps and all the little bullets that society fires at you if your skin colour is different. If you want to know how early these bullets begin to be fired, even infant mortality rates are higher in the US among black Americans.

Being poor is crucial when it comes to bad health. The life expectancy of women in the most deprived areas of England is more than seven years lower than that of women living in the least deprived, according to the most recent data published by the ONS. For men, the gap is more than nine years. And it has got worse over the past decade.

Poverty overlaps with race, but not entirely. And this means that, as more data comes in, we must also acknowledge that some of the factors that make ethnic minorities more vulnerable also make certain white Britons and Americans more vulnerable, too. As of June, the region in England with the highest death rates from Covid-19, overtaking London, is the north-east, which has terrible levels of deprivation and child poverty – and among the whitest towns in the country.

Individual disadvantage, as much as we may want to view it as a simple formula, operates in complicated ways. An affluent black Briton may well have better living conditions and diet than a working-class white person living in a former mining town, but then they are also more likely to face racial discrimination when they go to a hospital. There are layers of complexity here, each of which has to be unpicked. Going forward, what we need is fewer knee-jerk official reports and more slow, careful research.

In the end, this is also about power. The levers of capitalism have widened inequality between the rich and poor; funds drained from the NHS and local communities have left them less resilient; and populist politics have pitted people against each other. The issue is not just racism, but how racism plays out in a society that is already brutalising its citizens. Tackling racism is just one crucial part of the enormous task of making life fairer for everyone – but it is a necessary one, because a nation that is able to view some of its people as less human than others will never have the moral strength to resolve its other problems.

11 JUNE

A catchy slogan alone won't defeat racism. We need action

JOSEPH HARKER

If I hear one more white person say 'Black Lives Matter' I think my head will explode. The phrase, powerful when first popularised by black people after the shooting of Trayvon Martin in 2012 in the US, has now become so ubiquitous as to have lost almost all meaning. When even Boris Johnson can say 'Black Lives Matter' – the same Boris Johnson who talks of African piccaninnies, of 'bank robber' burqa wearers, who leads a party riven by Islamophobia but refuses a proper investigation into it, and who was part of a government that deported black British citizens, and continues the injustice of the hostile environment to this day – well, you know the slogan's cultural appropriation is complete.

Even racists hate racism. That's why they're always looking for ways to excuse what they do. 'It's not my fault – black people are just a bit more criminal than white people.' 'I'm not being racist – it's just that a lot of Muslims are terrorists.' 'I'd love to recruit a black person – it's just that they're not quite the right fit for this role.'

'It's just that ...' You won't find this chanted in a city square by thousands of protesters, but these are probably the three most powerful words in the history of institutional racism. They're the words people say in private – or don't say – when they're making the decisions that really matter. They are the words that determine whether someone gets that job, or that business contract, or that university place, or that rented room.

Over the past few days I've wondered, why now? Why, after all we've known about police brutality against black people, are people only now saying, en masse, that enough is enough? I think there are two core reasons. First, given the lockdown, there's not a lot else for young people to do. It's the first time in months that they have been able to be part of a group activity.

But the other factor is more fundamental: and that is white guilt. While black people have raged about the shootings and asphyxiations, for most white people there's always been a get-out. 'It's just that [those words again] ... he was maybe being too aggressive ... maybe the officers thought they were under threat ... it was a spur-of-the-moment pull of the trigger.' It's allowed white people to believe that, though the outcomes were all horrific, a white suspect in the same situation could have suffered the same fate.

The George Floyd video crashed through that delusion. A subdued and incapacitated suspect; a knee pushed down on his neck as he pleaded for breath; passersby screaming for his life as it ebbed away; officer Derek Chauvin blithely ignoring it all, cocksure that he'd face no consequences for his actions; a fellow officer standing guard to prevent anyone coming to Floyd's rescue. For almost nine minutes, many of them after he had passed out. Nine minutes. No white person could believe this could happen to them. That an officer of the law could be so callous, so unconcerned about the life of a white man.

That's why, this time, there have been unprecedented numbers of white people declaring their allegiance to the anti-racism cause. On the streets, even in the US, most protesters have been white. It has to be a positive thing that at last they're starting to notice. This was nowhere more apparent than in Bristol this weekend. If it had been a black-only crowd, would the statue of notorious slavemaster Edward Colston really have been allowed to topple, let alone be dragged through the streets and dumped in the River Avon?

Many British people were upset at what they saw. And I have some sympathy: mob rule is generally a bad thing, and risks getting disastrously out of hand. But what a glorious moment. It's an image that will last years in the memory, as the moment that people in one English city said the ritual humiliation of black lives was no longer acceptable. You can say 'Black Lives Matter' a million times but it will change nothing. This action changed things.

When I saw Floyd's life drain slowly away, I wondered why so little had changed since the Black Lives Matter movement swept across the US in 2014. Surely all US police officers should know they will be held accountable for any transgressions, especially when caught on camera? Chauvin clearly feared no repercussions.

There are 18,000 separate police forces in the US. In the UK there are 43. If we're going to bring about change we need to find a way to get into them all, change them all, and make those changes stick. It won't be by simply calling for more black police officers. That's been tried before, and any change is glacially slow. It won't be just by rooting out 'bad apples': a system that allows them in unchecked in the first place is already rotten to the core. It won't simply be by giving all officers 'diversity training': a couple of weeks on the streets after completing such a course, and they're back in the old routine, acting on instincts and stereotypes.

On the day of the first major UK Black Lives Matter protest last Wednesday, the Metropolitan police commissioner, Cressida Dick, was giving evidence to the London assembly. She was talking, coincidentally, about the disproportionate number of fines handed out to black people during the coronavirus lockdown – double the rate for white people. This, she explained, was partly because more officers have been operating in high-crime areas. To which the response must be, what has the lockdown got to do with high-crime areas? It's just another way in which black people (more likely to live in poorer areas, which are more likely to have higher crime rates) continue to be disproportionately targeted by the police. And then Dick added, as if trying to defend this: 'We've said again and again, be sensitive, be careful. And I think [our officers] have been. But I have to be honest, I haven't gone back to them to say, think about your unconscious bias.'

So there it is: we have officers disproportionately targeting black people, and nothing said to them in advance about being aware of the danger of racial stereotyping. This is where leadership really counts: the day-to-day decisions, at the most senior levels, that affect thousands of lives. To make lasting change, we ultimately have to get off the streets and into the rooms where these decision-makers operate.

Black Lives Matter is a catchy slogan. But right now, action is what really matters.

26 June

Calm in a sea of emotion: to make history, Klopp's Liverpool had to let it go

JONATHAN LIEW

In a way, it was one last joke at Liverpool's expense. Right, you've won the league for the first time in 30 years on a baking summer's evening: now everybody, stay at home! And of course, most did. They're the ones you probably didn't see. They stayed at home in Kinshasa and Kuala Lumpur, in Malmö and Manhattan, in Wallasey and West Derby. They gathered in WhatsApp groups and Zoom watchalongs and sat in their living rooms and bedrooms, quietly savouring.

Meanwhile, a few went out. They're the ones you probably did see: the ones waving their red smoke canisters, holding up their replica Premier League trophies, tooting their horns. In recent weeks there was a strange pseudo-debate over the prospect of Liverpool fans descending on Anfield to celebrate their title win. On one side we were presented with the idea of football fan as brainless beefcake, drawn irrevocably to revelry like a fly to shit. On the other, the football fan as noble and pious martyr, whose intrinsic virtue must never be questioned, let alone impugned.

Perhaps it ultimately should have surprised nobody that football fans are neither superior people, nor inferior people, but simply people. In moments of triumph or moments of trauma, football offers something we all need from somewhere: shared pride, a common emotional canvas, a sense of belonging at a time when we have scarcely felt more apart from each other. Winning your first championship since 1990, an achievement that for many will have been a lifelong consumption: is the urge to seek out companionship at a moment like this really so strange?

Of course, at most clubs, '30 years of hurt' that also generated 14 major trophies – including two Champions Leagues – is the sort of drought fans would happily sign up for. Yet Liverpool has never judged itself by the standards of most clubs, or indeed by the standards of most cities. Partly this is a question of geography, partly a question of culture, partly a question of politics. A proud port town that has traditionally looked outwards to the high seas, rather than inwards to its own country, for inspiration and kinship. You didn't need to be a Militant-voting, flag-waving scouse separatist to feel the disconnect. The sense that England was some other place, over there, and that on some level the feeling was entirely mutual.

The unashamed exceptionalism that has fuelled some of Liverpool's proudest achievements as a city has also turned it into a target. It's 16 years since the infamous *Spectator* leader that chided the people of Liverpool for wallowing in their 'victim status', for 'an excessive predilection for welfarism', for refusing to 'accept that they might have made any contribution to their misfortunes'. And yet to this day you will hear those very same tropes. The editor who published the article, meanwhile, just so happens to be the prime minister.

And so, with the possible exception of Manchester United, there is no other club in English football in whom rival fans are more emotionally invested, no club whose failures and calamities are more eagerly awaited or celebrated. The unbridled glee with which many fans still celebrate their title collapse in 2014 is hard to imagine ever being replicated for, say, Chelsea or Tottenham or Manchester City.

Perhaps inevitably, Liverpool's modern narrative has been built on resistance, of overcoming the odds, of taking on greater powers: whether over Hillsborough, or the tide of new money that transformed English football in the early 2000s, or even in protesting against their own owners. Above all, they have been railing against the idea that this is a place with more past than future, that their golden era has gone for good. That hurricane of rage, of irresistible just cause, has fuelled some of their greatest triumphs on a football pitch: Olympiacos 2004, West Ham 2006, Barcelona 2019. But over a gruelling 38-game season, it has more often proved a millstone.

The crowning achievement of Jürgen Klopp, therefore, has been to overcome the challenge that ultimately sank every one of his predecessors: to block out the noise. To set history to one side. To shout down the cynics and the doubters with a new cry of their own. There is a widespread perception of Klopp's team as an essentially emotional vehicle. In fact, this season Liverpool's football is more accurately defined as the pursuit of immaculate control.

In order to make history, first Liverpool had to let it go. It's tempting to spy parallels between the Liverpool of the 1980s – a city scarred by discord and decay – and the Liverpool of 2020, a city labouring under a decade of austerity. But at the very least, the red half of Liverpool will cherish this rare moment of communion: one of those times when everything else seems to fall silent, and all you can hear is singing.

28 June

There's another pandemic stalking Britain: hunger

JOHN HARRIS

In more than three months of reporting about the Covid-19 outbreak and the social crisis it has sparked, one subject has come up in my conversations far more than most: food. Or rather, an increasing number of people's familiarity with the experience and prospect of hunger.

As the recession that will surely explode by the autumn takes shape, food bank providers report surges in demand of, in some places, around 300 per cent. When the footballer Marcus Rashford took on and beat the government over the provision of free school meals during the summer holidays, he was shining a light on the same soaring want.

At the heart of this is something a lot of people understood well before the outbreak: that, from our immigration rules to the punitive benefits system, people have been deprived of the most basic security by deliberate policy. Of late, I think I have spoken to a different project every week, and the same themes have been echoed by everyone involved. A seemingly endless array of people have recently lost work, in both the formal and informal economies – and, if they are entitled to benefits, have suddenly discovered that the money they eventually receive in universal credit fails to cover even the merest essentials. For many who still nominally have jobs, the daily lottery of zero-hours contracts often increases their precarity, something worsened in many cases by coronavirus-related problems with childcare and public transport.

Now, with the government encouraging the misapprehension that the country is somehow returning to normal, it is clear what is coming next. Despite Boris Johnson's promise in the *Mail on Sunday* of a 'building blitz' and 'opportunity guarantee', when his chancellor Rishi Sunak's furlough schemes end and such temporary protections as the moratorium on evictions fade away, we will be hit by a social crisis that will be almost unprecedented, as people at the social grassroots well know.

In early April I spoke to Robin Burgess, who co-runs the Northampton Hope Centre, which provides hundreds of people a week with emergency food help. At that point, he was faced with declining public donations and skyrocketing need, and was unsure whether supplies would last much beyond a fortnight. Last week, he told me that the threefold increase in referrals that had materialised back then was unchanged. 'This is a lull before the next storm,' he said.

Thanks to a new government scheme called the Food Charities Grant Fund, Burgess's food bank will soon have received a total of £46,000, under terms that restrict its use to food, leaving storage, staffing and transport costs untouched. ('It's really a blank cheque for food retailers and wholesalers,' he said.) According to the scheme's terms, food bought with this money must have been fully distributed to people in need by 9 August, and there is so far no word on what will happen after that.

Particularly in cities, another huge issue is now inescapable. As the pandemic has ground on, attention has belatedly been paid to the million or so people in Britain who have what official-speak terms 'no recourse to public funds', or NRPF: that means no access to benefits, notwithstanding the right to live here at least temporarily. It is a condition established in law in 1996, hugely extended by Theresa May when she was in charge of the Home Office – and recently deemed unlawful in the high court, though the policy remains in place.

In the London borough of Newham, a food bank run by the Bonny Downs Community Association once used to help 15 or 20 households a week, a figure that has now risen to around 140, entailing a weekly bill of £1,000 that organisers say is simply unsustainable. Angie Allgood, a social worker who was one of the association's founders, reckons that 80 per cent of these people fall into the NRPF category. 'Before the outbreak, I didn't really know that part of our community,' she told me last week. Until late March, most of them worked long hours, often in hidden parts of the labour market. 'When Covid-19 hit and they lost their jobs,' she said, 'everything fell apart.'

I also spoke to Maruf and Tasnova, a couple who volunteer at the food bank. They are unable to get work, barred from benefits, and living with their six-year-old son and three-month-old daughter in a single room. Food is at the heart of their family's plight – not just because they have so little of it, but also in the way their anxiety is playing out in the daily rituals of mealtimes. Their son has been so unsettled – by lockdown, the suspension of school and his family's awful circumstances – that he often refuses to eat.

This is what structural racism looks like up close: cruelties deliberately targeted at the same people of colour who have been disproportionately affected by the virus, visible as a matter of everyday experience, and definitely in the minds of many of the people in our cities who have rallied to Black Lives Matter protests. What is strange, perhaps, is that issues as stark as these have been almost drowned out by noise about the latest events at Oxford University, rancorous TV debates about statues, or the way that corporations which had barely mentioned the condition of society before are now suddenly affecting to be conscientiousness incarnate. Such, it seems, is the tenor of this strange summer.

The prime minister, meanwhile, continues to behave as if he is in a Gilbert and Sullivan operetta, addressing a country that is enduring only a minor mishap, and ordering the pubs to open while warning of 'writhing scenes in the beer gardens'. Ministers tell us it's now our solemn duty to – as a *Daily Express* headline recently put it – 'spend for our country'. What seems to escape them is not just the awful gravity of Britain's coronavirus story, but the fact that increasing numbers of us have very little to spend on anything, including life's absolute basics.

There are ways out of these injustices that are not nearly as inconceivable as some people would have you believe: a minimum income guarantee or universal basic income, an end to the immigration rules that mean so many people live in a state of constant panic, and the long-overdue abandonment of the thinking whereby people are threatened with destitution as a matter of policy.

Slowly and uncertainly, these things seem to be rising to the political surface. But everything has to start with a basic acknowledgment: that there is no stronger challenge to the cruelties of the status quo than the reproach of hunger.

Summer

Britain beyond lockdown: can we make more space for nature?

JONATHAN WATTS

The first post-lockdown crops of the land army have been harvested. The food – chard, spinach, lettuce and radish – is being parcelled out to the needy. Now the volunteer labour force has its sights on a new goal: a land-use revolution that will make UK farming more nature-friendly, plant-based and resilient to future shocks.

At Machynlleth, a bucolic town on the southern fringe of Snowdonia, the recently formed Planna Fwyd! (Plant Food!) movement is encouraging sheep farmers to convert hillsides to vegetable production for the first time in decades. Once or twice a week, teams of volunteers fan out across the slopes to sow new crops of potatoes or tend gooseberry bushes, peas and squash. Others distribute seeds to local families and run online classes on growing plants at home.

'If the whole coronavirus experience has taught us anything, it is that we should be more self-sufficient. It was terrifying seeing the empty shop shelves,' said Chris Higgins, a retired academic. 'It's very enriching. Growing and cooking food and working together is a great way of engaging with the local community and nature.'

In the not-too-distant past, eco-farming in rural communes was considered a fringe activity, but many of its core concepts – local distribution, diversity and ecosystem management – have become mainstream concerns in the wake of a pandemic that has made the public appreciate the vitality of nature and the fragility of global supply chains.

For many, the greatest upside of the crisis has been the respite for other species – deer on the beach in Hartlepool, mountain goats wandering the streets of Bangor, more dolphins and porpoises in the harbour at Fishguard.

As the lockdown eases, Boris Johnson says the 'nation is coming out of hibernation', but unless more space is found for nature in the government's recovery plans, wildlife will once again retreat, the soil will degrade and the climate destabilise.

History shows the folly of trying to return to business as usual after a pandemic. In the 14th century, the Black Death disrupted trade, left crops unharvested and prompted devastating famines. The aristocracy attempted to regain lost revenue and authority with higher taxes and more restrictions. This created the conditions for Wat Tyler's Peasants' Revolt and the Welsh war of independence led by Owain ap Gruffydd. Today's rebels want greater food security, lower carbon emissions and healthier commons that can provide clean water, fresh air and a stable climate for everyone. This is not just the Landworkers' Alliance and Extinction Rebellion Farmers, but academics and former ministers who say it makes good business sense.

Machynlleth – the first seat of government for Gruffydd in the 15th century – is today among the most progressive rural communities in the UK. The small population of 2,200 people is home to a disproportionate number of influential thinkers, including Jane Powell, the coordinator of the Wales Food Manifesto. The writer and activist said Covid-19 had instigated a clamour for food democracy. 'It has mobilised people. There is a huge uprising of people volunteering to distribute or grow food. They've seen the fragility of global supply chains. I think it has given people a sense of: "Gosh, it's up to us." We'd like to be better prepared next time. We need more control and knowledge.'

In Wales – as elsewhere in the UK – the pandemic exposed the risks of excessively specialising in sheep and cattle for export. This was already a concern due to Brexit, which will end subsidies and reduce markets, and the broader consumer trend away from meat. Lockdown brought a sudden dearth of vegetables and a glut of lamb. Shocked consumers are calling for a more reliable local supply. Welsh hill farmers are looking for new revenue streams by planting crops or charging for ecosystem services such as flood control and peatlands that absorb carbon dioxide.

Helen and Keith Lessiter run the vegetable, fruit and flower stalls at the farmers' market in Fishguard town hall. They have seen a surge in demand for seeds and plants. 'We haven't been so busy in 10 years,' said Helen. 'Everybody wants to do their own growing. That is great. The more local production, the better.

'I hope this experience has made people appreciate what goes into food production. It has been classed as menial work for so long. Now people can see that it is not just a case of stick it in the ground and wait.'

A change in land use is essential to get the UK back on track towards its climate goals. Returning peatland, bogs and other habitats to their natural state could absorb as much as a third of the UK's CO_2 emissions, according to the Wildlife Trusts. Clive Faulkner, chief executive of the Montgomeryshire Wildlife Trust, said the region had proved it is possible to reskill farmers as environmental stewards. 'Twenty years ago, people thought we were kooky, but now many are following.'

Faulkner urged the government not to neglect the countryside. 'I worry about who will support the farming community,' he said. 'Covid-19 is an amazing catastrophe, but it is not as systematic a threat as our broken relationship with the landscape.'

8 July

A Scottish independence crisis is on its way – and English politics is in denial

RAFAEL BEHR

A virus that doesn't care about nations or history can still spread borders across the map like a rash. Different European countries' pandemic responses restored boundaries meant to be submerged for the cause of continental integration. That effect was less pronounced within the UK, but public health is a devolved matter, so lockdown has probed the tender line where England meets Scotland.

There is no Scottish plan to quarantine visitors from England, but Nicola Sturgeon has refused to dismiss the notion completely. Opining on the subject in parliament last week, Boris Johnson offered the untrue and crass assertion that 'there is no such thing as a border' between the two nations. The inane gauntlet was taken up by a handful of pro-independence activists over the weekend, who stood at the sign on the A1 welcoming motorists to Scotland with a banner urging the coronavirus-carrying English to stay away.

Sturgeon condemned the stunt as not 'sensible or helpful', and no doubt she meant it. The first minister is a nationalist but not an Anglophobe. Her method for dismantling the union has been to entrench SNP control of institutions until it is hard to distinguish party and state. The pursuit of independence then becomes a fact about what it means to be the government of Scotland, thus disqualifying pro-union parties.

It is working. The defeat of the yes campaign in a referendum has faded in the historical record more than it should, for something that happened only six years ago. That whole world looks hazy now through the volcanic ash of subsequent political eruptions: Brexit, which a majority of Scots opposed, then the pandemic.

The coronavirus emergency boosted the standing of incumbents in most countries, but that 'rallying to the flag' effect has been stronger and lasted longer in Scotland than in England. Even many of Sturgeon's critics privately concede that she has had a good crisis, leavening executive authority with humility and sincerity – qualities the Tory leader has only read about. Opinion polls show regular majorities for independence, although that masks a common lack of enthusiasm for re-enacting a referendum battle that divided families and polluted friendships. Sturgeon has to appeal to a mainstream that prefers the rhythm of normal government to the relentless beat of the separatist drum, while at her back is an impatient SNP faction that suspects her of getting too cosy with the status quo.

It is a sign of how badly the pro-union side failed to embed its victory that the independence debate is a three-way tussle between 'yes, now', 'yes, later' and 'let's not have this argument'. No party is challenging the SNP for control. Labour's ambitions are limited to winning back second place from the Tories, who have stagnated since losing Ruth Davidson's leadership. Between now and next May's Scottish parliament elections, Britain must pass through more Brexit turbulence; transitional arrangements expire on 31 December. In every scenario, the SNP then complains that English Tories have wrenched pro-European Scots from their home continent without consent. Barring some unforeseen political accident, Sturgeon will then be confirmed as first minister, arguing that her refreshed mandate compels Westminster to legislate for an independence referendum.

Johnson will refuse, thus vindicating the view that Tory England always represses the will of Scotland. But the prime minister might prefer that charge to a gamble on having his remaining time in office consumed by a battle to save the union, and possibly ending up in posterity as the man who broke the kingdom.

Downing Street's plan A to dampen the clamour for independence was hosing Scotland with public money, but competition for that resource is getting more intense and areas with Conservative MPs are the priority. If there is no sign of a Tory revival north of the border, an even more cynical path may appeal: letting the flames of resentment roar in Scotland, igniting a Johnson-supporting English nationalist backlash. All the better if that sustains the toxic question of whether Labour needs SNP MPs to support a coalition come a general election. It would take an exceptionally irresponsible prime minister on a streak of constitutional pyromania to pursue such tactics. Johnson is qualified.

A conflagration in Scotland might not be the next crisis to destabilise Britain, but it is in the queue. It is also unnerving how little England is prepared, when Scottish politics is a rolling rehearsal. That bodes ill for the pro-union cause. English voters who support neither a Tory government nor Scottish independence have no purchase on a debate that is existential for their country, if that country is identified as the UK. Theirs is the queasiness of the spectator with emotional investment in a contest and no influence on the result. That is how my French and German friends described Brexit, which is disturbing because the comparison feels both apt and ridiculous. There is eerie familiarity in the way the pro-union cause is floundering, but it is madness to imagine a cultural border between England and Scotland analogous to the Channel.

But the arguments against separation have atrophied from lack of exercise, and the nationalist songs have catchier tunes. The

SNP strategy is to make independence feel inevitable. It needn't be, but divergence is the easier trajectory to plot. Meanwhile, the unionist cause has not evolved beyond hoping Sturgeon is wrong, while deferring the moment of asking Scotland the question directly – which is an admission of fear that she is right.

11 JULY

The best interviewees? Give me an actor in their winter years with a few scores to settle

HADLEY FREEMAN

It was just by chance that I was the last person to interview comedy legend Carl Reiner, who died last week, four months after I spent an evening with him and his best friend, Mel Brooks, at Reiner's home in Beverly Hills. This was not my first final interview: I'm pretty sure I was the last journalist to interview Burt Reynolds, and I was surely the last to interview Kirk Douglas, 100 when I met him, in his home, just down the road from Reiner's.

It's possible there were more. It's a professional peril if you prefer to interview the old rather than the young, as I do. Once a celebrity gets over 70, they shake off whatever shackles of propriety once contained them and really enjoy themselves. If you imagine it's people like Johnny Depp or Mickey Rourke who give publicists headaches, you've never met a celebrity in their winter years with a few scores to settle.

Just looking back on interviews I've done in the past three months, there was Woody Allen (84), more than happy to not bother promoting his movie and talk for an hour instead about his battles – to put it mildly – with his ex-partner Mia Farrow, which fascinated me, less so the film distributor, which later made its displeasure known. Then there was the royal memoirist Anne Glenconner (87), eagerly – despite her publisher's warnings against it – dishing the dirt on Meghan Markle.

But this is not to flatten older people into a twinkly-eyed, cheeky, homogeneous whole. Reynolds, then 80, arrived limping, leaning heavily on a cane and in palpable pain. As I said hello, he took his soon omnipresent bottle of pills out of his pocket, crushed two on the table between us with his fist, and snorted them. The pills soothed his pain but addled his mind, and, during our interview, in which he dutifully trotted out anecdotes as though he were a dancing monkey and I the baying crowd, he started to cry. He was, it was said, bankrupt, and all he had left were his memories, and even those he had to flog. It was a heartbreaking glimpse into how pitiless life can be, even – maybe especially – to the once golden and beautiful.

Reiner, 98, was in every way the opposite. He faced his later years with no regrets. One of his last tweets, posted 48 hours before his death was: 'Nothing pleases me more than knowing that I have lived the best life possible by having met & marrying the gifted Estelle (Stella) Lebost, who partnered with me in bringing Rob, Annie & Lucas Reiner into to [sic] this needy & evolving world.' Evidence of this best life was apparent from the moment I walked into his home, where he had lived since the 1960s with Estelle, who died in 2008. Every available surface seemed to be covered with photographs of four generations of Reiners, and his daughter, Annie, was just leaving, having come over for a visit. Brooks, his best friend of 70 years, was waiting in the living room for their nightly dinner date in front of the TV gameshow, *Jeopardy!*

'Relationship goals' is what people say on social media about pictures of beautiful, loved-up celebrities. Reiner and Brooks are my relationship goal. I can think of no purer bliss than knowing, even at 98, I will never be alone because my best friend is right beside me in the armchair next to mine, every night. Sitting opposite them, Brooks and Reiner's friendship looked even more enviable; it was, simply, a love story. Reiner's body – that annoying outer casing with cruelly built-in obsolescence – was starting to let him down, but he and Brooks still got such a kick out of each other. Afterwards, Reiner sent me some beautifully written messages about his forthcoming projects, and we talked about getting him a column in the *Guardian*. He seemed so unstoppable, I worried what he and Brooks would watch over dinner if they outlived *Jeopardy!* Last year its host, Alex Trebek, announced he has cancer. It turned out, I didn't need to worry.

When I heard about Reiner, I thought of Brooks, left behind. I don't know if Reiner realised he was probably giving me his last interview, but I suspect Brooks did. 'The thought of being without him – the world would be too bleak!' Reiner said, and Brooks looked down and took his hand. When I interviewed Kirk Douglas I caught glimpses of another man watching us anxiously through the back window; I later found out it was his son, Michael, visiting his dad and keeping an eye on proceedings. This is the downside to interviewing older people: while they have generally come to terms with their proximity to the end, you see that those around them have not.

I never regret the interviews I've done, only those I haven't. Katharine Hepburn, John Hughes, Robin Williams, Harold Ramis, Robert Evans, Bea Arthur, Nora Ephron – all were alive when I started working as a journalist, but by the time I realised

I ought to interview them, it was too late. Interviewing someone towards the end of their life is an unforgettable gift: they have little to gain, but they are giving you their time, and there is no commodity more valuable. In a corner of my heart, I will always be watching Reiner and Brooks laughing together in their armchairs. What more could any heaven offer?

11 JULY

Sex, drugs, trauma, racism: no subject is off the table

HANNAH J DAVIES

There is a moment in episode one of *I May Destroy You* likely to send the heart rate of anyone who has ever procrastinated into over-drive. Author Arabella, played by Michaela Coel – also the series' creator, writer and co-director – is about to pull an all-nighter at her agent's Soho office. The agitated rap of Little Simz's 'Picture Perfect' soundtracks her journey on a bus, windows typically filthy, through the streets of London. A Twitter star, she has been signed up to write a follow-up to her hit debut *Chronicles of a Fed-Up Millennial*, a book you imagine could have been glibly sold as 'a black, British *Sex and the City*'.

Except, the all-nighter never happens. Arabella assembles her belongings, which include caffeine tablets, into a neat pile. She opens her laptop. The scene turns silent, soundtrack on mute. She stares at her screen, and stares a little more, restarts her music, smokes a cigarette. She glares at the pat sentence on the screen: 'So Tina, being in her thirties, couldn't understand why you, Terrell, also thirties, would take her there on a first date. Nor could I.' The cursor blinks. She Googles a phrase that solidifies both hers and the viewers' panic: 'How to write quickly.' So she takes a break. A Technicolor blur of pink hair and multicoloured cardigan, she meets her friends at a bar named Ego Death – that is, a total loss of one's identity. A procrastination nightmare becomes a fun night out and then something far more serious. Drugs are taken. A drink is spiked. The next morning she remembers nothing bar a figure looming over her, raping her. She stuffs it down but, as such ordeals have a habit of doing, it bubbles up again.

Coel's dramedy – about a group of young, black Londoners navigating friendships, dating and the ubiquity of sexual abuse – has been billed by critics on both sides of the Atlantic as the show of the year. It was inspired by Coel's own experience of sexual assault, while she was making the Channel 4 sitcom *Chewing Gum*, her Bafta-winning, pastel-bright comedy, an incident she revealed in her 2018 MacTaggart lecture at the Edinburgh international television festival.

Delving into the feast-or-famine world of London's creative industries, *I May Destroy You* shares a central premise with *Girls* – where Lena Dunham's protagonist memorably declared that she 'may be the voice of my generation. Or, at least, a voice of a generation' – but minus its privilege, set instead in a London where its socially mobile but materially lacking protagonists dance to 00s garage in a gentrified bar, visiting a council flat one day and a shiny publishers' office the next. Novelesque is overused when it comes to the post-*Wire* TV landscape, but here Coel gives a feeling of moving between different worlds within the same city à la Hanif Kureishi or Zadie Smith, each contrasting vision of London fizzing with realism.

It is, at its heart, a series about control. It's about whether self-determination – that ideology central to the neoliberal

Britain of Coel's adolescence – is enough to transcend your past. (In one gut-wrenching scene, Arabella speaks about how the feminist cause didn't appeal to her when she was younger, because she had been too 'busy being black and poor'.) It's about whether you can stop the people around you making grave mistakes. It's about whether you can have control over your body, when people do terrible, half-remembered things to you – and maybe even things both you and they can remember, but which are equally terrible. It's about whether you can have control over your mind, as well, by leaning into self-care, or whether that also is punctuated by painful memories. As the series unfurls, Coel manages to keep control, too, of our emotions, meting out and reining in the trauma as is necessary.

While sexual assault is not the focus of every interaction, or every scene, it does provide the backdrop from which everything else emerges. Its quiet presence shows sexual abuse as something that exists inside our world rather than a threat from somewhere far away – something you or I or anyone else may have experienced without even realising it was happening. It happens to Kwame (Paapa Essiedu), a gay man seasoned in the art of the Grindr hookup. It happens to Arabella again, in seemingly safer circumstances. It happens to Terry in a scenario she initially sees as empowering. It's traumatic. It's boring. It's bureaucratic. It's subtle.

This is, of course, not the first show to smartly tackle the horror of sexual assault. *Unbelievable*, Netflix's 2019 adaptation of a Pulitzer-winning article about a young woman who is treated as a suspect in her own rape case, was praised for showing the injustice inherent in the US justice system as regards sexual assault. However, where *Unbelievable* was an overwhelmingly dark series – one in which a whole episode could be devoted to the search for a 'Bad Man' – *I May Destroy You* has a rare lightness of touch, with

Coel acknowledging that sometimes the Bad Man, or Woman, is already in our field of vision.

Other scripted shows have managed that, too: *Orange Is the New Black*, where an inmate, Pennsatucky, continues a relationship with the prison guard who rapes her, and *Euphoria*, where transgender teen Jules is propositioned by a classmate's father, spring to mind. But few portrayals have been this comprehensive. In the wake of a storyline between Arabella and Zain (Karan Gill), where he removes a condom during sex – Arabella later describes him as 'not rape-adjacent, or a bit rapey: he's a rapist' – conversations about this practice of 'stealthing' were ignited on Twitter. Meanwhile, viewers wondered if there might be more to a story where one character, Theo, appeared to lie about being assaulted by a fellow school pupil in a flashback.

Questions are asked about representation, too. Coel couldn't have known that 2020 would be as marked by Black Lives Matter protests as it has been by Covid-19; that conversations about everything from defunding the police to racism on the *X Factor* would be prompted by George Floyd's killing. Nor could she have predicted that, simultaneously, a bad-faith culture war would emerge. And yet, unknowingly, she wrote the perfect show for a time when notions of blackness are once again being dissected by a white majority.

A few weeks ago, the journalist Allison Pearson wrote a highly pilloried *Daily Telegraph* column praising the series for showing her black characters who are 'human beings equipped with the full repertoire of virtues and vices', adding that 'people don't object to great work that is truly colour blind'. But, rather than being colour blind, *I May Destroy You* is just not centred on the usual colours, as scenes focused on 'white girl tears' and whether veganism is a type of white saviourism lay bare. While Coel was adamant in a pre-show interview with the *Guardian* that race wasn't her focus here, her lived experiences mean that this is arguably the kind of series that could only have been made by a black woman.

The Covid-19 era has posed important questions in regard to friendship – another area Coel couldn't have predicted but that gives the show an extra layer of timeliness. Who are our friends? What can we ask of, and expect from, them? Are some friendships a convenience rather than a necessity? The juddering, non-linear narrative helps manipulate our perception of the friendship between the trio. As in real life, nothing is static, and sometimes it isn't wholly clear whose side we should be on. There are no cliched antiheroes, or deus ex machinas; Susy Henny, the high-flying publisher who Arabella can't believe is a black woman, is the same woman who sends her out of her office empty-handed when she tries to get an increase on her book advance, and who declares 'rape – fantastic!' when the writer considers using her own experiences in her work.

I May Destroy You feels like a gamechanger for British TV: ambitious and radical, the kind of programme that percolates in your head between its weekly drops (a risk in the age of the binge that has undoubtedly paid off). Understandably, it may be too triggering for some survivors of sexual assault and rape to watch. But for those who are able to, it has an important message: what doesn't kill you may not make you stronger, but perhaps it won't break you, either.

13 JULY

Naomi Klein: 'We must not return to the pre-Covid status quo, only worse'

KATHARINE VINER

KATHARINE VINER: There is a great quote in one of your recent essays from a tech CEO, who says: 'Humans are biohazards, machines are not.' It chilled me to the bone and made me fearful for the future. And you have written interestingly about the 'Screen New Deal'.

NAOMI KLEIN: Silicon Valley had this pre-existing agenda before Covid that imagined replacing so many of our personal bodily experiences by inserting technology in the middle of them.

So, for the few spaces where tech is not already mediating our relationships, there was a plan – to replace in-person teaching with virtual learning, for instance, and in-person medicine with telehealth and in-person delivery with robots. All of this has been rebranded, post-Covid, as a touchless technology, as a way of replacing what has been diagnosed as the problem, which is the problem of touch.

And yet, on a personal level, what we miss most is touch. And so we need to expand the menu of options about how we live with Covid, because we do not have a vaccine; it is not about to arrive. Even if there is a breakthrough, it's going to be many, many months, possibly years before it can be rolled out at the scale we would need it.

So how are we going to live with this thing? Are we going to accept the pre-Covid 'normal', only much diminished, without the relationships that sustain us? Are we going to allow our kids to have all of their learning mediated by technology? Or are we going to invest in people?

Instead of pouring all of our money into a Screen New Deal and trying to solve problems in a way that diminishes our quality of life, why do we not go on a teacher-hiring spree? Why do we not have twice as many teachers with half-the-size classrooms and figure out a way to do outdoor education?

There are so many ways we can think about responding to this crisis that do not accept this idea that we have to return to the pre-Covid status quo, only worse, only with more surveillance, more screens and less human contact.

KATHARINE VINER: Do you see any governments talking like that?

NAOMI KLEIN: I was heartened to hear Jacinda Ardern talk about a four-day working week as a solution to the fact that New Zealand is very dependent on tourism dollars, and yet New Zealand is probably the country that has dealt with the pandemic better than any others in terms of its fatality rates. It can't fling its doors open to tourists in the way that it has in the past, so there's this idea that maybe New Zealanders should work less, be paid the same and have more leisure time to be able to enjoy their own country safely.

How do we slow down? This is what I am thinking a lot about. It feels like every time we slam our foot on the accelerator marked 'business as usual' or 'back to normal', the virus surges back and says: 'Slow down.'

KATHARINE VINER: We all love those moments of slowing down, but the UK government is hellbent on getting back to normal, come what may. There is an urgency not to change anything about how we live, just get back to how it was before.

NAOMI KLEIN: And it is madness. It is a very small percentage of the population that wants to just fling the doors open. It is a majority that actually is much more concerned about returning to work before it is safe, sending their kids to school before it is safe. It's sometimes framed as giving people what they want, but this is not what the polling shows.

There are similarities between the way Donald Trump has handled it and the way Boris Johnson has handled it. They are turning it into some test of masculinity, even in Johnson's case after having the virus. Jair Bolsonaro was talking about how he was an athlete so he knows he will handle it [the Brazilian president revealed he has coronavirus shortly after this interview took place]; Trump was talking about his good genes.

KATHARINE VINER: I was interested in your views on why you think the civil rights protests, in light of George Floyd's death, have happened now. It seems intriguing, in the midst of one crisis, that, around the world, there are these huge demonstrations against racism.

NAOMI KLEIN: This is not the first uprising of its kind. But I think there were certain aspects of it that were unique because of Covid and the outsized impact of the pandemic for African Americans in cities like Chicago where, by some counts, 70 per cent of the fatalities from Covid were African Americans.

Whether it's because they are the ones performing those at-risk jobs, without protections, or because of the legacies of environmental pollution in their communities, stress, trauma, unsafe workplaces and discriminatory healthcare, black communities are bearing a disproportionate burden of the fatalities from the virus, defying this idea that we were all in this together.

In the midst of this moment of profound trauma, those killings – of Ahmaud Arbery, of George Floyd, of Breonna Taylor – slice through that.

But then there is a question that a lot of people are asking, which is what are all these non-black people doing at the protests? That is what is new, certainly at this scale. Many of these demonstrations are truly multiracial; black-led multiracial demonstrations. Why is this time different?

I have a few ideas. One has to do with the softness that the pandemic has introduced into our culture. When you slow down, you can feel things, when you're in that constant rat race, it doesn't leave much time for empathy. From its very beginning, the virus has forced us to think about interdependencies and relationships. The first thing you are thinking about is: everything I touch, what has somebody else touched? The food I am eating, the package that was just delivered, the food on the shelves. These are connections that capitalism teaches us not to think about.

I think that being forced to think in more interconnected ways may have softened more of us up to think about these racist atrocities, and not say they are somebody else's issue.

KATHARINE VINER: There's a great line in the new introduction to *On Fire*, your latest book, when you say: 'whatever was bad before the disaster downgraded to unbearable' – it's an unbearable situation the way black men are treated by the police.

NAOMI KLEIN: There is always this discourse whenever disasters hit: 'Climate change doesn't discriminate, the pandemic doesn't discriminate. We are all in this together.' But that is not true. That is not how disasters act. They act as magnifiers and they act as intensifiers. If you had a job in an Amazon warehouse that was making you sick before, or if you were in a long-term care facility that was already treating you as if your life was of no value, that was bad before – but all of that gets magnified to unbearable now. And if you were disposable before, you're sacrificial now.

And we are only talking about the violence that we can see. What we have to talk more about is the violence that's hidden, and that's domestic violence. To put it bluntly, when men are stressed, women get it in the face and so do kids. These lockdowns are so stressful because families don't have any reprieve from each other and even the best family needs a little bit of space. Then you add layoffs, economic stress. It's a very bad situation for women right now.

KATHARINE VINER: I know you spent a lot of the last year working on the Green New Deal and the Bernie Sanders campaign. How does it all look now? Do you feel more or less positive about the potential?

NAOMI KLEIN: On some level, it is harder. You mentioned Bernie and certainly my preferred outcome would be a presidential candidate who is running a campaign with the Green New Deal at its centre. I do believe we will only win this with an interplay of mass-movement pressure from the outside, but also a receptivity from the inside. I think that we had that chance with Bernie.

It is harder with Joe Biden, but not impossible. At the end of *On Fire*, I gave 10 reasons in favour of a Green New Deal and why it is good climate policy. One of those reasons is that it is recession-proof. We have this really bad track record in the climate movement of winning gains when the economy is doing relatively well, because the kind of climate solutions we get from governments tend to be these neoliberal, market-based solutions, like climate taxes or renewable energy policies that are perceived to make energy costs more expensive, or carbon taxing that makes the price of petrol more expensive. As soon as you have an economic downturn, the support for these policies evaporates. We saw that after the 2008 financial crisis. Climate has got a reputation as being a bourgeois thing – the issue that you care about if you don't have to worry about putting food on the table.

What is important about a Green New Deal is that it is modelled after one of the greatest economic stimulus programmes of all time, during the greatest economic crisis of all time, and that is FDR's New Deal during the Great Depression. Because of this, the biggest pushback that I got when I released *On Fire* a little less than a year ago was: 'But we don't do things like this when the economy is doing well.'

The only times that we can point to – and this is a hard truth – when our societies have moved fast and changed big and catalytically are moments of great depression or war. Yet we now know we can change quickly. We have seen it. We have dramatically changed our lives. And we found out that our governments have trillions of dollars that they could have marshalled this whole time.

All of that is potentially radicalising. I do feel we have a chance. I would not describe myself as optimistic, because this is a future we have to fight for. But if we just look at moments in history when we have won big changes, they are moments like this.

This is an edited extract from an interview held at a Guardian Live event.

16 JULY

The power of touch: I miss football hugs. Now I long for a fetid, boozy embrace

SIMON HATTENSTONE

I crave a footie hug – or, even better, what we Manchester City fans call the Poznań. The football hug is a strange beast – usually, it involves a number of people, some of them strangers. It tends to be a bit stinky (BO, booze and fags) and is sometimes painful (when it goes wrong, it can go very wrong – you may end up in a different row, or even on the floor). Yet, despite the fetid, occasionally life-threatening nature of football hugs, they are a thing of wonder.

There is a shared ecstasy when the ball hits the back of the net – an unleashing of joy, passion, scarves and primal screams. You probably have nothing in common with your fellow huggers apart from supporting the same team and wearing identical replica shirts. In fact, you may dislike them in real life, and there is a good chance that you will never see them again. It is an extraordinary, unlikely bonding.

But the Poznań is something else. Fans of the Polish club Lech Poznań introduced it to Manchester City supporters during a Europa League match in 2010. They turned their backs on the game, wrapped their arms around the shoulders of the supporters on either side of them and repeatedly jumped up and down on the spot in unison. It was a beautiful sight – random, surreal, rhythmic, funny, collective – and utterly senseless.

The history of the Poznań is much debated. Some say it started in Poland in the early 1960s as a protest by fans against club management; others say it originated in Turkey and Greece, and was known as the Grecque. For Manchester City fans, though, it will always be known as the Poznań. After that match against Lech Poznań, we paid homage to its supporters by stealing their crazy hug-dance. We customised it by chanting 'Let's all do the Poznań' to the tune of 'Do the Conga'.

It was open to any number of meanings or none. We Poznańed in triumph after scoring, we Poznańed when we were bored, we Poznańed when we were rubbish. Turning our back on the football could be interpreted as supreme confidence (we knew we would win), despair (we knew we would lose) or indifference. Sod the footie, we were there for the craic. It was ludicrous, but it was also an act of love, trust and solidarity. A Poznań did not allow for party-poopers or mavericks (even though it was a maverick act). If one person broke the chain, the Poznań was ruined.

Even pre-lockdown the football hug was in danger of disappearing. VAR (the video assistant referee) has taken the spontaneity out of football: rather than hugging when our team scored, we started checking the TV screens to see if a goal really was a goal or just another shattered hope.

Meanwhile, the pandemic has robbed us of the opportunity to Poznań. Indeed, common sense may dictate that we never see it again. But football being football, and City fans being City fans, I have a sneaking feeling that when we are finally allowed back into football grounds, we may just celebrate with the most audacious, prolonged Poznań ever.

22 JULY

Serving the tea in a care home taught me to see old people anew

ARIFA AKBAR

For the past three months, I have been moonlighting as a tea lady. A few weeks into lockdown, and at the height of the Covid-19 crisis, my father's care home had become desperately under-staffed. Carers were going down with the virus, while cleaners were doubling up as kitchen staff, or vice versa. On the day I heard the manager's partner had had to come in to help serve the lunches, I felt embarrassed at standing by. So I volunteered for twice-weekly shifts.

This was not as altruistic as it sounds. I also wanted to keep an eye on my father; in the 15 years since he was diagnosed with frontal lobe dementia, he has been shuttled around numerous homes, some worse than others (one was shut down by the Care Quality Commission), and it has left me in a state of perpetual vigilance. So I turned up, put on a plastic apron and began wheeling a teapot around the ground floor.

It was a peculiar kind of second job, writing about theatre for this paper and then running around the corner to put the kettle on. It definitely felt the harder of the two roles at first. I saw how the carers were putting themselves on the line every day, and that they had little choice in the matter. But also, how do you ask a dementia patient who has lost almost all their powers of speech, hearing, or both, how many sugars they want in their tea? Or follow the instructions of a Sicilian woman telling you how to make her coffee in very precise detail, but also in Italian? I would often come away sweating. And saddened. The home lost a lot of patients to Covid-19 in a short span of time and seeing the suddenly empty beds was shocking. The shifts, in fact, were a small but humbling taste of the labour required in key work; all the more strenuous and risk-laden in these times, and coming in for 12-hour days that leave ankles swollen and backs permanently injured, but which still, evidently, hasn't earned its reward with a pay rise in the eyes of the government.

But it was also – surprisingly – good fun. There was the banter between carers and the stories the elderly residents told. The place grew on me until it became the highlight of my week, and then the highlight of my lockdown. I looked forward to seeing the women who would say 'God bless' and blow me a kiss every time I left them a cup of tea. Others who talked in snatches as I held their drinks up for them: one raged at her past, and her community for expecting her to marry when she preferred not to – and preferred women. Another who said she'd started painting later in life and now her work – serene scenes of green fields and big empty skies – hung all around her room. And a former university lecturer who had researched social policy around nursing and had never left a *Guardian* crossword unfinished until her eyesight packed in a few years ago, but who still had the paper delivered every day.

Until I began these shifts, these people had just been a background blur on my flight down the corridor to my father's room. His dementia seems slowly to be swallowing him up and there are days when it seems like there is a stone wall building up around him that is getting higher and harder to breach as the years go by. It can be sad or difficult to sit with him and at times it is hard to summon up the strength.

But now there was another reason to go in, and even he seemed cheered up at seeing me clatter around with the tea trolley. The prone figures I had passed so often, and felt myself pitying, had names and lives that I knew about and watching them taught me that sitting by a sunny window or dunking a custard cream in warm tea held its value and there was no cause for pity.

Writers such as Joyce Carol Oates and Haruki Murakami have written about the meditative effects of running and I found the same absorbing feeling in the ritual of making tea. It is simple, wholesome, and brings clarity and calmness. I know I would not feel that way if I had to do another 11 hours of it, but it has been lockdown's greatest gift – plus I now make a mean cuppa.

9 AUGUST

Time for a full clearout. Why we will not forgive the men who did this to Beirut

LINA MOUNZER

My eyes fly open and the horror is already there. The full range of it: what happened, and how, and who is responsible. It's 4am. My heart is pounding so fast I think I might throw up. Terrible images flash through my mind.

I've experienced debilitating grief before. It at least allows you short respite when you first open your eyes. Some seconds of oblivion just before you are slammed with the memory of how your life has been shattered. But there is no respite here. And it's not just my life that has been shattered. It's the whole world that sustains it, from loved ones to cityscape. I've barely slept. Just like the night before.

I think I'm not sleeping because I'm afraid of my bed. I think I'm afraid of my bed because I was in it when the explosion hit. I remember trying to leave the bed but it was listing like a ship. I had to climb off it. It took for ever.

We are, all of us in Beirut – and those who left Beirut but love Beirut – wrecked with exhaustion, grief and, increasingly, murderous rage. We can only think about, talk about one thing. What happened, and how, and who is responsible.

What happened: a massive explosion thundered through Beirut, its streets and homes, at 6.08pm on Tuesday 4 August. It was so huge it was heard in Cyprus. It was so huge it shattered glass and ripped doors off their hinges kilometres away. It incin-erated trees, tore the red roofs off centuries-old buildings and brought the blue sea inland. It left 5,000 injured and 154 dead – so far. There are many still missing under the rubble.

The best guess right now is there were 2,750 tonnes of ammo-nium nitrate being stored in hangar 12 at the Beirut port. Perhaps right next to a warehouse filled with fireworks. We don't really know how this ammonium nitrate, confiscated from a ship and stored in unsafe conditions in the middle of our city for six years, ignited. Because those who are responsible are actively rejecting an international investigation.

Let's be clear who they are, those responsible: every last grizzled warlord and their underachieving sons, nephews and sons-in-law who hold the highest seats of power. Every loyalist they have personally picked and manoeuvred into influential positions across every conceivable sector, public and private. Every minister and bureaucrat too self-interested or too craven to speak up. This mafia is what is broadly referred to in Lebanon as the 'political class'; the 'ruling elite'.

If I sound unhinged with anger, it's because I am. Equal to my grief over the devastation of the beloved city where I was born and raised, over the people dead, missing and injured, over the debris that now litters its streets – glass and stone, but also clothes and books and photographs and paintings, all the keepsakes of a life – is my rage at the men who did this to us.

Because this was no 'unfortunate accident' – it was lethal neglect. We've known for a long time that our safety, wellbeing and lives meant nothing to these men. They are the same people we tried to oust when we took to the streets in October 2019, in a wave of mass anti-government protests that exploded across the country. 'All of them means all of them,' we insisted, even when we were beaten by various party loyalists for the chant.

Sparked by a proposed tax on WhatsApp, the protests were in fact the result of years of accumulated frustration over public sector mismanagement and corruption so rampant it had sunk the country into $86 billion of debt. Thirty years after the end of the civil war, we still didn't have 24-hour electricity, proper water, proper sanitation or reliable rubbish collection. We had only endless construction sites, erecting posh real estate inaccessible to all but the ultra-rich.

We were angry then, but it was an anger powered by fierce joy. We danced and whooped and marvelled that so many of us had come together over sectarian and class lines. We managed to oust the government and we were elated in our victory. But it was short-lived: the new government appointed to take its place traded only names, not parties or policies.

Since then, our economy has fully imploded. Our currency has devalued more than 80 per cent. Banks limited our withdrawals while bankers smuggled $6 billion out of the country. Salaries and life savings have become worthless overnight. The government will not agree to the transparency measures necessary to unlock a loan from the IMF.

During the coronavirus lockdown, no aid was distributed to a population now destitute. The banks shut their doors to us for weeks on end. There were mass layoffs. Public suicides. People reduced to bartering their humblest belongings for baby formula and diapers.

And then the blast.

The blast caused by neglect so egregious, incompetence so spectacular, it would defy comprehension if we didn't already intimately know the callous disregard and contempt these men hold for our lives. Every authority figure, from the president down, denies responsibility, pleads ignorance, shifts blame. Nor has the state made any effort in the clean-up or retrieval of bodies. All of it has been undertaken by private citizens.

People are organising for mass protests. The anger I've seen is like nothing I've ever witnessed. I know because it boils in my own body too. Unlike the first time we took to the streets, there is no talk of grassroots overhaul or constitutional mechanisms that might be used to remove the ruling elite from power. The most ubiquitous hashtag accompanying the calls for protest is 'prepare the nooses'.

The state has already made the fatal mistake of neglecting flammable material, leaving it in unsafe conditions. A potential explosion just waiting for a spark. This time, when it blows up in their faces, they cannot plead ignorance.

10 AUGUST

This country sees itself as overcrowded and overgenerous – it is neither of those things

SUZANNE MOORE

On a clear day you can see ... the beach. And it is mobbed. I'm writing this on a glorious day in Kent and families, big gangs of teenagers and surfers are all making the best of it. The gulls are monitoring the chip situation and the girls in bikinis are proving that the underboob trend is actually real. Why shouldn't these people have fun? There is no school, no work; for many of the teenagers, their exam grades will be 'made up'. Can they not have their irresponsible youth for a summer? Isn't that a rite of passage and, despite everything, aren't they lucky to have it? This morning, before all the sunseekers flocked to the beach, another group of people will have arrived here: people who belong nowhere. Along this coast, cheap dinghies are arriving, carrying refugees. One day last week, 200 migrants arrived from Calais. Often, they can't swim; the luckier ones have paddles.

The stories I read here in the local papers make the situation more real, closer. This weekend, 20 people, including a small baby, arrived in one boat. A heavily pregnant woman arrived in Dungeness. She told Border Force officials she was eight months pregnant. Another person made it ashore, despite being in a wheelchair. Some brave soul rescued three migrants from their sinking kayak on the return leg of his charity Channel swim.

But is there any point tugging at heartstrings when hearts are hardened; when this crisis continues without end; when the cycle repeats and we learn nothing? It is five years since that picture of Alan Kurdi flashed around the world. A Syrian child of Kurdish descent, his body was washed up on a beach near Bodrum in Turkey. For a moment he was not seen as part of a demonic horde trying to invade 'us'. He was 'us' – a sleeping child whose death need not have happened.

Since then, all the issues that have made people cross continents and dangerous waters to leave everything they have ever known have intensified. Syria and the Kurdish people have been forsaken. War and persecution continue in many African countries. Libya is a failed state. Sudan is in crisis. The global movement of people continues; some seek asylum, some seek simply to make a living.

Still England holds itself up as tolerant, decent, an easy touch taken over by marauders. Nigel Farage has been urgently reporting the invasion near 'the white cliffs of Dover'. His tone does not reflect the truth: traumatised people in leaky inflatables. He has been throwing in his concern about them bringing the virus to the country – suddenly our leading voice for health and safety.

You have to hand it to the home secretary, Priti Patel, whose post appears to involve summoning contempt for migrants; to be fair, unlike Farage, she has been elected to do so. She always seems to be itching for something vaguely militaristic. To tackle this issue a new post has been created with what sounds like a made-up job title: Dan O'Mahoney is now the 'clandestine Channel threat commander'. Calls continue for the navy to be brought in. Once a vessel is 12 miles off the coast, it is in British waters. What are the navy expected to do? Shoot? Or just turn the refugees back, as the Australians do with phenomenal cruelty? It is hard to gauge sometimes who is the most hated when it comes to this particular situation: the migrants themselves, or the French. The French should stop these people gathering in Calais, goes the argument, and stop the people smugglers; the migrants should apply for asylum in France.

Actually, they do. The great majority of those seeking sanctuary in Europe don't get to Calais. Germany gets a quarter of all applications, France is next, then Italy and Greece. If someone has made it all the way to Calais, they have usually risked life and limb to do so and have some connection to the UK (often family or language).

This is not new. The Sangatte refugee camp was shut in 1992. The 'Jungle' encampment has been bulldozed. But still Calais is full of people sleeping in the woods.

I have never seen people living in such terrible conditions as I did at a camp near Dunkirk. And I have been to refugee camps in war zones. There was no water, no electricity, just mud and women trying to make hot food for their kids inside flammable tents. The men showed me their torture scars, their shoulders now dislocated, too, from trying to get over the wire fence. Some had bruises from French police who had first smashed their phones in front of them: their only connection to their past life and to the one they were desperately seeking. Some showed me films of sea crossings they had made and of those who had drowned and I understood why they would hang beneath a lorry, because they had been so near death so many times already. More than 70 million people are displaced worldwide and now we have Covid-19. One response is to shut down all borders, but the virus is already global. Social distancing has meant the setting up of strange, new, unintuitive borders. But desperate people will cross those borders because their lives are already at risk.

This island sees itself as overcrowded and overgenerous, but it is neither of those things. We can be better. We do not have to board up our imagination. We do not have to put up a 'no entry' sign to those who want a future.

It's not such a leap for me to see the boys playing football on a Kent beach, showing off to the girls, and to look just across the water and remember the young men and women I saw there, huddled in ditches, dreaming of a better life. Year after year, politicians pretend they can turn those dreams back, that we are not connected to the rest of the world except in the exact ways we choose. Surely we don't need to see more dead toddlers to know that that is a lie?

12 AUGUST

'Could I feel what they were doing? Yes': Rob Delaney on the pain and pleasure of his vasectomy

ROB DELANEY

I got a vasectomy a few months ago. A vasectomy is when they cut and tie off the vas deferens, which are these little tubes in your ball sack (scrotum) so that there's no sperm (sperm) in your jizz (semen) when you bust (ejaculate). I did this because my wife and I don't want her to get pregnant again. It doesn't mean we don't want any more kids, it just means that if we did have any more, they'd have to be adopted or stolen or left to us because friends or family with young kids died in a plane crash or had their brain stems blown apart by less-lethal rounds fired at them at point-blank range while they were waiting in an 11-hour line attempting to vote in the US election in November.

I figured after all my wife, Leah, and her body had done for our family, the least I could do was let a doctor slice into my bag and sterilise me. Leah had taken birth control for decades, which is a giant pain in the ass and also decidedly sexist pharmacological slavery. IMAGINE a man having to remember to not only take a pill every day, but also having to deal with employer-provided private insurance prescription plans in the US, who drop you or sell your plan to another company without telling you, among other crimes. And messing up once could land you with – for example – an ectopic pregnancy that isn't diagnosed soon enough because you're afraid to go to the doctor due to your high deductible, so you literally die and are dead, in a cemetery. I think I speak for my bros when I say: 'No thanks!'

Plus, Leah had been pregnant for almost three of the previous eight years, resulting in four beautiful boys. Which, incidentally, is my fault, since the sperm determines the sex of the baby. That's 166 weeks spent pregnant. Holy Christ is that bananas. As I was pregnant for zero weeks, Leah heartily agreed that a doctor should scalpel around in my balls so that she didn't become pregnant again – by me, anyway.

When Leah was pregnant with our third, we started talking about me getting a vasectomy.

I raised the idea with an older couple we're friends with and – in front of Leah – the guy said: 'Oh don't do that; what if things don't work out with you and Leah and you meet a younger girl and she wants to have kids?'

'That's EXACTLY why I'm doing it,' I said. I love Leah and I hope we die within minutes of each other in 2071, but if she left me or got hit by a meteor, all other women within a few miles of me need to know that I shall not sire (stud) again. We can go to the movies together and even attempt coitus after I've grieved for a sensible period (not less than three weeks), but I know my limits, and raising one brood as well as I can is all I have in me.

My vasectomy was the first surgery I've had in the UK with the NHS. Nice and easy preliminary process. I got a referral from the GP in my neighbourhood, then had an appointment with a balls guy. Nice Italian doctor named Bartolo, who gave my sack a confident grope and found my tubes easily and said he could do it with local anaesthetic.

I went in early one morning a few weeks later and was given a hospital bed. Hospitals make me sad, but also give me a deep peace, as I spent so much time in hospitals while our son Henry was being treated for brain cancer. Starting just after his first birthday, he lived in hospitals for 14 months. He visited them often after that while he lived at home for the final seven months of his short, beautiful life. I fantasised about them telling me I'd have to stay in the hospital for a while, and I could just think about Henry and feel closer communion with him. But I was also glad it would be an outpatient procedure, so I could get home to my alive kids and wife, who need me.

After a while, they wheeled me into the operating theatre and shaved my balls. I apologised for not having done so myself, but the doctor said it was better I didn't since I probably wasn't as good at shaving balls as he was and might have cut myself.

Then they shot some novocaine into my sack. I didn't like that, but I figured I'd be glad they'd done it in a few minutes. Then they set to work slicing into my pouch and clamping and cutting my vas deferens. If you're wondering if I could feel what they were doing, the answer is yes. I informed them of this and they gave me more novocaine. Since I'm not proud, I will tell you that at this point I asked for drugs or laughing gas or anything else they had handy. The nurse in turn asked me if I'd eaten breakfast that morning. The answer was yes, because it didn't say *explicitly* not to in the literature they'd given me beforehand and I'm a bit of a breakfast guy. Thus, they couldn't sedate me, lest I vomit up my breakfast and then choke on it.

So I just had to ride that pain wave, baby. I 'comforted' myself with the knowledge that what I was enduring would probably feel like a pleasant respite compared with what my wife went through four (4) times to bring our chunky sons into the world.

After maybe 30 minutes, they were done and they slid a cotton-wool-filled jockstrap on me and I was wheeled into a recovery room. I felt reasonably OK and was allowed to leave after my first successful pee. The pee came out of the correct hole and it didn't hurt to produce.

Maybe a week later, my wife discovered me masturbating in our living room at 3am. I explained that my post-op literature said that my first loads after surgery could contain blood and I didn't want her to have to see that. She appreciated that. God is good sometimes, however, and there was no blood. Thus, we could resume having sex.

I'm happy to report that, barring a couple of weeks of waning discomfort, there were absolutely no side-effects from the surgery. No lingering pain, no reduced libido, no reduction in dreams where I watch chubby women struggle in and out of wetsuits through a hole in a barn wall. You can't even see the scars, since they're on my horrible wrinkled scrotum.

I am sad sometimes that I won't get Leah pregnant again. Our youngest recently turned two and it hurts to think that we won't make more chunky little nuggets together. We really love babies. Our older two were present at the birth of our youngest, who was born at home, and they're amazing big brothers. So everyone at our house, including the baby, loves babies. But Leah and I both want her to be able to work and travel more easily and have a bigger world again, after an insane six years of being pregnant and breastfeeding, and sometimes doing those things while caring for a dying child. So, on balance, we're glad I did it.

After your vasectomy, you're supposed to ejaculate 20 times (at your own pace) and then bring a load into the doctor to be tested, so they know if the vasectomy worked. To keep track, I drew an eagle on a piece of paper and put a graph with 10 spots on each wing. Each time I skablorped, either with Leah or just by my lonesome, I put a little coloured sticker on a spot. I labelled it 'The Eagle of Sexual Freedom'.

You're also instructed to wear condoms until you have your semen tested, which Leah and I absolutely never once did. And since the coronavirus lockdown struck at the exact time I would've gone in to have my semen tested, I never did! So maybe it didn't work and we'll have more babies. Our field research (sexual intercourse to climax without pulling out) suggests that the vasectomy did work, since Leah used to get pregnant with the speed and purpose with which I run to the gas station when we're out of peanut butter. (It's the closest place that sells peanut butter.)

Apologies to the NHS staff whose post-op procedures we've so flagrantly violated, but if we do have another baby, we'll name him Bartolo after the lovely doctor who messed around in my big, ugly balls.

14 AUGUST

My pandemic epiphany: watching the world open up for disabled people

FRANCES RYAN

When lockdown began, chronic illness meant I'd already been stuck at home for a couple of years. It was my own self-isolation before self-isolation was in the lexicon, except with less sourdough. I won't say I was used to missing the world outside my bedroom because it is never a thing you truly get used to. House plants are not great conversationalists. A glass of wine in a restaurant is a thing of beauty to long for. But you adapt, because circumstances are demanding like that.

If the pandemic created one shared experience, it was this sense of missing out. Fomo went global and the world got creative to cope. Theatres went online. Museums hosted virtual tours. Work held meetings over Zoom. Musicians streamed gigs live to fans. As a disabled person, the weeks that followed lockdown were like going through Alice's looking glass.

Overnight, parts of everyday living – work, the arts, education, socialising – that had disappeared from disabled people's lives due to a mix of poor access or health conditions were available again. At a time in which the general population – including disabled people – had never been more restricted, there was a paradoxical sense of freedom. Suddenly, everyone was a little housebound and life opened up because of it.

Lying in bed, YouTube glowing on the screen, I watched the first play I had in years, transported in a flash to New Orleans and King George's court. Friends and family launched quiz nights; if I wasn't going out on a Friday night, no one else was either. Art galleries with multiple steps – and no ramp – opened their doors through the laptop. Anyone who has ever been deprived of normal life knows regaining it is about more than simply being able to see a play or gig. It is akin to finding something you've lost, as if a part of you comes back with it.

I began to speak to other disabled people experiencing similar things: bosses that had turned them down when they got ill now let employees work from home, universities that banned virtual learning were putting their degrees online. It was frustrating and joyful, obvious and revelatory. The secret was out: the world could be accessible. Inequality was actually a choice.

I'm not sure that realisation was my own personal pandemic epiphany – perhaps it would be more accurate to say it was the world's. Disabled people, after all, always knew life could become accessible with just a few changes. It just took a global pandemic for everyone else to notice.

As bars, the office and museums are slowly reopening across the world, it would be easy to go back to business as usual – to forget what society has learned, to abandon the minority now that the majority are catered for. Major theatres have already stopped their online showings. Employees working from home are starting to feel insecure about losing their jobs. But if we all have to go through this crisis, society may as well make some gains along the way. The new normal could be more accessible than the old.

14 August

As we come blinking into the light, leave a space in your life to make art

GRAYSON PERRY

We are often told that the arts are good for us: they improve our mental health; help us to empathise with different people; they entertain, educate, soothe and enthuse us; they make us better citizens. But who gets the most out of the arts? Is it the 'creative industries', the army of cultural workers who help make all the glory happen? Is it the academics who study, interpret, assess and talk about it? It must be the audience visiting the galleries, theatres and concert halls, mustn't it? The arts are *for* them, surely?

I have long argued that the people who get the most out of the arts are the ones who make them. Be it visual art, music, drama, literature, dance, moving image or comedy, making art gives us a place to distil our human experience. I am best known for visual art and TV, but have worked in all the aforementioned genres. I have participated with inept amateurism and sat at the top of the professional tree, and everything in between. I have shed tears of joy creating all of them, too.

In lockdown, we have been made to think about what is important to us, and we have had a lot of time to do it. What better recipe for making art can there be? What we found when making *Grayson's Art Club* for Channel 4 was a huge outpouring of creativity: every week, thousands of people from every background sending us their artworks. As we come blinking out into the light, now is the time to leave a space in our lives to make art, whether we join a choir, a writing group, a quilting bee, a dance class, set up a studio in the shed or make funny videos on our phones. Make a little nest for your feelings about being alive, nurture them that they may fledge and fly.

Most of the infrastructure to support this is in place: there are thousands of groups already set up to share and encourage. The Arts Council could help fund this, and employers could subsidise cultural activity, like a 21st-century equivalent of colliery bands. Any group activity is good for mental health, but making art together is doubly so.

The professional cultural sector will recover from this terrible blow; there is a deep hunger for the cream of human creativity. I feel it is just as important that everyone knows that making art is for them, and that the rewards increase with commitment, as with any relationship. Making art is good for you.

14 AUGUST

'We can only help ourselves': women in Belarus take protests into their own hands

SHAUN WALKER

The first chain of women appeared on Wednesday: a few hundred brave souls, dressed in white and holding flowers aloft, in a quietly powerful response to the gruesome violence inflicted on thousands of Belarusians over the previous days. By the next afternoon, columns of flower-waving women were everywhere, parading along the broad avenues of Minsk smiling, laughing and resolutely demanding change.

'We are here to show solidarity with all our men who were beaten up and abused,' said Tatyana, a 31-year-old waitress who was at the very front of a column of about 1,000 women – one of many such groups walking through Minsk. She and her friend were holding a white flag, which she said was a sign of their desire for an end to the violence.

On Friday evening, thousands of protesters descended on the Belarusian parliament, potentially setting the scene for a new showdown with riot police. As the demand for change intensifies, and reaches even the factories that are the pride of Alexander Lukashenko's neo-Soviet economy, the authoritarian ruler ended the week clinging on to power in defiance of an ever-broader coalition of opponents. But from the start, this has been an uprising inspired and led by women.

After several male presidential candidates were arrested or fled in the run-up to the vote, Svetlana Tikhanovskaya, the wife of one of them, stepped in. She and two other women formed a trio offering a simple programme that inspired many Belarusians: swift new elections that would be free and fair.

Lukashenko, misreading the nation's mood, laughed at Tikhanovskaya, suggesting she should focus on cooking dinner for her children. The attacks only made people admire her resolve more.

'The three of us were able to show that we had taken responsibility for what is happening and for the future of Belarus,' said Maria Kolesnikova, the only one of the trio who remains in Belarus, in an interview in Minsk this week. 'The west won't help, Russia won't help, we can only help ourselves. Our female faces became a signal for all women – and for the men too – that every person should take responsibility.'

No one knows the real result of Sunday's election, but it seems unlikely that Lukashenko won anything close to a majority, and certainly not the claimed 80 per cent. Authorities responded to protests with some of the most egregious police violence in modern European history. On Sunday and Monday, riot police fanned out through Minsk as if they were playing a computer game, scooping up anyone wearing protest ribbons or chanting, and many random bystanders.

Those snatched were subjected to brutal violence, and no one was immune. Not the 47-year-old man on his way home to his wife, arrested and later given an extended ritual beating by police while he was forced to lie face down on the floor. Not the 51-year-old reporter in the city of Grodno who shouted 'journalist' and waved his accreditation in the air, only to be kicked in the face and lose four teeth (and then be detained, and fined). Not the man dragged away by riot police, shouting in disbelief: 'I fucking voted for Lukashenko!' And not the 6,700 others detained. The locus of terror was a detention centre on the outskirts of Minsk: two imposing buildings, one white and one terracotta, behind high walls and barbed wire.

Weeping relatives waited outside, desperate for information about missing children, siblings or partners. A long line snaked back from a grey metal door, which had a tiny hatch that would open briefly every few hours. When it did, those waiting could give the names of their missing and wait for a *yest* or a *nyet* to be barked at them from an unseen person inside.

By day, snipers patrolled the rooftops, and appeared to be communicating with thinly disguised plain-clothed watchers stationed among the relatives. By night, anguished cries of pain could be heard from behind the walls. Occasionally, ambulances arrived to carry away those whose injuries from beatings had become critical. Judges arrived in minibuses to perform sham trials inside the prison, with many captives saying they were forced to sign papers with fabricated information about where, when and how they were detained.

By Wednesday morning, it seemed the protest had been crushed. The reappearance of the internet, crudely switched off nationwide just after the vote, seemed a sign that the authorities felt back in control of the situation.

As prisoners began to be released, thousands of graphic videos of their injuries and testimony were shared with disgust on messaging apps. The mood changed again, as the country began to appreciate the scale and brazenness of the abuse.

Marina, a 28-year-old musician who took part in a protest by women on Wednesday, said that before this year she had not been interested in politics, simply living her own life without feeling restricted by the repressive state. However, she was energised by the campaign of Tikhanovskaya and disgusted at Lukashenko's violent response. 'Now when I see his face, I can't even explain the feeling. It's something worse than hatred, it's something black inside me I didn't even know was there,' she said.

As shock turned to catharsis, Minsk on Thursday and yesterday resembled a carnival, as large groups of women marched through the streets, with cars honking in support providing a constant backdrop of noise. Police retreated and the authorities launched a belated strategy of half-hearted reconciliation.

Tikhanovskaya may now be out of the country, but her video appeal yesterday calling for protests over the weekend, combined with growing resolve among protesters and the increasing number of striking factories, suggests the next days will be crucial.

There has been total absence of demonstrations of support for the dictator, with none of the flag-waving youth groups or angry grandmothers that presidents in Russia and Ukraine have mustered over recent years in attempts to showcase the depth of their support as protest movements flared. Lukashenko appears to be in control of little except the police and army.

Kolesnikova dismissed talk of things turning violent. 'I don't think there should be a revolution, and the only person who is using words like "revolution" is the current president,' she said. 'We always talked only about peaceful methods of protest,' she said on Wednesday.

But events in Minsk were moving fast, with crowds massing on Friday evening likely to be the biggest demonstration yet, and uncertainty about how riot police will respond. The demonstration planned for tomorrow could be the biggest in the country's history.

Nobody really believes in the prospect of dialogue with the dictator, leaving a bloody crackdown or the sudden fall of the regime as the most likely outcomes.

At an intersection of two broad avenues on the city's edge where a protester was killed on Monday night, and where the bloodstains are still visible, people who had never before dreamed of attending a protest came to pay their respects. 'I'm scared. Of course I'm scared. But I have a son, and I don't want him to live in this kind of country,' said Marina, 54, who started crying as she spoke. As she brushed away the tears, a young man passed on a scooter. 'Thank you, wonderful women of Belarus!' he shouted, handing each a flower as he passed.

18 AUGUST

The fake meritocracy of A-level grades is rotten anyway – universities don't need them

SONIA SODHA

The stories are heartbreaking, the sense of injustice utterly profound. The government had little choice but to U-turn on its decision to use an algorithm to dish out A-level 'results' to thousands of young people that had bafflingly little connection to their ability or the quality of their work.

Step back, and this whole fiasco exposes some uncomfortable truths about how fair the system is normally, and the true extent of and limits to meritocracy. We take it as given that dropping a couple of grades in a one-off exam should amount to the be-all and end-all in determining which university you go to. Have a good exam day, and you could be attending the university of your dreams; have a bad day and the anxious cycle of clearing begins. All this is predicated on the crazy idea that we need to avoid AAA students studying with ABB students, BBC students studying with BCD students at all costs, or ... what?

Rankings allow illusions of meritocracy and simple choices to prevail – obviously we should go for the AAA student over the ABB one – when the reality is they may be covering up a choice that is more random and arbitrary than we may like to think.

A-levels may be great at ranking the ability of students to take a particular exam on a given day. But how useful is that for predicting how well they will do at university, sometimes in an entirely unrelated subject? Or in any given job? There will be some link, but is it strong enough to justify a university system in which dropping a single grade can close off entry to your first choice?

If exams aren't perfect, perhaps there are other ways of assessing students. But the other options all come with their own problems. Teacher-based assessment tends to be biased against young people from disadvantaged backgrounds; coursework can be a more accurate assessment of a teacher's willingness to coax the work out rather than a student's true ability. There simply is no such thing as a perfectly accurate method for ranking young people's abilities that works for everything from university entry to job recruitment.

That's only bad news if we consider a failsafe assessment of a young person's future abilities at the end of school as the alpha and omega of the education system. But why should it be? Why do universities and employers even need this in the first place?

It's only important for universities if we believe that it is paramount that the young person who gets BBC in their A-levels should not study alongside the young person who gets BCC – that they must be sorted into different institutions. To see how bizarre this is, look at the school system, where experts have shunned the use of academic selection in light of evidence that creaming off the most able children into separate schools does barely anything for their learning and simply worsens outcomes for everyone else.

Yet for some reason, when it comes to post-18 education, we turn this on its head and go for extreme levels of academic stratification – which, because children from more affluent backgrounds are much more likely to attend good-quality schools, also produces a highly socially stratified university system.

This system works brilliantly for the most selective universities, who get to select the highest A-level performers who hail disproportionately from affluent backgrounds, then claim the kudos when – surprise, surprise! – those students go on to do well. But it also fuels unjustified elitism. Because universities essentially mark their own homework (a first from one university is not equivalent to a first from another) employers tend to use the university someone attended as a shorthand for their labour market potential, rather than the skills they actually developed there. The prophecy becomes self-fulfilling. We couldn't design a better way to entrench privilege if we tried.

Employers also deserve more scrutiny. Traditional recruitment includes screening CVs – with A-levels and degrees a key filter for entry-level jobs – followed by an interview. Not only is this method ineffective at selecting the best people for the job, it can be downright counterproductive. Experimental studies have shown that interviewers are notoriously unreliable at predicting someone's capabilities. And interviews are a reliable way to smuggle bias into the process: interviewers tend to go for candidates who look and think like them, leading to less diverse, more groupthink-dominated – and less successful – workplaces.

One real-world example comes from Texas in the late 1970s, where a doctor shortage pushed politicians to instruct the state medical school to increase its admissions, after it had already selected 150 applicants after interview. It took another 50 candidates who had been previously rejected at interview – after much of that pool had already been snapped up by other universities. Those 50 went on to perform just as well clinically and academically as the original crop: their success at interview made no difference at all; they might as well have been picked from the shortlist at random.

We don't need A-level results to provide a high-stakes ranking. If we were more honest about the limits of meritocracy, we would move to a more comprehensive-style university system – where, like at school, young people of different abilities learn alongside each other, with real academic benefit. More large employers would disregard A-level grades and degrees, running aptitude tests and assessment centres to assess the skills relevant to their workplaces, randomly selecting from those candidates who make a cut-off to ensure a more diverse intake than interviewing could ever allow.

We have extensively debated the fairness of an algorithm, but let's not fail to ask why we even needed one in the first place. The real reason is that the system as it stands shores up elitism and maintains the grip that the upper middle class – for no good reason – has on influential jobs. But this weak attempt to fake meritocracy is a harmful pretence that denies too many young people a chance in the first place.

25 AUGUST

'I feel she was abandoned': the life and terrible death of Belly Mujinga

SIRIN KALE

It is maybe three metres from the concourse in Victoria station to the ticket office. As Belly Mujinga ran, she would have been scared. It was 21 March, a Saturday. Victoria was a ghost of its former self. Hardly anyone was around to see Belly as she dashed for the ticket office, her breath shaky and uncontrolled, her hand reaching out to wipe the spittle from her face.

There are facts in the story of Belly – and there is a version of events that is disputed. Then there is the symbol that Belly has become to people who never met her or heard the sound of her voice, but who know her name and the story of what happened to her in those fear-filled days at the start of the coronavirus outbreak in Britain.

The facts: Belly Mujinga and her colleague Nadia (not her real name) were working on the concourse that morning when a 57-year-old man approached them. They talked briefly, then CCTV shows Belly recoiling. The man walked away, and Belly and Nadia made for the ticket office. Belly became ill with Covid-19 and died just over two weeks later, on 5 April. After a public outcry, a man was interviewed by the British Transport Police (BTP), but he was later released without charge after producing a negative anti-body test, indicating that he had not had the virus.

The version that is disputed: Belly and Nadia were on the concourse when a 57-year-old man approached them. The man yelled at Belly and Nadia: 'What are you doing here?' Belly responded: 'Can't you see we're working? We're wearing a uniform.' The man yelled again: 'You can't be here. I've got Covid – I'll give it to you.'

This next bit is the most disputed, and most difficult, part of the story. In Nadia's account of the event – which was relayed to me by a third party – spit flew out of the man's mouth as he shouted. Some of it landed on the women. It was as if he had no teeth, according to Nadia's description. According to Belly, who told the story to her husband, Lusamba Gode Katalay, and her cousin Agnes Ntumba, the man spat at them intentionally.

The symbol that Belly has become: a mother, dead at 47, leaving behind an 11-year-old daughter. A frontline worker assaulted while doing her job. A black woman whose death went uninvestigated until a global anti-racism campaign forced the British authorities to take note. A petition calling for Justice for Belly has been signed by 2 million people and counting. 'It's murder, plain and simple,' writes one signatory.

Was Belly, whose health issues meant she should not have been in close contact with the public, murdered by the man she met on the concourse that day? Almost certainly not. The threshold for murder is high and, besides, the man did not have Covid-19. Was she assaulted that day? Based on Nadia's story and from what Belly told her family before she died, it seems possible, although it is not proven. Did the commuter intentionally spit at the women? We do not know.

But does it matter? The result was the same. Nadia fell ill, but has since recovered. Belly is dead, Ingrid is motherless and Lusamba is widowed.

Belly was born in Kinshasa, the capital of the Democratic Republic of the Congo (DRC). She was the youngest of four brothers and three sisters. They were not exactly well-off, but not poor, either. Belly studied journalism at the University of Kinshasa and got a job working for RNTC, the national broadcaster. She was RNTC's first female sports reporter, but journalists in the DRC are badly paid and the industry is nepotistic. 'Journalists in the Congo always have to beg,' says Lusamba, 61. 'You have to know the right people. It's difficult to survive.'

In 2001, as the security situation in the DRC grew more unstable Belly moved to the UK. She worked at a post office in Edgware, north London, which is where Agnes, a 46-year-old healthcare assistant, met her in 2005. 'I didn't know anyone in London,' says Agnes. 'Belly became my family.' She used to call her Sissy, for sister.

In 2011, Belly married Lusamba, who is also Congolese. They met at a church in Hackney in 2006. 'When I arrived,' Lusamba says, 'I saw her.' He proposed straight away, but Belly said no. Lusamba kept asking and still she said no. 'She led me on for five years! I was getting discouraged.' He had almost given up hope when Belly relented.

Ingrid was their only child. Belly poured all of her love and devotion into her daughter, although, as a traditionalist, she could also be strict, especially when it came to homework. 'Everything revolved around Ingrid,' says Lusamba. But it was a loving discipline, not a harsh regime. 'Ingrid and Belly were friends,' says Lusamba. 'They were really friends.'

If, before 21 March, you had found yourself lost and friendless at Victoria station – perhaps if your wallet had been stolen or your phone had died – there would have been no one in the world better for you to meet than Belly. She befriended the waifs and strays of the London transport network. She was Saint Christopher in a polyester uniform and rubber-soled shoes. 'She was a good person,' says Lusamba. 'I am not just saying that because she was my wife.'

Once, Belly found an Argentinian woman in Victoria station in a state of distress. Belly brought her home. 'She spent two days in our house,' Lusamba says. 'She ate what we ate, we organised her transport, and we didn't ask her for any money.'

The family spent last Christmas with a French family whom Belly had befriended in the station. They did not realise that London was essentially shut on Christmas Day. So Belly said: 'Come to my house.'

Belly started working for Govia Thameslink Railway (GTR) in 2011, first on the ticket gates and then as a ticket office clerk, the role in which she was employed when she died. One of Belly's colleagues from that period, who prefers not to be named, says Belly always volunteered for overtime – she was supporting her mother back home in Kinshasa – and often helped elderly passengers with their bags. 'She was well known at Victoria station,' he says. 'Everyone liked her.'

Towards the end of her life, Belly was not having a good time at work. She felt that she was being bullied by a manager. In

September 2019, things came to a head. Lusamba says Belly told him that she had mistakenly left some cash on the desk in the ticket office when clocking out of her shift. This was a common mistake, and usually the person on the next shift would lock away the money for their absent-minded colleague. Belly, however, was suspended for three months. 'That was the worst period of her life,' Lusamba says. 'She was in a really bad state. We tried to be there for her, to keep her chin up, but it was terrible.' In December, Belly was allowed back.

Things got frightening and strange for London's transport workers on 16 March. Boris Johnson advised the public to work from home and, overnight, commuter traffic plummeted. On 17 March, Belly was sent to work on the concourse, directing passengers through the station. She recorded herself. 'Hello,' says Belly in the video, panning the camera around. 'Just to show you Victoria. One of the biggest stations in London! There's no people. People are afraid.' The station is as empty as it would be on Christmas Eve, only without the cheerful stragglers and workaholics bearing gifts, belatedly making their way home. 'People are at home, afraid of going outside,' Belly goes on. 'Stay home and stay safe,' she concludes. She is not wearing personal protective equipment (PPE). At the time, there was no government guidance requiring face coverings to be worn by railway workers. In May, the guidance changed, at which point GTR issued workers with masks.

Belly's union, the Transport Salaried Staffs' Association (TSSA), argues that she should not have been on the concourse at all that day. 'Belly was a ticket office clerk,' says the TSSA. 'All of her primary duties should have been in the ticket office building.' (GTR says that it was routine for ticket office clerks to work on the concourse when required.) Moreover, Belly had an underlying respiratory condition: she had had surgery on her throat in 2016, which her employers may have been aware of, because she had to go for frequent checkups at the Royal Free hospital in north London.

Belly was not on the shielding register. A few days after the alleged spitting incident, Belly's doctor called GTR and told them that Belly should be shielding at home. But by then it was too late. Belly already had Covid-19.

On 21 March, Belly was working an early shift. At some point that morning, she was sent to work on the concourse, where she met the 57-year-old man. Words were spoken. The disputed incident took place. The man walked away. There was a panicked scramble back to the safety of the ticket office. According to her union representative, Belly – scared for her safety – begged not to be sent back on to the concourse, but she was sent out to finish her shift. (GTR did not comment on this claim.) No one notified the BTP. This month, the Crown Prosecution Service (CPS) announced that it had reviewed a subsequent BTP investigation and concluded that the evidence was 'insufficiently clear' to show an attack.

The following day was Agnes's birthday. When Agnes got home, Belly was waiting to surprise her. She had cooked a birthday spread – chicken, rice, plantain, two types of fish – and bought a cake. But she seemed distracted, preoccupied. She told Agnes that a 'mad person' had spat at her at work and that he said he had Covid-19. Agnes was taken aback, but did not press her further. 'If you look at pictures from that day, she is just sitting there, staring, like she's not really there,' says Agnes. 'Like she was thinking. Like there was something in her head, disturbing her.'

Belly fell ill on 29 March. By 30 March, her breathing was laboured. Lying beside her in bed, Lusamba was anxious. 'When she breathed in, you couldn't tell when she was going to breathe out again,' he says. They knew she needed a doctor, but they were scared to go to hospital, convinced from what they had seen on

TV and social media that she was more likely to get ill there than to be cured. By 2 April, Belly could not breathe, so she called an ambulance. When it arrived, Belly walked down the stairs from her second-floor flat as Ingrid and Lusamba watched. 'She just waved,' he says. 'That's the last image I have of her, waving goodbye.'

At Barnet hospital, Belly refused to go on a ventilator. 'She didn't want that,' Lusamba says. 'Because before she went into hospital, on all the social media, they kept talking about ventilators.' Later, Belly and Lusamba talked on the phone. 'She said: "I have got to get out of here." I said: "It's impossible – I can't get to you because I don't know where you are – and they wouldn't let me come in anyway."' On 4 April, Belly called Agnes. 'She says to me: "Agnes, please look after Ingrid,"' Agnes remembers. 'I say: "Sissy, I don't want to hear that. You are not going anywhere. We are all praying for you."' Later that evening, Belly video-called Lusamba, but would not turn on her camera. 'I said: "Why don't you want me to see you?"' Lusamba remembers. 'She said that she didn't want Ingrid to see her in this state.' But she seemed a little better – she was speaking clearly – and Lusamba was pleased. He told Agnes that Belly sounded stronger. That evening, they slept soundly, thinking that Belly was on the mend.

Lusamba received a call from the hospital early the next morning. He did not understand the call exactly – his first language is French – so he phoned Agnes and asked her to speak to the doctor. 'She called and got the news,' says Lusamba. He cries and wipes his face with a towel. There is a long silence.

'I feel, in a way, that our dead were abandoned,' Lusamba says. 'In my head, it's like that. When you are scared, you want to touch a person who is there. We left them there to die, and then we just disposed of them. It's really bad. There's this person you shared time with and you weren't there to see them die. I wasn't abroad. I was here. Nobody was with her when she died. Nobody.'

Lusamba does not like to think about Belly's funeral. It was not the funeral she would have wanted or the funeral she deserved. 'We were only allowed 10 people at the funeral,' he says. 'We have a large family and community. Not everyone could be there.'

Worse than the funeral, on 29 April, was the fact that Lusamba was not allowed to see Belly's body after she died, not even if he wore PPE. Not seeing his wife's body means that Lusamba struggles to accept that she is gone. 'When they brought the coffin, I didn't know what was inside,' he says. 'Was it really her? That is the question that haunts me.' It will be Ingrid's 12th birthday in September. 'When the other girls call for their mothers, she thinks about her mother,' says Lusamba. 'You can see. That's when it's tough. But she plays.'

It was at the funeral that Lusamba realised that he should not drop Belly's case. Two of her colleagues came to lay flowers on the grave. Lusamba noticed them, but did not think much of it. A few days later, he received a phone call from a friend who also knew one of the colleagues. The friend asked: 'Are you ready to hear the full story of what happened that day?' Lusamba was ready.

The Press Association broke the story on 12 May. By 13 May, Belly was on the cover of the *Guardian*, the *Metro* and the *Daily Mail*. 'This seems to me to be a murder,' Piers Morgan thundered on *Good Morning Britain*. On the same day, Johnson referenced Belly in prime minister's questions. 'Yesterday, this house learned of the tragic death of Belly Mujinga,' said Johnson. 'The fact that she was abused for doing her job is utterly appalling.' A GoFundMe appeal to cover Belly's funeral costs raised more than £230,000. The BTP launched an investigation, as did GTR and the Office of Rail and Road's Railway Inspectorate.

By this point, Covid-19's impact on black people was becoming increasingly clear. Data from the Office for National Statistics showed that black people were four times more likely to die of

Covid-19 than white people. 'You started to see the visual imagery of who was dying of Covid,' says Yvonne Field, an anti-racism campaigner from the Ubele Initiative.

Belly's story was enraging because it was a familiar one: a story of contempt for black people, especially black women. 'We know that black women work night and day to support their families,' says Field. 'They are the black family's backbone. The way she was disrespected makes me shudder.'

Public anger was at boiling point, but it had nowhere to go. And then, on 25 May, George Floyd was killed in Minneapolis and everything erupted. Anti-racism campaigners took to the streets in the US and the UK. On 29 May, the BTP concluded its investigation. Detectives told the press that the 57-year-old man they identified from CCTV had produced a negative antibody test, showing he did not have the virus, and was not responsible for Belly's death. Detectives visited Lusamba to give him the news. 'I don't like to use the word racism,' says Lusamba. 'But on the day the police told me they were stopping the inquiry, inside myself I felt it was racist.'

In response to Lusamba's claims, the BTP referred me to a public statement, which stated that the BTP had 'comprehensively reviewed all the available evidence and have not identified any offences or behaviour that meets the threshold for prosecution'.

It all seemed too convenient; too neat. The public was angry, and so they did what people do when they feel that justice has not been served. They took to the streets.

An 18-year-old student, Aima, from London, doesn't know how many Justice for Belly Mujinga posters, placards and banners she saw at the Black Lives Matter protest in Hyde Park on 3 June. 'Oh my gosh,' she says softly. 'There were hundreds.' Belly is one of the reasons Aima went out that day. 'After what happened to Belly,' she says. 'I thought: "We've had enough. We can't be silent."'

Lusamba was at the protest, too. 'It was one of the days that I will never forget until my death,' he says. 'It was a very good day. To see so many white and black people together ... I could see Belly on that day.' He is gratified by the public outcry around her death. 'When the public talks about it, I feel justice is being made,' says Lusamba. 'In a way it's kind of reparations.'

Most of the public anger is directed at Belly's assailant. But the story is bigger than that. 'I can understand the excitement of a criminal case about someone assaulting someone else,' says the TSSA. 'And that possibly being how she caught the virus. But that was never really the story for us, although it has caught people's imaginations. The real story is, why was she out there?'

'Belly was a dedicated and much-loved colleague at Victoria station and we are heartbroken by her passing,' says Chris Fowler, the customer service director for Southern (part of GTR). 'While the BTP's investigation and CPS's independent review have concluded that Belly's tragic death was not caused by this alleged incident, it does not detract from the tragic loss of our colleague from coronavirus. It has shaken us all and is a painful reminder of how deadly this virus is.'

Almost every aspect of the Belly Mujinga story is upsetting. Layers of injustice are buried inside each other, like Russian dolls. There is the alleged assault, which is straightforwardly contempt-ible. Then there is the question of why a woman with underlying health conditions was working in a public-facing role in the midst of a pandemic, rather than remaining within the relative safety of the ticket office. Why wasn't she listened to, if, as her union representative says, Belly told her supervisor she had been assaulted, and did not want to go back out to work? Why wasn't a report made to the police immediately? The list goes on.

Belly Mujinga has become a symbol. No one can bear the weight of decades of institutional racism, apathy and contempt towards low-paid workers, and emerge with their personhood fully intact. Their edges get smoothed out. To her family and her friends, though, she is still the Belly they knew. Someone who worked overtime to send money home, someone who loved to find a bargain online, someone who would meddle, because she thought she knew best. Someone who would reach out a helping hand under the fluorescent chill of the station lights, in the hurried capital she had made her home: London, a place where hardly anyone ever stops to assist a stranger in need.

If you were to find yourself lost and friendless in Victoria station today, there would be no Belly to help you.

4 SEPTEMBER

The eight secrets to a (fairly) fulfilled life

OLIVER BURKEMAN

In the very first instalment of this column, more than a decade ago, I wrote that it would continue until I had discovered the secret of human happiness, whereupon it would cease. Obviously, I never expected to find the secret, but on some level I must have known there were questions I needed to confront – about anxiety, commitment-phobia in relationships, control-freakery and building a meaningful life. Writing a column provided the perfect cover for such otherwise embarrassing fare.

I am drawing a line today not because I have uncovered all the answers, but because I have a powerful hunch that the moment is right to do so. If nothing else, I hope I've acquired sufficient self-knowledge to know when it's time to move on. So what did I learn? What follows isn't intended as an exhaustive summary. But these are the principles that surfaced again and again, and that now seem to me most useful for navigating times as baffling and stress-inducing as ours.

THERE WILL ALWAYS BE TOO MUCH TO DO – AND THIS REALISATION IS LIBERATING

Today more than ever, there's just no reason to assume any fit between the demands on your time – all the things you would like to do, or feel you ought to do – and the amount of time available. Thanks to capitalism, technology and human ambition, these demands keep increasing, while your capacities remain largely fixed. It follows that the attempt to 'get on top of everything' is doomed. (Indeed, it's worse than that – the more tasks you get done, the more you'll generate.) The upside is that you needn't berate yourself for failing to do it all, since doing it all is structurally impossible. The only viable solution is to make a shift: from a life spent trying not to neglect anything, to one spent proactively and consciously choosing what to neglect, in favour of what matters most.

WHEN STUMPED BY A LIFE CHOICE, CHOOSE 'ENLARGEMENT' OVER HAPPINESS

I'm indebted to the Jungian therapist James Hollis for the insight that major personal decisions should be made not by asking, 'Will this make me happy?' but, 'Will this choice enlarge me or diminish me?' We're terrible at predicting what will make us happy: the question swiftly gets bogged down in our narrow preferences for security and control. But the enlargement question elicits a deeper, intuitive response. You tend to just know whether, say, leaving or remaining in a relationship or a job, though it might bring short-term comfort, would mean cheating yourself of growth. (Relatedly, don't worry about burning bridges: irreversible decisions tend to be more satisfying, because now there's only one direction to travel – forward into whatever choice you made.)

THE CAPACITY TO TOLERATE MINOR DISCOMFORT IS A SUPERPOWER

It's shocking to realise how readily we set aside even our greatest ambitions in life, merely to avoid easily tolerable levels of unpleasantness. You already know it won't kill you to endure the mild agitation of getting back to work on an important creative project; initiating a difficult conversation with a colleague; asking someone out; or checking your bank balance – but you can waste years in avoidance nonetheless. When you expect that an action will be accompanied by feelings of irritability, anxiety or boredom, it's usually possible to let that feeling arise and fade, while doing the action anyway. The rewards come so quickly, in terms of what you'll accomplish, that it soon becomes the more appealing way to live.

THE ADVICE YOU DON'T WANT TO HEAR IS USUALLY THE ADVICE YOU NEED

I spent a long time fixated on becoming hyper-productive before I finally started wondering why I was staking so much of my self-worth on my productivity levels. What I needed wasn't another exciting productivity book, since those just functioned as enablers, but to ask more uncomfortable questions instead.

The broader point here is that it isn't fun to confront whatever emotional experiences you're avoiding – if it were, you wouldn't avoid them – so the advice that could really help is likely to make you uncomfortable. (You may need to introspect with care here, since bad advice from manipulative friends or partners is *also* likely to make you uncomfortable.) One good question to ask is what kind of practices strike you as intolerably cheesy or self-indulgent: gratitude journals, mindfulness meditation, seeing a therapist? That might mean they are worth pursuing. (I can say from personal experience that all three are worth it.) Oh, and be especially wary of celebrities offering advice in public forums: they probably pursued fame in an effort to fill an inner void, which tends not to work – so they are likely to be more troubled than you are.

THE FUTURE WILL NEVER PROVIDE THE REASSURANCE YOU SEEK FROM IT

As the ancient Greek and Roman Stoics understood, much of our suffering arises from attempting to control what is not in our control. And the main thing we try but fail to control – the seasoned worriers among us, anyway – is the future. We want to *know*, from our vantage point in the present, that things will be OK later on. But we never can. (This is why it's wrong to say we live in especially uncertain times. The future is always uncertain; it's just that we're currently very aware of it.) It's freeing to grasp that no amount of fretting will ever alter this truth. It's still useful to make plans. But do that with the awareness that a plan is only ever a present-moment statement of intent, not a lasso thrown around the future to bring it under control.

THE SOLUTION TO IMPOSTER SYNDROME IS TO SEE THAT YOU ARE ONE

When I first wrote about how useful it is to remember that everyone is totally just winging it, all the time, we hadn't yet entered the current era of leaderly incompetence (Brexit, Trump, coronavirus). Now, it's harder to ignore. But the lesson to be drawn isn't that we're doomed to chaos. It's that you – unconfident, self-conscious, all-too-aware-of-your-flaws – potentially have as much to contribute to your field, or the world, as anyone else.

Humanity is divided into two: on the one hand, those who are improvising their way through life, patching solutions together and putting out fires as they go, but deluding themselves otherwise; and on the other, those doing exactly the same, except that they know it. It's infinitely better to be the latter (although too much 'assertiveness training' consists of techniques for turning yourself into the former).

Remember: the reason you can't hear other people's inner monologues of self-doubt isn't that they don't have them. It's that you only have access to your own mind.

Selflessness is overrated

We respectable types, although women especially, are raised to think a life well spent means helping others. There's truth here, but it generally gets tangled up with deep-seated issues of guilt and self-esteem. If you're prone to thinking you should be helping more, that's probably a sign that you could afford to direct more energy to your idiosyncratic ambitions and enthusiasms. As the Buddhist teacher Susan Piver observes, it's radical, at least for some of us, to ask how we'd *enjoy* spending an hour or day of discretionary time. And the irony is that you don't actually serve anyone else by suppressing your true passions anyway. More often than not, by doing your thing – as opposed to what you think you ought to be doing – you kindle a fire that helps keep the rest of us warm.

Know when to move on

And then, finally, there's the one about knowing when something that's meant a great deal to you has reached its natural endpoint, and that the most creative choice would be to turn to what's next. This is where you find me.

Boris Johnson's 'oven-ready' Brexit had a secret footnote: we'll rehash it later

FINTAN O'TOOLE

Everybody knows Boris Johnson can lie for England. To his supporters, it was one of his best assets. They believed he could bamboozle the European Union into giving him the only Brexit deal that is really acceptable – one that gives Britain all the advantages of being in the EU without any of the botheration of being a member. The problem is that congenital mendacity isn't just for foreigners. If you lie for England, you will also lie to England.

This week, these two streams of fabrication finally became one. In openly admitting that it signed the withdrawal agreement with the EU in bad faith, Johnson's Vote Leave government also implicitly confessed that it lied wholesale to the electorate in last December's general election. The cross-contamination of domestic politics by the deceit that is Brexit's DNA is now complete.

On Tuesday, Northern Ireland secretary Brandon Lewis brazenly informed the Commons that a bill to amend the Irish protocol of the EU withdrawal agreement would 'break international law', albeit in 'limited and specific ways'. The qualification is nonsense. If one side can unilaterally change any bits of a treaty, nothing in it is binding. But, in any case, Lewis's declaration was part of a wider contention: that the British never quite understood what they were signing.

That same day, Johnson's court gazette, the *Daily Telegraph*, led with the headline: 'Brexit deal never made sense, PM to tell EU.' The story quoted 'a senior government source' as claiming that some of the treaty's consequences 'were not foreseen' and that it would have to be 'rewritten to protect the union'.

In itself, this claim is fraudulent. The idea that Johnson has suddenly realised that the protocol keeps Northern Ireland within the ambit of the EU's customs union and single market, and thus has negative implications for the union, is risible. This was what Johnson's close allies in the Democratic Unionist party were screaming about when he made the deal in October 2019. If Johnson didn't see that a radically different Brexit for one part of the UK would destabilise the union, he is an idiot. But in this case, he can be exonerated on that charge – he knew damn well and did it anyway.

He did it for the same reason he and his Vote Leave crew do everything else: because it suits their immediate interests. Theresa May's Northern Ireland backstop was threatening to bring the whole Brexit project crashing down. The Irish taoiseach, Leo Varadkar, offered Johnson a way out – the so-called 'border in the Irish Sea'. Johnson, the supreme opportunist, grabbed it, screwed the DUP, declared victory and the rest is history.

But this is where the real fakery starts. It is clear that Johnson and his most important confreres, Dominic Cummings and Michael Gove, never really saw this as anything other than a clever dodge, a tactical retreat. On his blog in March 2019, when May was in power, Cummings addressed 'dear Vote Leave activists': 'don't worry about the so-called "permanent" commitments this historically abysmal cabinet are trying to make on our behalf. They are not "permanent" and a serious government – one not cowed by officials and their bullshit "legal advice" with which they have herded ministers like sheep – will dispense with these commitments.'

In May this year, Steve Baker, former chair of the European Research Group, wrote in the *Critic* that Cummings 'said we should vote for the original withdrawal agreement without reading it, on the basis Michael Gove articulated: we could change it later'.

This idea that Britain could sign the withdrawal agreement with its fingers crossed behind its back and then just ignore it later on is, in a way, perfectly consistent with the larger mentality of Brexit. At the heart of its theology is the fantasy that there is such a thing as absolute national sovereignty, a complete unilateral freedom of action that had been taken away by the EU. Once Britain is 'unchained', it can do whatever it pleases. The withdrawal treaty is merely a route towards the obligation-free future that starts on 1 January 2021.

The Brexiters don't much mind that this trick requires Britain to expose itself as a rogue state that treats international agreements as disposable. They presumably haven't bothered to look up, for example, the membership of the United States House committee on ways and means that would control any US–UK trade deal. (It's chaired by Irish-American Richard Neal, who's highly engaged with Northern Ireland.) The catch is that all of this doesn't stop at smartarse duplicity towards other countries. It involves the flagrant deception of English voters. More perhaps than any modern election, Johnson's campaign in December was reduced to a single issue: Get Brexit done. This was to be achieved by electing a parliament that was committed to passing the 'oven-ready' and 'excellent' withdrawal agreement.

There was always one level of spuriousness in this – the withdrawal agreement was not the end of anything. But it is now clear that there was a much deeper and even more cynical level of fakery. It was not just that Brexit would not be 'done' when the withdrawal agreement was duly passed, it was that Cummings and Johnson intended all along to undo it.

Brexit is a promise that was made to be broken because the best of all worlds the voters were offered in 2016 was always a mirage. But that breach has widened over time. It is now an open chasm in British democracy.

Index